The Spirit of Hidalgo

Latin American and Caribbean Series

Waking the Dictator
Veracruz, the Struggle for Federalism, and the Mexican Revolution, 1870–1927
Karl B. Koth

The Spirit of Hidalgo
The Mexican Revolution in Coahuila
Suzanne B. Pasztor
Co-published with Michigan State University Press

Clerical Ideology in a Revolutionary Age
The Guadalajara Church and the Idea of the Mexican Nation, 1788–1853
Brian F. Connaughton, translated by Mark Alan Healey

Monuments of Progress
Modernization and Public Health in Mexico City, 1876–1910
Claudia Agostini

THE
SPIRIT
OF
HIDALGO

The Mexican Revolution in Coahuila

Suzanne B. Pasztor

University of
Calgary Press

&

Michigan State
University Press

University of Calgary Press
2500 University Drive NW
Calgary, Alberta
Canada T2N 1N4
www.uofcpress.com

Michigan State University Press
1405 South Harrison Road
25 Manly Miles Building
East Lansing, MI 48823-5202
www.msupress.msu.edu

National Library of Canada Cataloguing in Publication Data

Pasztor, Suzanne B., 1964–
    The spirit of Hidalgo

    (Latin American and Caribbean series, 1498-2366 ; 2)
    Includes bibliographical references and index.
    ISBN 1-55238-047-5   University of Calgary Press
    ISBN 0-87013-626-7   Michigan State University Press

    1. Coahuila (Mexico: State)—History.
    2. Mexico—History—Revolution, 1910-1920. I. Title. II. Series.
F1266.P37 2002   972'.14   C2002-910772-5

 We acknowledge the financial support of the Government of Canada through
the Book Publishing Industry Development Program (BPIDP) for our publishing
activities.

 The Canada Council for the Arts
Le Conseil des Arts du Canada

Printed and bound in Canada by AGMV Marquis.
∞ This book is printed on acid-free paper.

Page, cover design, and typesetting by Kristina Schuring.

For my grandmother, Irene Halasz,
in loving memory

Series Editor's Preface

It is a very great pleasure to introduce the Latin American and Caribbean Series published by the University of Calgary Press. Not only does this series embrace a variety of historical, literary, and postcolonial themes; it is the only one of its kind in Canada. Our intention is to publish cutting-edge and revisionist studies that reinterpret our understanding of historical and current issues in Latin America and the Caribbean.

Christon I. Archer
Series Editor

Contents

Acknowledgments

This book began as a research project nearly a decade ago. Along the way, I have received valuable assistance from many individuals and institutions. A Graduate Fellowship and two research grants from the Institute of Latin American Studies at the University of New Mexico helped fund my initial research, as did a grant from the International Federation of Women's Clubs. More recent grants from the School of International Studies at the University of the Pacific, as well as an Eberhardt Foundation Fellowship from the same university, have enabled me to continue my research on Coahuila.

Several individuals have provided useful input, assistance, and encouragement during the production of this work. Linda B. Hall, John L. Kessell, Robert Himmerich y Valencia, and Christine M. Sierra of the University of New Mexico as well as Don M. Coerver of Texas Christian University critiqued the original dissertation and provided initial guidelines for turning it into a book. I am particularly indebted to Linda Hall and Don Coerver, who have continued to be gracious mentors. Peter V. N. Henderson of Winona State University kindly supplied the first external review of my work, Donald E. Worcester lent his masterly editing skills to portions of the manuscript, and Douglas Richmond shared photographs from his own collection, while encouraging me to pursue this project. I am especially grateful to Christon Archer, who provided valuable suggestions for the improvement of the manuscript, and who was instrumental in supporting its publication. A special thanks as well, to Walter Hildebrandt, John King, and the amiable staff of the University of Calgary Press.

The assistance and support of several people in Mexico, where I conducted the majority of my research, was invaluable. In Saltillo, Alfonso Vázquez Sotelo, director of the Instituto Estatal de Documentación, which houses the State Archive of Coahuila, generously accommodated my work even as his staff was in the process of reorganizing that archive. I am also grateful to Arq. Guillermo González, director of the Archivo General del Tribunal Superior de Justicia, who allowed me special access to documents in this little-used archive. Carlos Manuel Valdés Dávila, Ildefonso Dávila del Bosque, and the staff of the Archivo Municipal de Saltillo provided encouragement and a comfortable place to work. Martha Rodríguez García and José Luis García Valero gave additional support and suggestions. Finally, I wish to thank Elizabeth Gutiérrez Romero and the faculty of the Centro de Estudios Socioeconómicos of the Universidad Autónoma de Coahuila for including me in their institution as a visiting research scholar.

In Mexico City, the staff of several archives provided equally valuable assistance. Lic. Eutiquio Franco helped to orient me in the Archivo General de la Nación. At the Centro de Estudios de Historia de México/CONDUMEX, Lic. Josefina Moguel Flores and her staff aided my work in the archives of Venustiano Carranza and Bernardo Reyes. Beatriz Carrillo González of the Archivo de Relaciones Exteriores was especially helpful in guiding my research on the border region. I am likewise grateful to General Antonio Riviello Bazán, former Secretary of Defense, and General Eulalio Fonseca Orozco, who allowed me access to the Archivo de la Defensa Nacional on two separate research trips.

As any academic knows, archival assistance is only part of what makes the often lonely task of research worthwhile. The hospitality and friendship of several people in Mexico have made my work as a Mexican historian both enjoyable and rewarding. In Saltillo, Martha Rodríguez García and Alfonso Vázquez and his family have always provided a warm welcome. In Mexico City, Esperanza Fujigaki Cruz and Augusto Cardona Fujigaki have provided pleasant companionship and a comfortable place to stay. In California, Walter Brem of the Bancroft Library continues to be a friendly and helpful presence, and the hospitality of Debbie and David Keefe has been a refreshing addition to my Bay Area research trips.

On a more personal level, I thank my parents for never doubting my abilities, my brother Peter for being so wonderfully himself, and Timothy Keefe for sharing the joys of love, laughter, and baseball. Finally, I would like to express my gratitude for the following people whose paths have crossed mine over the past several years: Dwight Crowder, Deborah Buffton, Pam Radosen, Jaes Seis, Jan Dederick, Cynthia Ostberg, and Frances Kalfus. Their encouragement, inspiration, and wisdom have meant more to me than they will ever know.

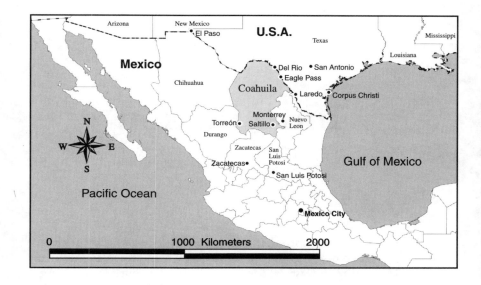

Coahuila and Surrounding Area

Introduction

This inquiry into the meaning and process of the Mexican Revolution grew out of research conducted in Mexico during the last decade of the twentieth century. The time was a volatile one for Mexico: the North American Free Trade Agreement (NAFTA) was completed, linking Mexico's economy with those of Canada and the United States; a rebel group in the southern state of Chiapas became more visible and soon came to occupy (at least for a time) centre stage; and Mexico continued to wrestle with problems of political corruption and financial instability.

It was amid such challenges that President Carlos Salinas de Gortari announced fundamental changes to the 1917 Constitution, the document that for many Mexicans continues to embody the spirit and ideals of the Mexican Revolution. In a 1992 speech commemorating the seventy-fifth anniversary of the Constitution, Salinas stood before a large picture of Emiliano Zapata, the Morelos rebel whose name has become synonymous with the Revolution, and spoke of the need for change. Asserting that the principles of the Revolution must change to meet Mexico's changing needs, Salinas announced reforms to Article 27 of the Constitution, effectively ending the institution of communal landholdings, or *ejidos*. Acknowledging the popular perception of Article 27 as one of the most representative outcomes of the Revolution, Salinas assured Mexicans that the spirit of the Revolution was still alive.

As Mexico drifts towards a global economy and attempts to dismantle not only its *ejido* system but also its network of state-run industries (both symbols of the country's revolutionary gains), it has become common to hear comparisons drawn between the current situation and the era of Porfirio Díaz, the man who dominated the country on the eve of the Revolution and whose policies brought an unprecedented degree of foreign influence and political centralization to Mexico. Amid changes to the Constitution, the advent of NAFTA, and recent challenges to the Mexican political system (most notably the 2000 election of Vicente Fox that ended the seventy-year political dominance of the Institutional Revolutionary Party), the Mexican Revolution that ended Díaz' reign has assumed a new relevance. What was the spirit of that Revolution? This book seeks to answer that question.

The state of Coahuila, located in northeastern Mexico, provides a unique setting in which to explore the meaning of the Mexican Revolution. The third largest state in Mexico, Coahuila was the home of two of the Revolution's most outstanding figures: Francisco I. Madero and Venustiano Carranza. By the end of the nineteenth century Coahuila was experiencing rapid modernization and an economic transformation that made the state a showcase of Porfirian Mexico. At the same time, this northeastern state clung to its federalist heritage through the periodic assertion of local autonomy and political independence in the face of Porfirian attempts at centralization. When the Revolution developed within Coahuila, it represented two things: popular reaction to economic modernization and the dislocations this engendered; and the shifting of Coahuila's political system in response to both popular discontent and pressures from the central government. Both of these components are explored in this book and both, I would argue, speak to the spirit of the Revolution.

To understand the meaning behind Coahuila's revolutionary experience, one needs to investigate the broader forces at work in the state on the eve of the Mexican Revolution. The first two chapters of this study explore these forces by examining the social, economic, and political context of Coahuila prior to the 1910 revolt that adopted Francisco I. Madero as its leader. As in many northern states, Coahuila's experience as a frontier encouraged the development of a tradition of local autonomy and helped shape an economy and society that largely reflected such autonomy. By the end of the nineteenth century Coahuila's transformation from a frontier to a dynamic and rapidly modernizing Mexican state was well underway. Yet the repercussions of that transformation were clear. Economic dislocations and the increasing tendency of Mexico's central government, under the leadership of Porfirio Díaz, to assert its authority at the state and local levels now became a part of Coahuila's historical process. Ultimately, these changes encouraged the emergence of several avenues of political opposition.

When the Mexican Revolution began in 1910 with Francisco Madero's call for the overthrow of the aging Porfirio Díaz, it was the popular classes that seized the initiative in Coahuila. Chapter 3 examines this popular revolt, which was both a response to specific events and a part of Coahuila's broader transformation. Chapter 4 continues the exploration of the popular movement that persisted beyond Madero's victory and explores the relationship between President Madero and Coahuila's other revolutionary native son, Venustiano Carranza. A persistent economic crisis as well as Madero's own lukewarm commitment to change set the stage for Carranza's Constitutionalist movement, which was largely successful in harnessing the popular revolution in the aftermath of Madero's death in 1913.

What were the characteristics and bases of support for Carranza's Constitutionalism? How did Carranza, in the face of persistent challenges from rival factions and in light of Coahuila's ongoing economic crisis, support his movement? Chapters 5 and 6 address these questions with examinations of Carrancista recruitment and of Constitutionalist efforts to finance military campaigns. Carranza's approach to Coahuila's popular movement as well as his cautious approach to reform bore fruit in the recruitment of a genuinely cross-class army, while his mastery of the Texas-Coahuila border proved crucial to the supply and financing of that army.

Perhaps the most viable challenge to Carranza's leadership of Coahuila's revolution came from Pancho Villa, whose tenuous alliance with Constitutionalism unraveled in 1914, and who controlled significant portions of the state for nearly a year before Carranza's definitive victory in September 1915. Chapter 7 explores the phenomenon of Villismo, which some Coahuilans embraced as holding out promise of more sweeping change, and which encouraged members of at least one of Coahuila's wealthiest families to reject Constitutionalism.

The final chapter analyzes the meaning of the Constitutionalist victory of 1915, which signaled the end of major fighting within Coahuila and paved the way for the adoption of a new state constitution. As Coahuila began a gradual reconstruction of its economy and political system, Carranza's designated governor, Gustavo Espinosa Mireles, embarked upon a program of moderate reform that acknowledged many of the demands of the past revolution, while at the same time reflecting the limits of that revolution.

How does Coahuila fit into the general picture of the Mexican Revolution? What can it tell us about the significance of that Revolution and its place in Mexico's history? These themes are also a part of this book. Coahuila's revolutionary experience, I argue, confirms the view of the Revolution as a process rather than an event. Rather than a sharp break with the past, Coahuila's revolution was part of a broader transformation that, in light of Coahuila's history, encouraged protest and rebellion.[1] And while the Revolution did bring significant changes to Coahuila, revolutionary outcomes were often far from radical, and revolutionary events should be seen as part of Coahuila's broader adjustment to modernization and its dislocations.

How does Coahuila's experience compare with that of other Mexican states? The continuing production of regional histories of the Mexican Revolution suggests that for many northern states the Revolution was experienced as a cross-class struggle for autonomy. The northern revolution was distinct from the more traditional peasant rebellions in areas such as Morelos, home of Emiliano Zapata. The revision of our view of the Mexican Revolution based on the idea of northern uniqueness has found its most complete expression in Alan Knight's two-volume work *The Mexican Revolution*. Knight introduces the concept of *serrano* revolt to refer to the experience of the north and other areas in which the authority of the state was tenuous and in which local autonomy was carefully guarded. Rather than seeking a restructuring of society, he claims *serrano* rebels sought to free themselves from the central government that encroached upon their independence, especially during the Porfiriato. Such movements contained a significant bandit element and often involved the mobilization of an entire community regardless of class. Particularly in the north, with its more mobile population and lack of a traditional peasantry, the Revolution had a logic of its own by which groups formed alliances, often against class or ideological interests. At the same time, and as in the case of traditional peasant rebellion, specific grievances were expressed through popular revolt.[2]

This study demonstrates the extent to which Coahuila's revolution was a "northern" experience. The social bases of support for Madero and Carranza, as well as the patterns of rebellion, targets of rebel violence, and concrete grievances and petitions for reform that surfaced as a result of the Maderista and Carrancista movements, tend to support the revisionist views of a cross-class rebellion that gave expression to a deeper desire for autonomy. An adequate explanation of Coahuila's revolutionary experience, however, must go beyond the *serrano* thesis. For while the sentiment of self-determination informed much rebel activity and rhetoric, the momentum of Coahuila's popular revolution was largely a product of the state's economic troubles, which began after 1900 and continued throughout the Revolution. And this economic crisis demonstrated the extent to which Coahuila, like many areas of Mexico, had become vulnerable to outside economic forces.[3]

This work then, is an exploration of the Mexican Revolution and of Coahuila's historical process during the years surrounding the turn of the twentieth century. It is a story that begins with rebellion, continues with popular revolt, and ends with both change and compromise. It is an account of adjustment and transformation, an account that underscores both Coahuila's frontier heritage and its struggle to cope with change.

1

The Spirit of Hidalgo

Nineteenth-Century Coahuila

In 1896 Bernardo Reyes, governor of Nuevo León and strongman of northeastern Mexico, puzzled over rumours of a revolt in central Coahuila. Some twenty-five men, most from the "lower elements" of Coahuilan society, were implicated in a plot against Mexico's president, Porfirio Díaz, that included plans to kidnap the aging dictator. Questioning of the suspected rebels revealed contacts with other malcontents in southwestern Coahuila and in the northern border town of Piedras Negras. Interrogated by local authorities, Manuel Sarabia, a spiritist[1] from the town of San Buenaventura and leader of the plot, spoke mysteriously of a revolution that "in the spirit of Hidalgo" would engulf the entire state of Coahuila and would eventually count among its supporters two men by the names of Madero and Carranza. The "Conspiracy of Monclova," as it came to be known, quickly sputtered out. Its adherents were imprisoned, with Manuel Sarabia, in the interest of Porfirian peace, sent to the federal prison at San Juan de Ulúa.[2]

The spirit of independence invoked by Sarabia and likened to the 1810 rebellion of Father Miguel Hidalgo y Costilla, which helped ignite colonial Mexico's struggle for freedom from Spain, was an indelible part of the Coahuilan social landscape. An Indian frontier during the colonial period and much of the nineteenth century, this northern state had developed a tradition of local autonomy. Geographical location encouraged the growth of a self-sufficient economy, while distance from central authority generated a tradition of political independence that made Coahuilan leaders among the foremost champions of federalism.

1

By the late nineteenth century, when the Conspiracy of Monclova surfaced, Coahuila was in the midst of a significant economic transformation that would gradually replace its traditional self-sufficiency with a highly integrated economy that was linked to and dependent on outside markets. The initial arbiter of this change was a new entrepreneurial class emerging in northeastern Mexico by the mid-nineteenth century, a class that was itself a product of the individual initiative and economic autonomy characteristic of northern Mexico. During the reign of Porfirio Díaz, this native "bourgeoisie" reluctantly accepted the advent of an aggressive group of foreign businessmen whose investments hastened the process of Coahuila's economic transformation.

The economic changes that began at mid-century and introduced a new capitalist class, both native and foreign, brought other significant changes in Coahuilan society. To meet the increasing demand for labour generated by the growth of various economic sectors, and to compensate for the lack of a sizable native labour supply, workers from central and southern Mexico poured into Coahuila. This new workforce, like the capitalist class that supported it, was distinguished by its modern nature. Rural as well as urban industrial workers enjoyed what were among the highest wages in Mexico, and more traditional work relations, such as debt peonage, common in central and southern Mexico, became increasingly rare.

The economic and social developments that were characteristic of Coahuila's history during the second half of the nineteenth century took place within a shifting and often unpredictable national context. In the decades after 1821, the year of Mexico's independence, the national government was characterized by political instability and financial insolvency. The definitive loss of Texas and of additional and substantial territories in the United States-Mexican War of 1846-48 underscored the young country's weakness. From 1858 to 1861 the War of Reform, which pitted Mexico's two dominant political factions, liberals and conservatives, against each other, dragged the country into a destructive civil war. On its heels came the humiliating French Intervention (1862-67), which began as an attempt by Mexico's European creditors to collect outstanding debts, and degenerated into the abortive effort of Napoleon III to establish an imperial base in the Americas. The French occupation seemed proof positive that Mexico had neither the unity nor the resources to protect its own sovereignty.

The promise of national integration and economic development finally emerged in 1876 when Porfirio Díaz, a career military man from Oaxaca, staged the successful Revolt of Tuxtepec. Díaz' rebellion brought an end to the liberal government that had been established by Benito Juárez at mid-century, and was sustained after Juárez' death by Sebastián Lerdo de Tejada. During the ensuing "Pofiriato," Díaz himself (from 1876-80 and 1884-1911) and his military colleague Manuel González (from 1880-84) governed Mexico. In many respects, Díaz and González continued along the course charted by Juárez, Lerdo, and other liberals during La Reforma. This crucial period of reform, which began in the 1850s and culminated in the 1857 Constitution, illustrated the growing conviction that economic development was the key to Mexico's future. While nineteenth-century liberals also embraced the idea of individual rights, it was this first conviction that became the central tenet of Mexican liberalism.

La Reforma included an assault on corporate property (including lands claimed by the Catholic Church and Indian communities) and utilized land reform in an attempt to make Mexico's agrarian economy more dynamic. Porfirian policies built upon this liberal foundation, and were reinforced and often inspired by the small but influential political clique known as the Científicos, so-called because of their "scientific" approach to political questions. Above all, the Porfiriato sought to usher the country into a modern industrial age, and it brought an unprecedented degree of centralization to Mexico.

Díaz and the Científicos embraced foreign investment as a key to economic growth, and new government policies opened up Mexico's land and other resources to development by Mexican and non-Mexican entrepreneurs. With the help of foreign money and management, the country's infrastructure, particularly its railroad system, began to take a modern shape. At the outset of the twentieth century, Mexico's economy was distinctly export oriented and strongly dependent on outside markets. Predictably, the fruits of Porfirian development were shared by relatively few, and economic policies often jeopardized the livelihood of Mexico's substantial lower class.

The impressive, if lopsided, economic growth that Mexico experienced during the Porfiriato was achieved with the help of a political system based on a combination of incentives to obey the central government and coercive measures to ensure such obedience among the recalcitrant. In each Mexican state, Díaz sought to manipulate local elites and strongmen, often playing them off against one another. He also used his military friends, including General Bernardo Reyes, as a counterbalance to local political machines. The army and a rural federal police force, the *Rurales*, helped provide the stable conditions needed for development, and stood ready should Díaz' more conciliatory political efforts fail.

The nineteenth-century developments that helped to transform Coahuila's economy and society, then, took place amid equally dynamic national events and trends. Some of those events, most notably the United States-Mexican War, had direct and significant effects on the state. Others, such as the modernizing policies of the Porfiriato, built upon already existing trends in the local economy, and contributed to economic and social dislocations that were already in evidence. Still others, particularly the attempts at political centralization during the Díaz years, provided a challenge to Coahuila's historical autonomy and eventually contributed to active resistance against the Porfirian regime. Encouraged by national events, nineteenth-century Coahuila was changing. The nature, extent, and consequences of that transformation were apparent in each region of the state.

Northern Coahuila

Four socio-economic regions emerged in Coahuila as a result of nineteenth-century growth: the north, centre, Laguna, and southeast. Northern Coahuila (which formed the political unit known as the Rio Grande District) was one of the first areas to feel the effects of economic change. The Mexican-American War, which ended the political unity of Texas and Coahuila forged after Mexican independence, also created an international border that would encourage the integration of this area into a broader economic sphere. Yet its historic position as the northernmost reach of Coahuila's Indian frontier had also encouraged independent development and ensured the persistence of a strong tradition of political and economic autonomy. More than any other area of Coahuila, the Rio Grande District was characterized by its vastness, isolation, sparse settlement, and vulnerability to Indian attacks. The historical weakness of central authority in this region had contributed to the emergence of a particularly independent spirit.

19th-Century Coahuila:
Regions, Districts, and Selected Municipalities

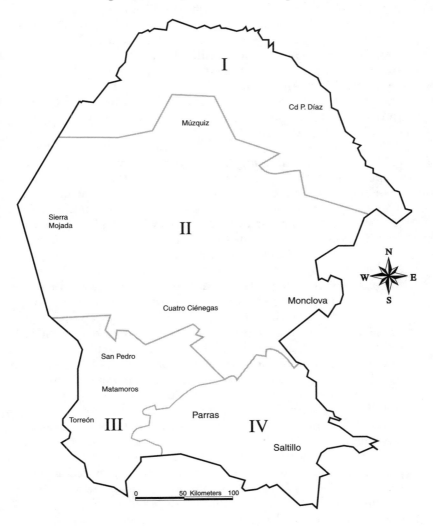

I North: Rio Grande District
II Center: Monclova District
III Laguna: Viesca District
IV Southeast: Saltillo and Parras Districts

Colonial settlement of this frontier had been the cautious and too often unsuccessful work of mission and *presidio* (military outpost).[3] By the mid-eighteenth century the Spanish crown had redoubled its efforts to settle New Spain's northern frontier, including the region of Coahuila, or Nueva Extremadura. Those who would defend such areas against Indian intrusions were granted their own lands, which they could freely sell or augment. These "military colonists" also enjoyed the rare privilege of carrying arms (a necessity on this Indian frontier), and they came to enjoy an unprecedented degree of local autonomy.[4]

A national decree revived the institution of the military colony in 1848, calling for the establishment of a new group of *colonias* along Mexico's northern border and the reinforcement of old *presidios* and *colonias*, many of which had been abandoned. This national initiative was a response to the continuing problem of raids by nomadic Indian groups, which had increased as colonization of Texas pushed them southward. It also reflected Mexican fears of Anglo-American expansionism. Several new *colonias* were established in the Rio Grande District and one in the *municipio* (municipality) of Múzquiz on the northern fringe of Coahuila's Central (or Monclova) District.[5] This new group of settlements, like those of the colonial era, enjoyed little success, falling victim to their traditional enemies: poor communications, Indian depredations, and weak state control.[6]

Despite the dubious achievements of *presidio*, mission, and *colonia*, these institutions played a significant role in determining the pattern of development in northern Coahuila. Small communities of independent farmers tended to develop near *presidios* and missions, and new population centres emerged around the military colonies as well. Furthermore, *hacendados* (owners of large rural estates) in northern Mexico had traditionally allowed independent cultivators to settle on their lands to help protect against Indian raids.[7] After 1850 these smallholders, accustomed to political autonomy and relative economic independence, were abruptly drawn into a national and international economic system.

The establishment of an international border in northern Coahuila increased the economic importance of the Rio Grande District. The town of Piedras Negras, established on the site of the military colony of Guerrero, became home to Coahuila's first customs house in 1855. Efforts to stem the flow of contraband and discourage other illegal activities characteristic of this frontier, provided a more stable environment for business. This, in turn, encouraged the development of Coahuila's cattle industry. At the same time Piedras Negras became a major point of contact with the United States. During the American Civil War it was the outlet for cotton grown in Texas and other southern states, as southern cotton growers exchanged their crops for arms and food for Confederate troops.[8]

Merchants in Coahuila, many of whom were part of a nascent entrepreneurial class emerging in northeastern Mexico after 1850, benefited enormously from these developments. Several built their fortunes on profits earned from the transportation of goods. Commerce remained rudimentary until the arrival of the railroad in the 1880s; until then transportation of goods was accomplished with mule trains. As well, an active and always colourful contraband trade persisted throughout the nineteenth century, and more than one Coahuilan merchant engaged in a combination of legal and illicit trade. Evaristo Madero, patriarch of the influential Madero family, used his revenue from trade and contraband as well as his personal connections in Texas and northeastern Mexico to build an economic empire based in Coahuila and including extensive interests in agriculture, mining, textiles, and banking.[9]

While the economic transformation of Piedras Negras and Coahuila's northern border region worked to the benefit of Mexican merchants, it also encouraged the American investment that helped seal that transformation. Commercial links between northern Coahuila and the United States, especially Texas, continued to be strong after the Civil War, when Americans established their own businesses on the other side of the international line. Some American companies even began to invest in the development of mines to the west of Piedras Negras, responding to rumours that the mountains were rich in silver and lead. An active trade existed between the towns of northern Coahuila and Texas, with corn, wheat, wool, raw sugar, hides, and goat-skins marketed in San Antonio and other Texas towns in return for raw cotton and manufactured goods. Despite the Texas-Coahuila border's well-deserved reputation as a lawless frontier still victimized by Indian raids, and despite American complaints of the arbitrary nature of the Mexican justice and taxation systems, American business interests continued to prosper.[10]

As the economic significance of Coahuila's border increased, so did the political importance of Piedras Negras and its customs

house. Events within Mexico demonstrated this new importance, and indicated the extent to which leaders of northeastern
Mexico would go to defy central control and to preserve their
economic and political independence.

This independent spirit was especially apparent during the
French Intervention, when the northeastern states of Nuevo
León, Tamaulipas, and Coahuila were incorporated into what
Mario Cerutti has referred to as an "economy of war."
The administrator of this self-contained system was Santiago
Vidaurri, who emerged as the fiercely independent strongman
of northeastern Mexico during the 1850s. Vidaurri used his
considerable influence to enlist the resources and support necessary to maintain a significant number of troops. His bold scheme
extended to the annexation of Coahuila, which remained part of
Nuevo León until 1864. To the further chagrin of the Mexican
government, Vidaurri controlled the customs houses along the
Rio Grande, and he even refused to give Benito Juárez customs
revenues needed to sustain the fight against the French intrud-
ers.[11] Only after the expulsion of the French did Juárez succeed
in breaking Vidaurri's control.

Under Vidaurri political and military power became linked
to the activities of northeastern Mexico's most important
businessmen. Merchants played a key role in financing local
armies during the mid-nineteenth century, and their support
was rewarded with favourable trading conditions. Vidaurri's
economy of war found especially strong patronage among
Monterrey's entrepreneurs, including Evaristo Madero (who had
established his transportation business in Monterrey in 1852),
Patricio Milmo, and the González Treviño family. These same
merchants became influential businessmen in Coahuila as well.
Support of Vidaurri's independent economic system soon translated into political power, and by the end of the nineteenth century several prosperous merchant families had come to occupy a
significant place in national society.[12]

In addition to Vidaurri's economy of war, there were other
obstacles to the imposition of central economic control. Chief
among these was the persistent contraband trade that had historically characterized the exchange of goods on both sides of the
Rio Grande, and that continued into the twentieth century. To
discourage this informal economic sector the Mexican government established a Zona Libre, or "free zone," in 1858. The
free zone allowed imported articles to enter Mexico free of

charge and was intended to enable residents of the border area to acquire basic necessities legally.[13] Yet instead of discouraging contraband, the Zona Libre apparently encouraged it by providing duty-free and therefore low-cost goods that became part of a lucrative trade beyond the borders of the zone itself. The northern border towns became mere "warehouses," providing illicit goods for points farther south. Even Evaristo Madero, once a participant in the contraband trade of the northern frontier, would later favour abolition of the free zone because it impeded regular commerce among residents of the Mexican border region.[14]

The government of Porfirio Díaz inherited the problem of contraband and general security on the northern frontier. Good relations with the United States hinged on protecting the legitimate transport of goods (and thus providing a favourable climate for American investment). American authorities frequently called for abolition of the Zona Libre. Finally, in 1905 Díaz abolished the free zone and established strict guidelines for inspecting and escorting all goods imported into Mexico. Coahuilan officials hailed the measure as a step that would help transform the border area into a productive economic region.[15]

In attempting to integrate Coahuila's border zone into the national economy and make it attractive to American investors, Díaz faced not only the defiance of border residents but also the determination of local officials to profit from the area's legitimate and informal economies. Local authorities, often with the sanction of the state government, extracted export fees to support the municipal government, and those fees often fluctuated in response to local "exigencies." Duties were collected on horses and cattle, but a merchant knowing the right people could make a private *arreglo* (arrangement) and receive a sizable discount.[16]

Coahuila's state government also attempted to appropriate customs duties for its own use. With its large areas of good grazing land, the Rio Grande District had attracted Texas cattlemen for many years. To encourage the development of the area Coahuilan officials had allowed these lands to be leased very cheaply and had forbidden the imposition of an export tax. When American property became abundant and more valuable, however, the state imposed a head tax on all exported cattle. Despite a national repeal of such "extraction" laws under the Díaz government, the Coahuilan legislature remained defiant and the state continued to collect its own cattle export tax. The determination of local and state officials to profit from the newly prosperous Rio Grande District and the inability of the central government to gain control of the situation ensured the persistence of an informal economic sector.[17]

Even in the contraband trade official connections were to be found. An interesting arrangement emerged during the governorship of José María Garza Galán in the 1880s. Relatives of the governor, apparently with his help and encouragement, did a brisk business passing various items across the border and beyond the Zona Libre, which still operated at that time. The efforts of Díaz and Bernardo Reyes to stop these activities revealed the involvement of local officials as well as members of the Mexican army entrusted with the pursuit and punishment of *contrabandistas*.[18] Reyes suggested that the governor's involvement may have been an attempt to deal with fiscal problems caused by Garza Galán's predecessor, who had left the state treasury empty, neglecting to pay government employees and perhaps the military as well.[19]

The extent to which members of the Mexican army were involved in contraband activities is impossible to determine. Yet the frequent complaints that military personnel were poorly paid and equipped in Coahuila lends credence to the claim that the army was a key player in this informal economic sector. In addition, national revolts and crises had a special character on this northern border. Military leaders as well as local officials tended to respond to such crises with opportunism rather than with genuine support of, or resistance to, the principals of the revolt itself.

Such was the case with Porfirio Díaz' revolt of La Noria in 1871-72, which sought to depose President Benito Juárez. Ill-prepared and provisioned, the Federal troops of Colonel Pedro A. Valdés were forced to evacuate Piedras Negras in 1871, leaving the town to Díaz supporters under Colonel Anacleto Falcón. As the newly installed officials lowered customs duties in an attempt to encourage imports and generate revenue, Valdés and his men retreated south. Yet rather than regroup for an offensive against Falcón, these soldiers used the opportunity to raid defenseless towns for money and goods. Valdés' men avoided confrontation with La Noria rebels. American Consul William Schuchardt remarked that Valdés and his men were acting more like enemy raiders than representatives of the government, and he explained such behaviour by the fact that these soldiers had not received their pay for a long time. Indeed, many soldiers apparently sold stolen goods on the other side of the international line, and after Falcón's troops forced him to cross into Texas, Valdéz attempted to recruit more men there with the promise that those who followed him back into Mexico could steal all they wanted.[20]

For the popular classes (rural and urban workers) living along Coahuila's border, economic integration, however grudgingly accomplished, meant a different challenge to their autonomy. Among smallholders in particular, the economic changes that occurred after mid-century and intensified during the Porfiriato constituted an attack on their very means of subsistence. This was especially the case after 1880, when the decrease in the incidence of Indian raids, and even more importantly, the coming of the railroad and the increasing value of land led to the expropriation of the lands of *campesinos* (peasants or rural labourers) throughout northern Mexico. The former military colonists and others who had benefited from the pattern of independent settlement in the region lost not only their lands but also their political autonomy.[21]

National and local laws promulgated between 1866 and 1883 promoted land concentration in several areas of Mexico, and especially in the northern states, which were less populated and integrated. Particularly during the Porfiriato, survey companies and businessmen were encouraged to claim and improve large tracts of undeveloped land. At the same time, Díaz offered free land and tax exemptions to those who would help settle such land. The real estate speculation that grew out of such national policies affected all areas of Coahuila. Stockholders of land survey companies took possession of large portions of *terrenos baldíos* (public lands), especially in the Rio Grande District and the central part of the state. Two such stockholders were generals Gerónimo Treviño and Francisco Naranjo, who received land in return for their services against the French and later in support of Díaz. Mexican businessmen and foreign entrepreneurs, including Evaristo Madero and Irishman Guillermo (William) Purcell, also acquired lands by taking advantage of Porfirian policies.[22]

As land values increased and foreign and Mexican investors sought to expand their holdings at the expense of communal properties (lands and resources available for common use) and smallholders, many in northern Coahuila lost their lands. As this process continued, disputes over scarce resources, especially water, also increased. In 1903 these disputes caused Governor Miguel Cárdenas, himself a beneficiary of land concentration, to pledge himself to the complete elimination of communal property.[23]

By the end of the nineteenth century competition for water in northern Coahuila was a major source of conflict among *hacendados* and between *hacendados* and smallholders. Range disputes were also common. In 1909 the *vecinos* (residents) of Gigedo in the Rio Grande District petitioned for the use of a road leading to the town of Nava that the agricultural company of the Garza Brothers had closed with barbed wire.[24] Complaints of this type were frequent as land became concentrated in fewer hands and as cattlemen in particular sought to enclose those lands. Some smallholders attempted to impose their own brand of justice, cutting newly erected barbed wire fences that deprived them of land or impeded their passage to other areas.[25]

The same competition for lands and water that displaced smallholders and produced discontent among the popular classes also affected the region's elites, and the increasing prevalence of foreign landowners in the area gave many disputes an anti-foreign tone. At the same time and despite the continuing transformation of the northern border, an informal economic sector continued to operate. Authority remained largely local, and even the army showed a remarkable flair for independence and entrepreneurship. This complex situation helped make Coahuila's northern border a centre of unrest and rebellion.

The political movement of Catarino E. Garza was emblematic of discord along the international frontier. In September 1891 Garza and his followers in the border regions of Coahuila, Nuevo León, and Tamaulipas published a revolutionary plan calling for the overthrow of Porfirio Díaz. Their revolt was to be carried out by a newly established rebel army that took as its banner the Constitution of 1857 and pledged to defend the principles of no re-election, political and economic freedom, and state and municipal sovereignty—principles that had been trampled upon by Díaz and his Tuxtepecan allies. The rebellion of the Catarinistas began with a small and seemingly insignificant raid from Garza's base in south Texas into Tamaulipas.

It continued sporadically throughout the rest of the year, with Mexicans on both sides of the border echoing Garza's call for revolt. The movement seemed to fade, however, with the capture by American officials of several Catarinista rebels and Garza's reported flight to Florida.[26]

A native of Matamoros, Tamaulipas, Garza had been educated in Texas and Mexico before entering the Mexican army. Charged with insubordination, he had fled to Texas, where he established himself as a journalist in several south Texas towns. In Eagle Pass, Garza had published a paper that regularly attacked José María Garza Galán, the Coahuilan governor imposed by Díaz in 1886. In 1887 Garza Galán had unsuccessfully petitioned U.S. officials for Garza's extradition. The Porfirian governor also attempted to have the border rebel assassinated.[27] Texas newspapers disagreed as to whether Catarino Garza was a "border ruffian" or a popular and well-educated journalist obsessed with overthrowing Díaz. Matías Romero, Mexican ambassador to the United States, dismissed the Garza revolt as the work of "fugitives, malcontents, seditious refugees, and idlers" who were found in abundance along the Mexican-Texas border.[28]

Garza's following in the Coahuilan border region, although difficult to document, was of some significance. It included Marcos Benavides, uncle of the young Francisco I. Madero and a prominent landowner not only in northern Coahuila but also in the southwestern part of the state. Benavides and other Coahuilans were eventually established as a contingent of the Garza "army" known as the "Guerrilleros de Coahuila." Catarinismo also counted among its supporters the journalist Paulino Martínez, who later became an ally of Francisco Madero and who endorsed the latter's efforts to end the Díaz regime.[29]

Although the Catarinista movement itself had sputtered out by 1893, other political and reform movements continued to find support in northern Coahuila into the next century. Indeed, the Rio Grande District would be an active centre of pre-revolutionary unrest and revolutionary fighting. Because the northern border zone, more than any other region of the frontier state of Coahuila, had developed a tradition of independent development and political and economic autonomy, further attempts of the Mexican government to centralize its control would here meet adamant resistance.

Central Coahuila

Central Coahuila, or the Monclova District, from which the 1896 Conspiracy of Monclova sprang, experienced much the same pattern of development as the northern region, and by 1900 was undergoing its own economic transformation largely due to development of mining. Sparsely settled by *presidio* and mission since late-colonial times, this expansive area was also home to at least a few military colonies during the nineteenth century, most notably the *colonia* located in the northernmost municipality of Múzquiz.

Throughout the colonial period most of this sparsely settled region had been given over to cattle ranching, which, along with agriculture, was the basis of Coahuila's economy during the Porfirian era. By the late eighteenth century much of this district had come under the control of the great *latifundio* (estate) of the Sánchez Navarro family, which supplied Coahuila's *presidios* and missions. This estate, formed by the heirs of one of Saltillo's original Spanish founders, came to encompass a large portion of Coahuila and, at over sixteen million acres, was the largest *latifundio* in all of Mexico. Its growth occurred through proper legal channels but often at the expense of small-scale farmers and ranchers. Despite their success as landowners, the Sanchez Navarros erred politically when they decided to support the French Intervention. They thus incurred the wrath of Benito Juárez and Mexican liberals, who ordered the confiscation of their *latifundio*. As the Sánchez Navarro estate began to dissolve, much of its land became the property of prominent political and military figures in northeastern Mexico. [30]

Land concentration continued to affect the Monclova District in the latter part of the nineteenth century, facilitated by national laws issued during the Porfiriato and the liberal governments that preceded it, and by concessions granted to survey companies. Such concessions provided generals Gerónimo Treviño and Francisco Naranjo with vast estates in central Coahuila. Survey companies also acquired lands for two of Coahuila's prominent Porfirian governors, General José María Garza Galán and Miguel Cárdenas.[31]

Land concentration in central Coahuila, as in the north, proceeded at the expense of smallholders and residents of communal lands. The vast *hacienda* La Babia of General Treviño came to supplant the military colony located in the municipality of Múzquiz, undoubtedly displacing the colony's inhabitants.[32]

The attempts of a new group of landowners to enclose their properties mirrored events in Coahuila's border area, as did the numerous disputes over water. The Nadadores River was a particular source of contention in central Coahuila. The appropriation of its waters by Governor Garza Galán in the late nineteenth century not only deprived owners of small agricultural holdings, but also caused disputes among the Monclova District's more prominent landowners. In 1895 Emilio Carranza, a farmer and cattleman in the region, petitioned General Bernardo Reyes for help in reclaiming the waters of the Río Nadadores. Several years later Reyes recommended that a commission be sent to resolve the Nadadores issue. Apparently no settlement was reached and conflicts continued.[33] In 1898 Martín Morales and Francisco García Letona brought suit against Guillermo Richardson, owner of the *hacienda* La Jalpa. Richardson was charged with changing the course of a local supply of running water, thereby depriving others of this scarce resource.[34] Quarrels over water and rangeland continued in the Monclova District throughout the Porfiriato.

As in the northern part of the state, resource disputes in central Coahuila were a product of the transformation of the local economy from one of largely self-sufficient agriculture and cattle ranching to one increasingly tied to international markets and gradually integrated into greater Mexico. This transformation was due to the development of mining after 1880, which was itself aided by the arrival of the railroad and by the subsequent influx of investment capital from Mexicans and foreigners. The exploitation of lead, copper, zinc, silver, and coal affected the entire region by spurring the development of new towns and the revival of older population centres. The mining of coal was of particular significance: by the turn of the century Coahuila was Mexico's main supplier of this resource.[35]

A revision of Mexico's mining code in 1884 transferred subsoil rights to those owning the land, breaking the colonial tradition that all minerals and precious metals belonged to Crown or nation. The new code allowed mining claims to be freely bought and sold. As a result José María Garza Galán was able to acquire all rights to coal contained in the area of San Juan de Sabinas. By 1905 he had sold his claim to the Compañía Carbonífera de Sabinas, which included members of the Madero family as principal stockholders, and thus was one of only a few Mexican-owned mining companies operating during the Porfiriato.[36]

The development of mining had a significant impact on other

aspects of the region's economy. It boosted agricultural and cattle production, which now responded to the increasing needs of the new mining sector. Carbonífera de Sabinas, for example, had numerous contracts with local *hacendados* who provided food for mining communities. Such arrangements were an added impetus to land concentration, as a few *hacendados* sought to monopolize this lucrative enterprise. Mines throughout northern Mexico became their own self-contained social and economic systems. Rosita, Coahuila, for example, had its own schools, hospital, and post office, all under the control of Carbonífera de Sabinas. Rosita also attracted merchants from surrounding areas, who brought their goods to the mining town for sale.[37]

In mining as in most sectors of Coahuila's expanding economy, competition between Mexican and foreign investors was often strong. By 1909 the most productive of Coahuila's coal mines were under the control of the American Smelting and Refining Company (ASARCO) of the Guggenheim family. Yet Mexican entrepreneurs continued to invest in this sector of the economy. Chief among them was the Madero family. Investors in coal mines and in most other sectors of the state's economy, the Maderos were staunch competitors and at times political opponents of ASARCO and other foreign companies. By the early twentieth century the Madero family was one of the few Mexican families still active in the mining sector, and they owned the only non-foreign smelter in Coahuila.[38]

The growth of mining in the Monclova District was accompanied by the development of the region's other resources. The exploitation of guayule, which was processed into an elastic rubber gum and exported to England, Germany, and the United States, became an important activity and, like mining, involved both foreign and national investment. The extraction and processing of this resource also became a virtual foreign monopoly. The Continental Rubber Company of the Rockefellers, based in New York, controlled most of the state's guayule resources. The chief Mexican competitor of Continental Rubber was, once again, the Madero family, which also engaged in the cutting and processing of guayule through its company Las Filipinas.[39]

In addition to generating often fierce competition between foreigners and Mexicans, Coahuila's mineral resources inevitably brought intervention by the central government. Discovery of the rich resources of Sierra Mojada immediately generated a jurisdictional dispute between Coahuila and the neighbouring state of Durango. The Díaz regime decreed this area a federal territory in 1879, naming General Francisco Zérega as its military commander. Sierra Mojada became a part of Coahuila in 1880, but because of continuing competition over its resources it remained under close supervision of the state and central Mexican governments.[40]

As one of Mexico's richest sources of lead and ores and a major supplier of these minerals to the United States, Sierra Mojada was of great interest to American investors. A U.S. consulate was briefly established there during the 1890s. Díaz attempted to encourage American investment throughout Coahuila's mining region, but not all Mexicans were receptive. Local officials, themselves involved in the lucrative business, blocked American efforts to engage in mining. Members of the Mexican army also attempted to profit from the situation, claiming American mining rights for themselves and helping Mexican companies jump American claims in return for part of the profits.[41]

As the central region underwent the transformation from a highly self-sufficient cattle and agricultural economy to a more modern, market-oriented economy, it became home to an increasingly modern workforce that distinguished northern Mexico from the rest of the country. Coahuila's mining region depended largely on migrant workers, who were attracted to labour-poor Coahuila by high wages. Foreign workers (predominantly Americans) were also present in some Coahuilan mines. At the same time, however, frequent fluctuations in international prices and markets made the workers' employment insecure, and frequent work stoppages occurred.[42]

In addition to being at the mercy of market forces, Coahuila's miners were also often at the mercy of the mining companies. Frequent complaints surfaced over the *tienda de raya*, or company store, which was often the only source of basic necessities for the miner and his family. Mining companies periodically attempted to pay workers in store coupons instead of cash, and advancement of store credits encouraged indebtedness. The safety of the mines was also a key issue, and discrimination by foreign companies against Mexican workers (blocking Mexicans from advancing into managerial positions) was another frequent cause of complaint.[43] Open conflict in Coahuila's mining region surfaced over wages, inadequate housing and living arrangements, and dangerous working conditions. Most commonly such conflicts took the form of strikes and pillaging of the company store, the latter form of protest often being led by the female relatives of miners.[44]

Miners' grievances were just beginning to be channeled into organized activity on the eve of the Mexican Revolution. Anarcho-syndicalism found adherents among some of northern Mexico's miners and offered a plan of action against mining companies and employers, as well as an outlet for the anti-foreign sentiment that was prevalent in many mining communities. Mine workers were especially drawn to the Mexican Liberal Party (PLM), which was established in 1905 and embraced a program of social and political reform that included benefits for workers. The proximity of the U.S. border, which was a main zone of PLM activity, also encouraged the penetration of anarcho-syndicalist ideas. Miners in northern Mexico may also have been politicized through their experiences working in the mines of the American southwest, where the Western Federation of Miners was active.[45] As the heart of Mexico's coal region, Coahuila itself was the home of one of the country's first miners' unions. The Unión de Mineros Mexicanos (UMM) was established in July of 1911, emerging out of a syndicate already established in Rosita, which became the seat of the UMM. Several members of the UMM would readily join insurgent forces during the Mexican Revolution.[46]

The Laguna

The 1896 plot against Porfirio Díaz that generated rebel activity in both northern and central Coahuila also had echoes in the Laguna region, situated in southwestern Coahuila and contained within the political district of Viesca. Manuel Sarabia, suspected instigator of the Conspiracy of Monclova, had apparently been in contact with Hilario Siller, a fellow spiritist from this area, and Toribio Regalado, a landowner of modest means.[47] In this corner of the state as elsewhere, the conspiracy was played out amid economic development and transformation. The Comarca Lagunera (encompassing the Coahuila towns of San Pedro, Matamoros, Viesca, and Torreón, as well as Mapimí, Lerdo, and Gómez Palacio in the neighbouring state of Durango) was emerging as a new socio-economic region, aided by the construction of irrigation works and by the breakup of large estates, both of which set the stage for the growth of the Laguna's cotton industry. The railroad arrived in the

1880s, connecting the zone to Mexico City and to the United States border towns of El Paso and Eagle Pass. The Laguna soon became the country's principal producer of cotton, helping to supply the growing textile industry in Porfirio Díaz' Mexico.[48]

The new economic importance of the Laguna generated increased competition over water and land. Resource disputes continued to divide the region's elite landowners throughout the Porfiriato. Competition also took the form of an ongoing struggle between the landed and the landless, making agrarian unrest part of the Laguna's modern history.

As in other areas of Coahuila, landowners in the Laguna had developed a tradition of allowing independent farmers to settle on their lands in order to help against nomadic Indian raids. The farmers of these collective settlements, or *congregaciones*, frequently demanded legal possession of the lands.[49] These shareholders, as well as small-scale farmers, also struggled to establish independent towns by legally acquiring communal (or *ejidal*) plots. In the 1860s President Benito Juárez had attempted to calm agrarian strife in the Laguna by carving the town of Matamoros out of the *latifundio* of Leonardo Zuloaga. San Pedro emerged in the same way: the confiscated lands of *hacendados* who supported the French Intervention of the 1860s were given to resident smallholders in 1870 by liberal governor Victoriano Cepeda. Other small plots in the Laguna went to loyal veterans of the struggle against the French.[50]

The establishment of independent settlements and the parcelling out of confiscated lands after mid-century was not a permanent solution to the Laguna's agrarian problem, particularly as competition for land and water increased. Although the breakup of the region's *latifundias* sometimes worked to the advantage of smallholders, it more often benefited northern Mexico's emerging business class. This group simply utilized lands from the Laguna's older *haciendas* to create more modern estates. During the Porfiriato, independent agricultural colonies like Matamoros and San Pedro faced additional obstacles in their battle for lands and water, as national policies encouraged further land concentration and as foreigners became the majority of landowners and renters in the Laguna.[51]

The Laguna's newly prosperous cotton industry likewise affected the region's large population of sharecroppers, or *aparceros*. With the influx of a new, mobile labour force from south and central Mexico, sharecroppers, once an important reserve labour supply, were no longer as useful. And as the Laguna's *hacendados* responded to the economic boom by placing more land under cultivation and expanding their irrigation works, less water was available for the small plots of sharecroppers. The fate of the Laguna's *aparceros* is unknown, but their discontent perhaps contributed to the agrarian unrest that continued to characterize this area.[52]

The cotton boom that contributed to this unrest also caused a burst of industrial development in southwestern Coahuila. After 1880 the textile, cotton-seed processing, guayule, and mining and smelting industries all found a home in the Laguna. Torreón, a town that emerged almost overnight as a railroad centre and crossing point of the Central and Mexican International railroads, became the region's bustling centre, replacing the older agricultural town of Matamoros.[53]

Rapid economic growth also made a significant mark on the society of this region. The sudden influx of capital and entrepreneurial talent from outside the region helped create a society of landowners and businessmen who were progressive and future oriented. Investment in the new economy flowed in from prominent families of northern Mexico, including the Corrals of Sonora, the Terrazas of Chihuahua, and the Maderos based in Coahuila and Nuevo León. Prominent national figures such as Francisco Bulnes (a Ceintífico congressman and apologist for the Díaz regime) and José Yves Limantour (another Científico who served as Díaz' finance minister) also played roles in the development of the Laguna. Above all, the Laguna became a centre of foreign investment. Italians, French, Belgians, Germans, Spaniards, Chinese, British, and Americans became landowners and engaged in a variety of extractive industries. German businessmen, as well as the American Smelting and Refining Company of the Guggenheim family, were prominent in mining; John D. Rockefeller's Continental Rubber Company was dominant in the guayule industry; and the British invested heavily in agriculture. Prominent Mexican landowners in the Laguna numbered only four: Práxedis de la Peña, Amador Cárdenas, Carlos González, and the Madero family.[54]

With its significant industrial growth accompanied by the development of commerce, banking, and the service sector, the Laguna was also fertile ground for the growth of a sizable middle class. Here too foreigners were prominent, dominating skilled urban and industrial jobs. Mexicans also found their places as craftsmen, clerks, managers, and professionals.

The increasing importance of the Laguna inevitably generated competition among regional elites. The interference of the central government, which began in earnest during the Porfiriato, complicated the situation and demonstrated that in this corner of Coahuila as well economic autonomy was a prized possession. This became particularly apparent in the spring of 1881, when over three hundred armed landowners and rural workers from southwestern Coahuila invaded the neighbouring state of Durango. Accompanied by the municipal president of San Pedro, Epitacio Sifuentes, and by Carlos González (*hacendado* and local political boss of Viesca), *hacendados* and owners of more modest estates, along with agricultural workers, moved swiftly to destroy the irrigation works of Durango landowner Ulpiano Lavín. When the invaders withdrew several days later, they had ruined several bridges and filled in irrigation canals that threatened to deprive them of water from the Nazas River.

Accustomed to such frontier justice tactics, and himself a landowner in Coahuila's Laguna region, which depended on the uninterrupted flow of the Nazas from the upper river zone in Durango, Coahuila's governor Evaristo Madero took no action, assuming the matter was "happily" ended. Indeed, Madero's only real complaint was that Federal troops had meddled in the affair. Similar invasions had occurred since the 1860s, reflecting the determination of Coahuilans to safeguard their share of the waters of the Nazas. The legal dispute that ensued in the aftermath of the 1881 invasion, however, involved not only the governors of Coahuila and Durango but also the federal government. By 1888 a new federal law had made the central government the arbiter of future disputes over the Nazas River, illustrating the extent to which that government was determined to inject itself into this newly prosperous region. One of the first significant products of central involvement was a sizeable concession of water rights to the foreign-owned Tlahualilo Company. This concession was intended to encourage the development of lands in Durango's Laguna region, and was destined to provoke anew the anger of the landowners of the lower Nazas zone in Coahuila.[55]

The 1881 Nazas dispute illustrated the resolve of local landowners to safeguard their rights to a scarce resource, but it also demonstrated a phenomenon that would recur during the Mexican Revolution: the co-operation of *hacendados* and their workers. This phenomenon was a product of the modern work relations that emerged in the Laguna, as well as an expression of the unique social milieu characteristic of the region by the late nineteenth century. Just as the Laguna's elite represented a progressive business class rather than a traditional regional elite, so too was the Laguna's workforce "modern" in the sense that it was mobile and lacked traditional ties to the region. Most workers came from central Mexico to work in the cotton fields, help in the cutting and processing of guayule, work in the mines along the Laguna's western border, and provide labour for other new industries. Because of the sudden and explosive demand for labour that could not be met by the Laguna's native population, and because of competition for labourers among the different economic sectors, workers in this region enjoyed some of the highest wages in Mexico. Labourers on the cotton plantations received the highest agricultural wages in Mexico, and were paid in cash rather than in coupons good only in the *hacienda* store.[56]

These agricultural workers, the largest sector of the Laguna's workforce, had not been deprived of their own lands, nor did they labour under the odious system of debt peonage. Indeed, in addition to their relatively high wages, unskilled agricultural workers often benefited from *hacendados'* enlightened approach towards their workforce, which included the establishment of schools and provision of health care and other benefits. Seasonal cotton pickers formed an additional element of the Laguna's agricultural labour force. Some forty thousand migrant workers poured into the Laguna between August and November to help with the harvest. For many, the Laguna was part of a continuing migration that also involved seasonal work in the United States. As different industries competed for their labour, this seasonal workforce became increasingly vocal, demanding higher pay and better conditions.[57]

Laguna society, modern and prosperous, characterized by an innovative, entrepreneurial spirit, was also reflected in the region's modern *hacienda*. Tied to regional and national markets, the Laguna's *haciendas* were run like specialized businesses, making use of new technology in irrigation and importing high-quality cotton seed from the United States. Mexican *hacendados* in the Laguna, moreover, personified the social mobility that characterized this frontier area. Many had started as merchants, moneylenders, miners, and industrialists in other areas of northern Mexico.[58]

Many other landowners began as *hacienda* administrators or as renters of *hacienda* lands. Such was the case with several of the employees of the *hacienda* La Concha of Carlos González Montes de Oca. Much like Evaristo Madero, González had begun to acquire land in the Laguna with the help of revenues from his family's transportation business. During the first years of La Concha, cash income needed for the construction of irrigation works and the initial development of the *hacienda* came from rentals of land. By 1910 many of La Concha's renters were owners of their own plots. In addition, several high-level employees of La Concha (administrators, accountants, office personnel) enjoyed a remarkable degree of social mobility during the Porfiriato. Many became landowners after the Mexican Revolution.[59]

The careers of Evaristo Madero and other Laguna entrepreneurs, as well as the existence of a well-paid, mobile, and increasingly vocal labour force, testified to the region's dynamism. At the same time, however, the northern tradition of independence still held sway, as private armies and justice systems prevailed. The persistence of such independent forms of control was apparent in 1881 when, as mentioned above, rural workers and landowners, including the newly prosperous *hacendado* Carlos González, defied the central government, and solved a water dispute by force of arms.

Southeastern Coahuila

The 1896 Conspiracy of Monclova, which found adherents in many areas of Coahuila, apparently had no echo in the state's southeastern region. Yet the southeast (including the political districts of Saltillo and Parras) was also affected by the economic transformation that began to occur after the mid-nineteenth century and that was sealed by the arrival of the railroad. Here too the transformation caused not only growth but also social change and unrest.

Although primarily an agricultural region through much of the nineteenth century, southeastern Coahuila also included the state capital of Saltillo, which since the colonial era had developed as a major commercial centre. Saltillo began as a *presidio* designed to aid Spanish efforts in pacifying the Indian frontier. Its good climate, abundant water, and strategic location (which served as a jumping-off point for those headed to Texas, Nuevo León, and Tamaulipas) ensured Saltillo's survival despite the continued threat of Indian attacks. In the aftermath of Mexico's struggle for independence Saltillo retained its importance,

and served as a link between the fertile Laguna region and
Monterrey, capital and industrial centre of the neighbouring
state of Nuevo León. During the Mexican–American War
Saltillo was briefly occupied by American troops, and at the
height of the French Intervention Benito Juárez established his
national government there. Juárez was well received in the
Saltillo area, and his popularity extended throughout southern
Coahuila, at least in part because of his attempts to address the
Laguna's agrarian problem. This popularity meant that Díaz'
initial revolt against the central government garnered no real
support in this region.[60]

The economic developments of the late nineteenth century
as well as its position as the seat of state government ensured
Saltillo and southeastern Coahuila a prominent place in Porfirian
Mexico. During the latter part of the nineteenth century, telegraph and railroad lines connected Saltillo to the international
border and to central Mexico. For a time, Saltillo was the
terminus of the Mexican International Railroad and thus a major
centre of Mexico's export trade. The city shipped goatskins, istle
(a coarse fiber from the agave plant used to make thread, rope,
and paper), and lead ore to New York; grain and vegetables to
San Antonio, Texas; and lumber gathered from the surrounding
sierras to Monterrey. By the turn of the century, an industrial
zone had emerged in the capital and its environs. The cotton
boom in the Laguna encouraged the growth of the textile industry, and several new textile factories sprang up. Paper factories
as well as wheat mills also helped fuel the growth of southeastern Coahuila, as did Guillermo Purcell's establishment of a metal
foundry in Saltillo in 1904. Nearby Parras, the other important
town of the southeast, emerged as a centre of viticulture. Along
with the Laguna and Monclova regions, the Saltillo-Parras zone
came to contain Coahuila's most important families. And like
Torreón, Saltillo became home to a sizeable foreign community,
consisting primarily of Americans but also including Spaniards,
Italians, British, Germans, French, and a few Chinese.[61]

The social and economic transformation of the southeast mirrored events in the rest of Coahuila. The dissolution of great
colonial estates during the mid-nineteenth century altered the
agrarian structure. The great estate of the Sánchez Navarros,
which extended into this area, was among those transformed
into individual *haciendas* and smaller *ranchos*. Progressive *hacendados*, several engaged in viticulture, came to replace the great

property holders of the colonial and early independence periods. Here too land concentration mixed uneasily with smallholdings, and a non-native (and more mobile) rural workforce increased in size. In the larger towns, and especially in Saltillo, a class of largely non-native urban workers also emerged, as did a growing middle class of shop owners, teachers, small-scale merchants, office workers, and government functionaries. Several entrepreneurial families, most from northeastern Mexico, were joined by increasing numbers of foreign investors as they sought to reap the benefits of Coahuila's transformation.[62]

Camarilla Politics and Porfirian Centralization

The economic transformation of Coahuila had already begun in 1876 when the Tuxtepec revolt brought Porfirio Díaz to power. The initial arbiters of this transformation were members of a new capitalist class mostly from northeastern Mexico. Injecting themselves into the Coahuilan economy at a time when political and economic autonomy was still the norm, these emerging elites built their fortunes without real assistance or interference from the centre. Economic development and solutions to economic problems remained matters of local initiative. While Porfirian policies and laws, specifically those encouraging land concentration, allowed many budding capitalists and ambitious military men to take better advantage of the situation, such policies simply complemented a process already underway. Nevertheless, the Díaz regime hastened this transformation and increased tensions already being fuelled by economic dislocation and competition. The imposition of the Porfirian political system also had repercussions.

Porfirian centralization arrived with a vengeance in 1884 when Díaz ordered the ouster of Governor Evaristo Madero. Patriarch of one of the most influential families in northeastern Mexico and a personal friend of former president Manuel González, Madero had developed a reputation for political and economic independence. To Díaz himself Madero was perhaps best known for his opposition to the Tuxtepec revolt. Indeed, Díaz was generally wary of Coahuila because of its tradition of independence and its lukewarm support for his 1876 rebellion. Concurrent with Governor Madero's expulsion, Federal soldiers attacked the Madero *hacienda* El Rosario, centre of the family's economic empire and birthplace of Francisco I. Madero.[63] This event marked the beginning of the political and economic persecution of the Madero family that would continue into the 1900s.

Díaz further increased his control over northeastern Mexico in 1885 when he named General Bernardo Reyes commander of the Third Military Zone, encompassing the states of Coahuila, Nuevo León, Tamaulipas, and San Luis Potosí. A native of Jalisco and veteran of the war against the French, Reyes had loyally served both Benito Juárez and Sebastián Lerdo de Tejada. And although he somewhat belatedly supported Díaz, he quickly emerged as the Porfirian strongman of northeastern Mexico. In Coahuila, Reyes became the key to the central government's manipulation of local politics.

By the late nineteenth century, Coahuilan politics was characterized not by formal institutions, but by informal arrangements based on kinship and business ties. Political participation was the province of a small group of extended families and economic partners, and by the 1890s three cliques dominated the state's political life. The oldest such clique, or *camarilla,* was led by Evaristo Madero, whose economic empire and political influence were concentrated in the southeastern municipality of Parras and in the Rio Grande District of northern Coahuila. José María Garza Galán, and the Garza Galán family itself, led a second faction based in the Monclova District of central Coahuila and centred in the municipality of Múzquiz. The third and newest group was led by Miguel Cárdenas, a lawyer and *hacendado* from the Monclova district, who was emerging as the progressive leader of choice for Coahuila's growing professional class and for many of the state's *hacendados.* The Cárdenas *camarilla* was also based in the state's mining region, and it came to include members of the Carranza family.[64]

While each of these cliques was a product of local ties, each also had connections with national political life. Despite an uneasy relationship with Díaz himself, Evaristo Madero maintained good relations with José Yves Limantour, the Científico finance minister who served the aging dictator. The Garza Galán faction also had Científico connections, with Díaz' father-in-law Manuel Romero Rubio. The Cárdenas faction, in turn, was increasingly identified with Díaz' strongman in northeastern Mexico, General Bernardo Reyes.[65]

Coahuila's cliquish and informal political system came under increasing assault during the Porfiriato. While Díaz and Reyes worked within the confines of *camarilla* politics in an attempt to manipulate Coahuilan elites, the broader effect of their efforts was to undermine local political arrangements, and to challenge the state's political autonomy. This was particularly clear during state elections, which Coahuila's prominent families and entrepreneurs had become accustomed to orchestrating. Now, under the watchful gaze of Reyes, such elections became mere formalities. Municipal and state officials were imposed, and Reyes often made use of his military subordinates to ensure electoral outcomes.[66]

The erosion of local political arrangements began in the immediate aftermath of Governor Evaristo Madero's ouster. In 1886 Díaz and Reyes imposed José María Garza Galán, a veteran of the Tuxtepec revolt, as governor. Garza Galán's administration continued many of the personalistic practices characteristic of nineteenth-century Cohauilan politics. But the governor was also increasingly obliged to do the bidding of the central government. The Garza Galán governorship marked the beginning of a new political era, one in which Coahuila's highly localized and informal power relationships would be compelled to adapt in the face of centralization.

In the spirit of *camarilla* competition, Garza Galán used his new-found political clout to extend his personal influence and that of his political faction beyond his family's base in Múzquiz. Encouraged by Reyes and Díaz, Garza Galán also made use of the institution of the *jefatura política*. In Coahuila *jefes políticos* (or political bosses) had been employed during the early nineteenth century as a means of increasing state authority over municipalities. Designated and removed by the governor, they had extensive formal and informal powers, including control over elections, armed forces, the military draft, taxation, public security, and the allocation of water, land, and mining rights. Abolished by the 1869 state constitution, the institution had been revived in the 1870s. In Coahuila, it became a key to the centralizing efforts of both Díaz and Garza Galán.[67]

During the governorship of Garza Galán jefaturas existed in the five political districts of Coahuila: Saltillo, Parras, Viesca, Monclova, and Rio Grande. The governor also established five new *jefaturas*, all within the booming mining region of the Monclova District. Here a population of increasingly vocal miners, railroad workers, and other labourers contributed to an atmosphere of political unrest.[68] Not surprisingly, given the intimate connection between political and economic activities in late-nineteenth-century Coahuila, Garza Galán designated friends and family as *jefes*. These men used the posts to their personal benefit. In Sierra del Carmen, Garza Galán's uncle and half-brother shared the post of *jefe político*, using their position to enjoy the profits of this important mining region. In the strategic border town of Piedras Negras (which was renamed Ciudad Porfirio Díaz in 1888) another uncle held the post, and received land and a streetcar contract in the bargain.[69]

For many Coahuilans imposition of *jefes políticos* during the governorship of Garza Galán represented the ultimate affront to local autonomy. Although the institution was not new, its most recent incarnation significantly undermined the *camarilla* system and its ability to direct local or municipal political arrangements. Many of Garza Galán's *jefes* nullified municipal elections (an 1891 federal law even allowed governors to name *jefes* instead of holding local elections), and *jefaturas* were sometimes crafted with the intent of undermining the influence of rival political groups. This was particularly the case in Parras and the Laguna region, where *jefaturas* became a means of weakening the influence of the Madero family, one of Díaz' main political objectives. Further insult was added in 1890 when Garza Galán placed the financial burden of supporting Coahuila's *jefaturas* on the municipalities themselves.[70]

Adding to the strain of political centralization were the economic policies imposed by Díaz and Garza Galán. Taxes on mid-sized urban and rural properties hurt the nascent middle class, while an 1894 state law ordered privatization of all communal lands, which were immediately grabbed by large landowners, especially foreigners. Federalization of water rights in the 1890s also had a significant economic and political impact. Finally, economic concessions and tax exemptions under Garza Galán increasingly excluded significant elements of Coahuila's economic elite.[71]

State and national economic policies, as well as the political centralization that alienated many Coahuilans, helped generate conflict and ultimately rebellion. When Garza Galán began a second term as governor after the electoral farce of 1889, an opposition society was established in Coahuila. Rebellion finally broke out in several parts of the state when the Porfirian governor announced his intention to run for yet another re-election.

The revolt of August 1893 involved important elements of Coahuilan society. In the Monclova District the Carranza brothers played a major role. Emilio Carranza led the attack in Ocampo, while Jesús and Sebastián rallied mine workers and ranchers in Sierra Mojada. Venustiano Carranza helped coordinate strategy but took no part in the fighting. In the Río Grande District and the Laguna region the Madero clique was active, with Evaristo threatening to revolt and relative Marcos Benavides providing arms to the rebels of northern Coahuila and joining them in their depredations for a few days. Planters of the Laguna's lower river zone, disgruntled over the Tlahualilo concession and the central government's increasing control of water allocation, joined the call for Garza Galán's ouster.[72] The Catarinista movement, which had faltered after its abortive rebellion of 1891-92 enjoyed a brief resurgence in Coahuila's northern border region at the beginning of the year. Many of its adherents joined in the uprising against Garza Galán.

Although intended as a revolt to unseat Garza Galán, the rebellion itself involved a series of strikes against local officials, the symbols of a new era of Profirian and Galanista central-ization. In several towns, members of Coahuila's elite political factions led local inhabitants in deposing those imposed author-ities and replacing them with leaders of their own choosing. The rebellion also caused a brief wave of banditry.[73] Both of these patterns would surface again in the 1910-11 revolution of Francisco I. Madero.

Díaz and Reyes moved quickly to end the rebellion without alienating key members of Coahuila's cliquish political and eco-nomic system, whose support was still a critical part of the Porfirian regime's delicate game of control. Rebels achieved the ouster of Garza Galán; the emerging and increasingly impor-tant *camarilla* led by Miguel Cárdenas, who himself had been a candidate for governor in 1893, emerged as the overall winner. Cárdenas would soon become Coahuila's governor with the help of Bernardo Reyes. The Carranza family, supporters of Cárdenas, was also rewarded with certain concessions. The family was allowed political control of its home base of Cuatro Ciénegas, and Emilio Carranza and others were given legis-lative posts. Emilio's brother Venustiano, who had established himself as an *hacendado* of modest means in central Coahuila, enjoyed another stint as municipal president of Cuatro Ciénegas after being removed from that position under the Garza Galán administration. He would also serve brief terms as state senator and interim governor. The Carranza family received economic concessions as well in the form of lower taxes and grants of federal lands.[74] Not surprisingly, the Madero family received few concessions after the revolt. While Díaz recognized that the Madero *camarilla* was still a significant force, he continued his attempts to undermine its political power, often by stalling when the Madero family requested economic favours.[75]

Significantly, too, Díaz and Reyes quietly worked to retain the support of the Garza Galán faction. Through his willingness as governor to do the bidding of the centre, José María Garza Galán had proved himself pliable. He (and his *camarilla*) continued to be an asset to Díaz, and could potentially serve to offset the growing strength of the political faction led by Miguel Cárdenas and including the Carranza family. Thus economic aid (primarily in the form of tax exemptions) continued to flow to the Garza Galáns, and Reyes chose five delegates from the Garza Galán clique to serve in the state legislature in the aftermath of the 1893 revolt. Even after Garza Galán's death in 1902, his son Andrés (who assumed control of the family businesses) continued to enjoy the assistance of the Díaz regime.[76]

Reyes and Díaz also responded to grievances against the *jefes políticos* that had surfaced with the rebellion and were a major impetus for revolt. Except in the important economic centres of Sierra Mojada and Torreón, *jefaturas* were abolished. Informally, however, the practice of manipulating municipal politics from the centre continued. Indeed, as governor, Miguel Cárdenas assisted Reyes in designating *jefes* to govern at the local level. Thus while the 1893 rebels achieved both the ouster of Garza Galán and the official abolition of the hated *jefaturas*, Reyes and Díaz continued to erode Coahuilan autonomy. Immediately after the revolt Reyes prepared electoral slates for Coahuila's municipalities to ensure the victory of desirable candidates. Meanwhile, Miguel Cárdenas, aware of the changing political climate, looked increasingly to the central government (and to Reyes) for patronage.[77]

As an Indian frontier far from the centre of power, nineteenth-century Coahuila developed a tradition of local autonomy, political independence, and economic self-sufficiency. The emergence of a new entrepreneurial class, the growth of a substantial middle class, and the steady increase in foreign investment began to transform the state's economy after 1850. A modern and largely non-native workforce was also central to this transformation, which would link Coahuila to outside markets and transform its society. At the same time, however, older forms persisted, clashing with the modernizing mission of the Porfiriato. Dislocations were inevitable, especially in northern and central Coahuila, with their heritage of communal landholding. The Laguna too had retained its shareholders and independent farmers, who would resist land concentration through banditry and rebellion.

Coahuila's economic growth was accompanied by the development of a political system dominated by three cliques that incorporated a small group of extended families and business partners. While these political elites welcomed modernization, they were, like the popular sectors, affected by the increasing competition for resources that such modernization created. Porfirian political centralization, moreover, was not always welcomed by local elites, many of whom had built their fortunes in the absence of central control or regulation. The rebellion of 1893 and the key role played by the opposition to *jefaturas* demonstrated the extent to which local autonomy was an issue that would drive Coahuilans to revolt. The more shadowy Conspiracy of Monclova, which took place three years later, invoked the same desire for independence in its call for a revolution "in the spirit of Hidalgo." By 1900 the issue of self-determination had become a rallying point not only for many of Coahuila's elites but also for members of the popular classes and the emerging middle class. The grievances caused by centralization, as well as the dislocations resulting from economic and social transformations, would find expression in the reform movements emerging after 1900.

2

Porfirian Politics
and the Growth
of Maderismo

Coahuila's political situation remained volatile in the aftermath of the 1893 revolt. The overthrow of José María Garza Galán did not significantly weaken his *camarilla* or dampen the political aspirations of its members. Díaz and Reyes took pains to placate the Carranza family, but those efforts did not ensure loyalty to the central government. And just as the aging dictator had failed to accommodate the Madero clan, so eventually would his insistence on centralization alienate members of the Cárdenas faction. Meanwhile, the exclusive nature of Porfirian politics, coupled with the effects of national economic policies, caused frustration among Coahuila's popular classes and growing middle class. Even as Díaz shrewdly orchestrated Coahuila's cliquish political system, the limits of the Porfirian model were increasingly apparent. Those limits would help to encourage the growth of three major reform movements: Reyismo, Magonismo, and Maderismo.

Reyismo

The revolt of 1893, which reaffirmed the central government's control over Coahuilan politics, highlighted the political importance of Bernardo Reyes in northeastern Mexico. By the time of the rebellion, Reyes had already begun to build a personal power base in Nuevo León. He became governor of that state in 1884, a year before Díaz named him commander of the Third Military Zone, and he gained a reputation as a progressive reformer who supported municipal autonomy, workers' rights, the expansion of education, and other liberal causes. Yet while he was indispensable to Porfirio Díaz' control of the northeast, Reyes' own political ambitions generated suspicions among the president's inner circle, the Científicos. This was especially true after 1900, as speculation mounted over who would eventually succeed the dictator. In 1904 Díaz had agreed to designate a vice-president. His choice of Científico Ramón Corral was an unpopular one. As the 1910 election neared, and with Díaz approaching eighty, Reyes came to be seen (particularly by opponents of the Científicos) as a more suitable vice-presidential candidate.

The significant role Reyes played in ending the Coahuilan revolt of 1893 and successfully negotiating the deposing of Científico-supported governor Garza Galán increased Científico antagonism, as did the spectre of Reyes as a presidential contender. More alarming to Díaz himself was the increasing political support for Reyes that had begun to emerge in north-eastern Mexico. In 1900 Díaz tried to check Reyes' popularity by calling him back to Mexico City to serve as minister of war. Despite his removal from Nuevo León, and Reyes' outward reluctance to challenge the Científicos or appear disloyal to the Porfirian regime, Reyismo had a life of its own. It appealed to the growing middle classes, excluded from Porfirian politics, and to labour groups and members of the Mexican army. In 1909 the Partido Democrático was established in Mexico City to challenge Científico political dominance. Reyes was presented as a vice-presidential candidate for 1910, and a progressive party platform that included the principles of direct suffrage and municipal autonomy was drafted.

Reyista clubs emerged in many areas of Coahuila, including Saltillo, Torreón, Múzquiz, and Parras. Particularly in the Laguna, several prominent landowners and businessmen joined the Partido Democrático. Many of these men had also served as volunteer officers in the Second Reserve of the Army, a controversial group that Reyes had created during his two-year tenure as minister of war. In Científico eyes, the Second Reserve was yet another indication of Reyes' thirst for power. As the jousting between Reyes and the Científicos continued, Díaz played to both parties, abolishing the Second Reserve and returning Reyes to Nuevo León.

Reyes himself never accepted the candidacy of the Partido Democrático. Yet his ambition was still evident, and his attempts to assure Díaz and the Reyistas of his personal support for the re-election of Vice-President Ramón Corral in the coming election were lukewarm. In July 1909 General Gerónimo Treviño arrived in Monterrey as the new commander of the Third Military Zone, charged more specifically with keeping an eye on Reyes. Finally, in October Díaz acted definitively, sending Reyes to Europe to study military tactics and thus imposing political exile on the former strongman of northeastern Mexico.[1]

Díaz' growing suspicion of Reyes extended to the influential Coahuilan Venustiano Carranza. Born in Cuatro Ciénegas in 1859, Carranza was the descendant of a Basque family that had come to Coahuila during the colonial era. His father, José de la Jesús Carranza was a successful cattleman in central Coahuila who distinguished himself in the struggle to halt the Indian raids that plagued the state throughout the nineteenth century. Jesús' political and economic clout steadily increased, aided by his open and generous support of the liberal cause. The post of *jefe político* of the Monclova District was Jesús' reward for a loan made to Benito Juárez during the French Intervention, and the Coahuilan also acquired additional lands that Juárez seized from his Conservative enemies. By the end of the nineteenth century, Jesús Carranza was among the wealthiest Coahuilans, able to use his economic power to obtain political favours, including an exemption from state taxes during the first term of the Garza Galán administration. In 1890 he divided his now substantial properties among his fifteen children, including Venustiano.[2]

Venustiano Carranza was educated in Mexico. He received his secondary schooling at Coahuila's prestigious Ateneo Fuente, located in the capital of Saltillo, and then completed three years of medical training at the Escuela Nacional Preparatoria in Mexico City. When eye problems forced him to end his studies, Carranza returned to central Coahuila and the municipality of Cuatro Ciénegas to help with the family ranches. He inherited a modest plot from his father and gained a reputation as a good rancher and successful member of Coahuila's new entrepreneurial elite. A progressive businessman, Venustiano insisted on pursuing and preserving his economic interests. He was also critical of Porfirian centralization and disgruntled over foreign domination of the Mexican economy.[3]

Family influence enabled Venustiano to claim at least a tentative place in the Porfirian system. He assumed a leadership position in Reyes' Second Reserve, and himself trained some of its units, which then found a place within the Federal Army structure. In 1887 Carranza was elected municipal president of Cuatro Ciénegas after a brief stint as a municipal judge. Beginning his political career during the unpopular regime of Garza Galán, Carranza witnessed the effects of political and economic centralization. Indeed, during Garza Galán's second term, Carranza was summarily removed from his post as municipal president. As local government was progressively undermined by Porfirian politics, and as economic policies intensified social divisions, Carranza was increasingly attracted to the reformist and nationalistic tendencies that had come to characterize the Reyista movement. In the aftermath of the 1893 revolt Carranza worked closely with Reyes to reach a political settlement to the dispute. José María Múzquiz briefly occupied the post of governor before Carranza's political ally (and 1893 gubernatorial candidate) Miguel Cárdenas assumed the post. His fifteen-year regime was marked by improvements in education and infrastructure, but the pace and nature of economic growth continued to strain Coahuilan society.[4]

With the political clique led by Cárdenas now dominant, the Carranzas began to enjoy greater economic prosperity and political clout. Venustiano served as municipal president of Cuatro Ciénegas for another three terms, and served in the state legislature. With the help of Reyes, he assumed the role of federal senator from 1903 to 1908. Brother Emilio found a place in the state legislature and later served as the municipal president of Ocampo. Favourable economic treatment also allowed Venustiano and other members of the Carranza family to expand their holdings. For Profirio Díaz, the political changes in Coahuila after Garza Galán's ouster came to represent a double threat. Not only was the Cárdenas faction identified with the growing political movement of Reyismo, but the Carranzas, particularly Venustiano, proved increasingly intransigent in the face of Porfirian attempts to control the political and economic life of Coahuila. Economic concessions such as tax breaks and land grants to the Carranzas did not always bring the expected support for the Porfirian regime. At times Venustiano seemed more intent on supporting Reyes than the dictator who was largely responsible for Reyes' power. He refused to officially endorse the re-election of Díaz, and his brother Emilio was an outspoken critic of the socio-economic disparities caused by Porfirian policies. Even towards Reyes Venustiano Carranza exhibited a remarkable degree of independence and a determination to preserve his personal political autonomy on the local level.[5]

The triumph of Miguel Cárdenas and the Carranzas in 1893 was accompanied by the continued decline of the Madero faction in Coahuilan politics. As part of the effort to centralize control over Coahuila, Reyes took care to impose local officials in the Laguna and in Parras (headquarters of the Madero family economic empire) who were not connected to the Madero clan. And while the family's fortune continued to grow throughout the Porfiriato, Evaristo was not always granted the economic favours that he requested. Indeed, the Maderos were assessed higher taxes.[6]

In the realignment of Coahuilan politics, the followers of José María Garza Galán also found themselves in the uncomfortable position of political "outs." While Díaz and Reyes took care to placate the Galanistas (even attempting to bribe the ousted governor) this still-powerful political faction became openly belligerent. When Miguel Cárdenas arrived in Saltillo to campaign for election, a brief scuffle and exchange of bullets occurred between the police and Garza Galán's henchmen.[7] Although Garza Galán retired to his *hacienda* in Múzquiz, he continued to be a source of concern for Reyes.

Garza Galán's *hacienda* became the headquarters of a Galanista campaign to unseat Cárdenas in 1896 and to provoke disorder during elections. Reyes sent Federal troops to guard the Garza Galán estate and to serve as a warning to supporters of the undermined *cacique* (political boss). The Galanista campaign generated some support in central and northern Coahuila, but Reyes' harassment prevented an effective challenge to the re-election of Cárdenas.[8]

Galanismo also found echos in the Rio Grande District of northern Coahuila, a centre of revolt in 1893 and an area now controlled by Reyes' military subordinate Colonel Fructuoso García. Sent to help pacify this restless frontier zone, García eventually became president of the important municipality of Ciudad Porfirio Díaz and began to enjoy economic privileges as well.[9] Local resentment of García, who now represented the unwelcome intervention of Reyes and who served as a reminder of Coahuila's increasing subordination to the Porfirian regime, took the form of Galanismo among some of the more prominent residents of the Rio Grande District.

Upon his arrival García noted that the local administration

was full of frustrated Galanistas whose lackadaisical work and scandalous behaviour were a constant concern. Municipal Council member Rafael Múzquiz, who had served several terms as municipal president of Ciudad Porfirio Díaz during the Garza Galán administration and was both a local official and state legislator at the time of García's arrival, was particularly troublesome. Múzquiz and other local officials, including federal officers of the Ciudad Porfirio Díaz customs house, met frequently in Eagle Pass, Texas, to express publicly their support for Garza Galán and to complain about Coahuila's lack of autonomy and continued subjection to Reyes.[10]

Reyes also faced the opposition of former *jefes políticos*, several of them relatives of Garza Galán. Manuel Rosas, uncle of Garza Galán and former *jefe* of the Rio Grande District, was especially intractable. He remained in northern Coahuila after his dismissal and was frequently associated with Galanista plots.[11]

Galanista opposition continued throughout the Cárdenas administration, but in the end it was Díaz himself, beset by Científico demands and increasingly concerned with Reyes' popularity, who effected the governor's departure. When Cárdenas announced that he would not run for re-election in 1909, his close political ally Venustiano Carranza (who in 1908 had been allowed to replace Cárdenas during the governor's absence) became a candidate. Carranza defied Díaz' demand that he withdraw from the contest. Díaz then determined to check Carranza and remove the Cárdenas faction, now considered firmly in the Reyista camp, from Coahuilan politics. Laguna landowner Práxedis de la Peña was installed as interim governor and then helped rig the election, ensuring that Jesús del Valle, a former *jefe político* and Galanista who enjoyed Científico support, was installed as Coahuila's executive. Despite an impressive show of support for his candidacy, Carranza was helpless to act. And as Reyes was shipped off to his European exile, Carranza's hopes of clinging to his already precarious position in the Porfirian system disappeared.[12] He would soon be forced into an uncomfortable alliance with Francisco Madero.

By the end of 1909 the political profile of Coahuila, and indeed of northeastern Mexico, had changed dramatically. Reyes, the hope of progressive reformers such as Carranza, had been sent into exile and Díaz had refused to accommodate his supporters. With the Garza Galán clique reinstalled, the growth of a new reform movement led by the grandson of Evaristo Madero gained momentum.

Maderismo and the Anti-re-electionist Movement

As the revolt of 1893 drew to a close and Reyes and Díaz worked to strengthen central control over Coahuila, Francisco I. Madero returned to Coahuila. Born in 1873 in Parras, centre of the family economic empire, Madero was the first child of Francisco Madero and Mercedes González Treviño. A slight and rather nervous young man, Madero completed several years of schooling in France (at the Lycée of Versailles and the School of Advanced Commercial Studies) and in the United States (at the University of California-Berkeley), receiving a thoroughly practical education in business and agricultural management. While studying business in Paris, Madero received his first exposure to spiritism. Madero's eager embrace of spiritist ideas would infuse his political career with a moralistic, quixotic quality. After completing his education and returning to Mexico, Madero pursued several other interests that, like spiritism, contributed to his reputation as a rather unusual fellow. He developed an interest in homeopathic medicine, and after a spiritual crisis brought on by his mother's long illness Madero swore off smoking and drinking and became a vegetarian.[13] One family friend described Madero as a man of impeccable hygiene (who bathed and changed clothes at least twice a day) and of tremendous physical strength (who relished long horseback rides and who had braved freezing waters during the wintertime to swim across the Rio Grande).[14]

With his adoption of French spiritism while abroad and his later adherence to such practices as homeopathy and vegetarianism, Madero was unique among his Mexican peers. In his educational path and the application of his knowledge and skills to the family business, however, Madero was typical of the new entrepreneurial class that had begun to emerge in northeastern Mexico before his birth. Furthermore, Madero's political activities in Coahuila did not simply operate within the confines of his personal beliefs and convictions. They also occurred within the context of, and were largely guided by, the exigencies of a local political system characterized by elite competition, family and kinship loyalties, and a traditional resistance to central control.

Upon his return to Mexico Madero became manager of family properties in San Pedro. In 1903 he married Sara Pérez, daughter of Marcario Pérez, a landowner in central Mexico. As both an agriculturalist and an administrator Madero proved himself an outstanding member of the Laguna's class of modern *hacendados.* His accomplishments included the improvement of cotton cultivation through the introduction of different varieties of cotton seed and the use of modern machinery. In his relationship with workers Madero also became known as one of the region's more progressive businessmen. Some of his attempts to foster good relations with his workers, including the application of his personal knowledge of homeopathic medicine to help cure their ailments, were seen as impractical by other members of the Madero family. Yet while his often unique personal convictions may have compelled Madero to extend his services beyond the ordinary, in his provision of medical care and education to workers and their families he was not alone. The scarcity of labour that was characteristic of Coahuila, and particularly the Laguna, as well as the increasing competition for workers among the various new industries of northeastern Mexico made such efforts necessary to attract and retain labourers. Madero's own father, whose activities included management of the family textile factory in Parras, was known for his conciliatory attitude towards workers as well as his provision of good salaries, free medical services, and schools.[15]

Madero's business dealings also reflected the inter-elite competition that was especially characteristic of the Laguna region. As a member of a family that was often the only significant Mexican representative in economic activities increasingly dominated by foreigners, Madero continued a tradition of resisting foreign domination over resources and markets. In 1906 he established a syndicate of local cotton growers to protect planters against the artificial lowering of prices by the cotton industry. Madero also became involved, as had his grandfather Evaristo and his father Francisco, in the explosive dispute over the waters of the Nazas River. He championed the cause of property owners of the lower river zone against the foreign-owned Tlahualilo Company, and in 1907 he published a study of the water issue.[16] It was in fact the elite competition and conflict in which Madero participated that made the Laguna a centre of opposition to Díaz and an important base of support for several opposition movements. In addition to the water issue, the virtual monopoly of the guayule industry by Rockefeller's Continental Rubber Company divided Laguna elites, as did the attempts of Mexican and foreign industrialists to manipulate the cotton seed and soap industries, to the detriment of the region's cotton planters.[17]

Francisco Madero's participation in the political life of Coahuila was guided not only by his personal convictions and strong belief in democracy but also (and perhaps more importantly) by his experiences as a member of an elite family that had witnessed the gradual erosion of its political and economic power and autonomy. Madero's grandfather Evaristo and other members of the Madero clan were politically active throughout the Porfiriato, although the family's political influence began to wane after Evaristo's removal from the governorship in 1884. And while the Madero coffers continued to prosper during the Porfiriato, the family's ability to secure special economic favours declined after Evaristo's fall. In sum, the Madero clan was increasingly disenfranchised, and this clearly affected Francisco's political activities and contributed to his evolution as a political figure.

Madero's initiation into the volatile world of Coahuilan politics began with the municipal election of San Pedro in 1904. After forming a local political club that became the basis of a broader political movement and that included other San Pedro farmers, Madero worked for the election of local planter Francisco Rivas. Electoral fraud resulted in Rivas' defeat, but the Club Democrático of San Pedro soon devoted its efforts to impeding the re-election of Governor Cárdenas in 1905.[18]

As a participant in local politics Madero was frequently, and often reluctantly, compelled to operate within the cliquish political system of Coahuila—a system that often necessitated uneasy alliances between otherwise contentious political factions. In the 1905 governor's race, Madero thus agreed to support Frumencio Fuentes, the candidate of the Garza Galán clique and of Científico Ramón Corral. Maderista and Galanista clubs met official resistance at every step of their campaign, and the expected Porfirian machinations again resulted in the re-election of Cárdenas. Madero, harassed by local authorities and threatened with arrest, briefly retired from Coahuilan politics, a victim of the local political system that counted him and the entire Madero clan as political outcasts.[19]

By 1909 Madero was again a prominent figure, but his attention was now focused on national politics. As the 1910 elections approached, Díaz granted an interview to American journalist James Creelman of *Pearson's* magazine in which he indicated his wish to retire from politics and his intention to welcome opposition parties in the electoral contest. Díaz' words encouraged a flurry of political activity and emboldened many of his rivals.

Madero, skeptical of Díaz' recent talk of the impending arrival of a new democratic era in Mexico, published *The Presidential Succession of 1910*, a commentary on Mexico's problems. The country's unfortunate history of absolutist rule, which had reached a new height under Díaz, was the focus of this bold but poorly written book. Madero warned that absolutism would continue under either Ramón Corral or Bernardo Reyes, the two most likely inheritors of the Porfirian throne. He called for a definitive end to the Porfirian era, and for the formation of a party that represented the democratic principles suggested in the phrase "effective suffrage and no re-election." Díaz himself had earlier employed this same phrase to protest against the re-election of Benito Juárez, which he considered a violation of liberal principles and of the spirit of the 1857 Constitution.

The Presidential Succession also addressed a few social concerns, lamenting the treatment of Mexican workers, whose attempts to fight for better conditions and treatment were met with brute force by the Díaz machine. Madero also criticized Díaz' neglect of education, noting that some 84 per cent of Mexicans were still illiterate. The immediate need for political reform, however, was the primary focus of *The Presidential Succession*. Madero was clearly emerging as a political democrat rather than a determined social reformer.[20]

In the spring of 1909 Madero helped to establish a national Anti-re-electionist club in Mexico City. Reflective of Madero's own limited political goals, the Anti-re-electionist program emphasized respect for the democratic process and for municipal autonomy. Madero's focus on the latter, an idea often expressed with the phrase *municipio libre*, was significant. For much of Mexico's post-colonial history, the independent municipality had been the key to local survival, particularly in frontier areas like Coahuila. In the absence of an effective central government, municipal leaders raised the local forces that protected against Indian raids, raised local revenue, and attended to the economic survival of the community. The *municipio libre* was also a key to Coahuila's *camarilla* system, itself premised on self-determination and ready access to local power and resources. Madero's determination to safeguard municipal autonomy was as much an attempt to protect Coahuila's cliquish political system as it was a protest against a national regime that increasingly threatened local sovereignty.

Echoing *The Presidential Succession* and the needs and experiences of a modern elite, specifically that of northeastern Mexico, the Anti-re-electionist platform endorsed legal reform to help workers as well as policies that would assist businessmen by restricting monopolies and supporting agriculture, industry, and commerce.[21] The Anti-re-electionist movement soon began to spread, and branches were established in several Mexican states, including Coahuila and Nuevo León. As the new party's vice-president, Madero, accompanied by party secretary Felix F. Palavicini, set off on a speaking tour. Anti-re-electionism was gaining momentum just as Bernardo Reyes was sent into his European exile. Madero made a direct appeal to the leaderless Reyistas, many of whom were willing to consider Madero as an alternative to the Díaz-Corral ticket. In April 1910 the Anti-re-electionists, joined by some Reyista supporters, formally endorsed Madero and Dr. Francisco Vázquez Gómez as their presidential and vice-presidential candidates. Madero set out on a campaign trail that would eventually cover most of the country.[22]

While Madero's focus was now on the presidential election of 1910, he was also a participant in the 1909 elections of his native state. With the Científico strategy of diminishing Reyes' influence bearing fruit in the overthrow of Miguel Cárdenas, members of the nascent Maderista movement supported the candidacy of Carranza. Once again the outcome was predictable: using strongarm tactics, Díaz ensured the victory of Jesús del Valle, a member of the Garza Galán faction, and he actively persecuted members of the opposition.

By the end of 1909, with Bernardo Reyes still in exile, many Reyistas, including Carranza, began to drift into the Anti-re-electionist ranks. The alliance between Reyistas and Maderistas, however, was always tense. Madero had a personal dislike for Reyes himself, and he voiced opposition to the Reyista movement.[23] Reyes in turn had expressed animosity toward the young Coahuilan and had taken steps to crush his political ambitions. On the eve of the 1905 gubernatorial election Reyes warned Díaz of Madero's activities and described him in particularly unflattering terms: "of all of his family, [Francisco Madero] is the only one to whom nature has not been kind, for he is rachitic and exceptionally ugly, which inclines him to a certain melancholy ... and which predisposes him to become easily upset."[24]

While Madero publicly endorsed Carranza's bid for governor in 1909, he distrusted Carranza for his earlier support of Reyes and failed to provide him with any real support, a fact that caused many Reyistas to resent Madero. Madero was convinced that Carranza's bid for the governorship would fail and his support for Carranza was of secondary importance to his efforts to expand the activities of the Anti-re-electionist cause.[25] In turn, although Carraza himself was eventually drawn into the revolutionary movement led by Madero, he remained skeptical of Madero himself. A feeling of mutual distrust plagued the relationship between Madero and Carranza from the start and proved to be an obstacle after the overthrow of Díaz.[26]

As Madero extended his political activities to the national level, the Anti-re-electionist movement in Coahuila continued to grow. This local Maderista movement built upon the San Pedro Anti-re-electionist club and developed within the context of a political system dominated by elites and characterized by strong family and kinship ties. Prominent landowners and businessmen directed most local clubs.[27] Madero also counted among his supporters several relatives. The San Pedro club included uncles José María Hernández and Angel and Catarino Benavides, the latter a landowner and businessman in northern Coahuila who included among his rebel credentials leadership in the 1893 revolt and connections to the Mexican Liberal Party.[28] Maderista sympathizers also included Marcos Benavides, another relative who had participated in the rebellions that were common to the state's border region.

As the Anti-re-electionist movement grew, Maderista clubs in Coahuila began to attract other elements of Coahuilan society. The local club in Cuatro Ciénegas was led by Cesáreo Castro, owner of a small transportation business, and Vicente Flores, former professor and administrator of a local school, who had recently been dismissed. Both men would play prominent roles in the revolution of 1910-11.[29]

As national phenomena Reyismo and Maderismo represented two of the major liberal reform movements that had arisen by the early 1900s to challenge the Díaz regime. In Coahuila both garnered their initial support primarily from members of the elite, and both operated within the context of an already existing system of cliquish state politics. Elite support for Reyismo tended to come from people like Carranza who, while not truly disenfranchised by Porfirian politics, supported the progressive reformism that had come to characterize Reyes' administration of the neighbouring state of Nuevo León. Maderismo, on the other hand, included several elite Coahuilans whose political and in some cases economic fortunes declined following the ouster of Governor Evaristo Madero.[30]

Both movements also gained adherents among members of Mexico's growing middle class. Middle-class support was an expression of the aspirations of a group that had emerged with and profited from the economic modernization of Mexico. This group, which included teachers, lawyers, clerical workers, and other educated professionals, as well as shopowners, merchants, and in some areas *rancheros* (smallholders), was primarily a product of industrialization and urbanization—a process especially apparent in northeastern Mexico by the end of the nineteenth century. Reyes in particular gained adherents among the middle classes in the rapidly growing cities of northern Mexico, including Monterrey, Parras, Torreón, and Múzquiz. But the rising middle class, motivated by the desire to match its economic clout with political power and, in many cases, by its commitment to nineteenth-century liberal ideals, also found a new voice in Francisco Madero.[31]

Although Reyismo and Maderismo included in their ranks some politically disenfranchised Coahuilans, these political movements primarily represented the views of groups who were beneficiaries of the economic growth that reached its height during the Porfiriato. The more radical movement of Magonismo, however, found support not only among disgruntled members of the middle class but also among the working class, which, after 1900 was increasingly politicized by and vulnerable to an economic system heavily dependent on outside forces.

Magonismo and the Mexican Liberal Party

Magonismo, which found formal expression in the Mexican Liberal Party (PLM), endorsed the principle of no re-election and other moderate views. Formally established in 1905 by brothers Ricardo and Enrique Flores Magón, the PLM emerged from a 1901 gathering of intellectuals dedicated to the preservation of nineteenth-century liberal ideas (including the principle of individual rights) and critical of the Porfiriato. In its early days, the PLM enjoyed the support of Madero and other Anti-re-electionists. But as the movement developed, and as its members faced persecution by Díaz, it became increasingly radical. From St. Louis, where they sought refuge from Porfirian repression, the Flores Magón brothers in 1906 issued a call for the overthrow of Díaz. The PLM party platform embraced more extreme ideas, including agrarian reform and protection for Mexico's Indian peoples, than the more clearly reformist movements of Reyismo and Maderismo. When the Magonistas openly endorsed violence as a tool for bringing about change, they lost the support of Madero and other more moderate crusaders.[32]

Coahuila, as well as the other northern states of Sonora and Chihuahua, was a centre of PLM activity, and the Rio Grande District was the area of most PLM activity within the state. Del Río, Texas, located just across the border from the Coahuilan town of Las Vacas, was the southwest Texas headquarters of the PLM; Magonista leaders had established party newspapers there. Coahuila itself was part of the PLM's "Third Military Zone," which included Tamaulipas, Zacatecas, Chihuahua, and Texas. Several PLM groups emerged in northern Coahuila, and Torreón and Saltillo were also home to Magonista clubs.[33]

Although little record exists of specific PLM groups, many in Coahuila were located in areas where mining was the main activity. Group leaders in these areas tended to be businessmen, sometimes Mexican industrialists adversely affected by the expansion of foreign influence. PLM members also included small and mid-sized merchants whose businesses were hurt by the commercial monopoly held by foreign mining companies such as ASARCO. An important PLM group existed in one of the mining communities of the wealthy Sierra Mojada region, where ASARCO used its control of the local water supply to secure mining labour, offering water in return for work.[34]

While local PLM leadership often had a distinctly middle-class character, Magonismo also generated significant support among miners and other industrial and agricultural workers,[35] especially in northern Coahuila and the Laguna. It was in these two regions that the PLM staged small-scale revolts in 1906 and 1908.

On September 26, 1906, a small group of PLM rebels crossed into Coahuila from Del Río, attacking the small town of Jiménez. After sacking several houses, kidnapping the municipal president and other local officials, and extracting forced loans, the rebels appropriated guns and horses from local residents. They then scattered with the approach of Federal forces.[36] The Jiménez attack was led by Juan José Arredondo and Calixto Guerra, both natives of northern Coahuila who were well known to residents on both sides of the border. While little information is available on Guerra, the fifty-six-year-old Arredondo was a former captain and commander of the Rio Grande District and had served as municipal president of the northern population of Morelos. Perhaps a victim of the abolition of military colonies and the land concentration that displaced many smallholders in northern Mexico, by 1906 Arrendondo had become a resident worker of a *hacienda* in northern Coahuila and a member of an underground PLM club in Jiménez.[37]

Mexican consular official Francisco Villasana was quick to downplay the attack on Jiménez, describing it as purely an act of banditry with no revolutionary overtones. He insisted that the sensationalist press of the border region had inflated the event and emphasized the report of a conservative newspaper that likened the PLM rebels to Christian Scientists who were "conducting their revolution by absent treatment."[38] Despite such claims, Mexico's unsuccessful attempts to extradite the apprehended rebels highlighted two difficulties that had plagued Mexican authorities throughout the nineteenth century and would continue to hamper their efforts to control Coahuila's border region: the rebel sympathies of residents on both sides of the Coahuila-Texas border and the reluctance of many Texas officials to prosecute rebel groups. The support of the largely Mexican and Mexican-American population of Del Rio made that town a convenient meeting place for the PLM. County judges and other local Texas authorities were less than zealous in prosecuting rebel activity, succumbing to political pressure and the need for the votes of the sizeable Mexican-American population.[39]

As part of an attempt to begin a general revolt, the Jiménez raid ultimately failed. PLM leaders regrouped, however, and in June of 1908 staged two attacks—one on the Laguna town of Viesca and one on the border town of Las Vacas. In Viesca, some fifty rebels assaulted and robbed the local bank and post office, temporarily imprisoned municipal officials, tore up railroad tracks, and committed other depredations before fleeing north into Matamoros. A few rebels were captured, and local officials responded by arresting and in some cases executing suspected workers and members of the middle class.

In Las Vacas, rebels carried out a haphazard assault on the town's military barracks before taking refuge in Texas. And although Calixto Guerra and Patricio Guerra (both participants in the 1906 revolt) were detained in Texas, Mexican prosecutors were again forced to wrestle with south Texas politics as they sought extradition of the Magonistas.[40] Las Vacas insurgents

also included Guillermo Adam, a day labourer from northern
Coahuila who was lured into the PLM ranks in Del Rio (offered
a one-peso daily wage by a PLM recruiter) while on his way to
work on the Texas railroads. Adam soon found himself back in
northern Coahuila, where he was armed and given instructions
for the ensuing PLM raid.[41]

Although the 1908 Las Vacas and Viesca raids failed to generate the broader rebellion planned by PLM leaders, Magonista
activity continued in the form of guerrilla movements based in
the mountains of northern Coahuila.[42] While it is difficult to
document the provenance of most PLM rebels, Adam's situation
was probably common by 1907, when Mexican workers began
to feel the brunt of an international economic crisis. Indeed,
in its continued ability to attract workers, the PLM opposition
rode the crest of broader economic forces that had begun to pro-
duce a sizable group of unemployed and restless labourers. Like
Guillermo Adam, these workers provided ready recruits.

With an economy largely dependent on foreign capital and
markets Coahuila—like the rest of Mexico—was vulnerable to
market forces. The steady contraction of cotton and guayule
markets after 1900, coupled with periodic droughts, flooding,
and a grasshopper plague, especially hurt the Laguna region.
Jobless workers left the area in large numbers, searching for
work elsewhere. On the eve of the Mexican Revolution the
town of Matamoros was almost bankrupt, having lost harvests
to drought and frosts for three consecutive years. The mobility
of the labour force had already caused a labour shortage in
the Laguna, as workers left to seek better jobs in the mines
and industry. *Hacendados* became so desperate that they were
compelled to import Chinese and Japanese workers to pick the
cotton crop.[43]

Other sectors of Coahuila's economy experienced recession
after 1900. A downturn in the silver market forced several
Coahuilan mines to shut down, causing problems for related
enterprises. Between 1901 and 1910 Coahuila's textile workforce dramatically declined. Outside of the Laguna, drought
affected *hacendados* and smallholders alike. Members of independent farming communities and residents of several municipalities of northern Coahuila complained of a lack of water and
food, and many asked for a revision of taxes on their properties,
noting that drought had made their lands almost worthless.[44]

By 1907 Coahuila (and Mexico itself) was facing an agricultural crisis in which basic commodities were scarce and prices inflated. Recession heightened the danger of unrest, particularly in the Laguna, as thousands of migrant workers returned from the United States in search of work. Many of them had already been politicized by exposure to American unionism and to the PLM. Those wandering across the border in search of work provided ready recruits for the sizable PLM contingency along the border.[45] Economic problems also had repercussions for the middle class of northern Mexico. Inflation and higher taxes took their toll, and discontent was increasingly expressed as resentment towards foreigners and foreign investment.[46]

On the eve of the Mexican Revolution, Francisco Madero penned a note to a friend in San Pedro commenting on the failure of the PLM to generate a more substantial movement. He insisted that the failures of the Jiménez, Las Vacas, and Viesca revolts were proof that Mexicans wanted not revolution, but a more democratic movement.[47] Madero's comments downplayed the significance of Mexico's economic troubles just as they demonstrated the strength of his political convictions. Those convictions would soon be challenged by Porfirian persecution, and Madero's faith in peaceful reform shaken. While he continued to endorse a program of moderate change for Mexico, Madero was forced to move beyond formal political competition to realize his goals.

By 1909 the political machinations of Díaz and the Científicos had alienated a large sector of the Coahuilan elite. Reyismo, which gave expression to the aspirations of Mexico's middle and labouring classes, and which garnered the support of Venustiano Carranza and other Coahuilan elites, had faded. The Anti-reelectionist movement, meanwhile, continued to grow, attracting some Reyes supporters in an often uneasy alliance. Like the Reyes movement, Madero had an elite core of support including several of his relatives. Madero's plan for change, with its advocacy of progressive economic reforms, reflected his background as a member of northeastern Mexico's entrepreneurial elite. At the same time, Madero's insistence on the political goals of effective suffrage, no re-election, and municipal autonomy echoed the sentiments of several Coahuilans who, like the Madero family, had been relegated to the edge of the Porfirian power structure.

Finally, the increasingly radical PLM, with its middle-class leadership and significant following among Mexican workers, found a home in northern Coahuila, the border zone, and the Laguna. Magonismo, moreover, was an important reflection of Coahuila's economic vulnerability. After 1900, economic crises and dislocations generated popular unrest and provided recruits for rebel movements. These same factors would help give the Maderista revolt of 1910–11 its unique quality.

3

Regions and Rebellions

The Maderista Revolt of 1910–11

In June 1910 Madero passed through Saltillo on the campaign trail. In anticipation of his visit, members of the local Anti-re-electionist club Francisco Martínez Ortíz, Serapio Aguirre, Adolfo Huerta Vargas, and Benigno Ramos Fuentes circulated flyers inviting people to meet Madero at the railroad station. Censured by local officials for failing to get permission to publicize the event, each man was fined. Although the visit caused no real unrest, local authorities tormented Madero and his supporters. By the end of the summer, all Maderista demonstrations and publicity on behalf of the Anti-re-electionist cause were banned.[1]

A few days after his Saltillo visit, Madero was arrested in Monterrey on trumped-up charges and transferred to prison in San Luis Potosí for safekeeping during the approaching elections. Vázquez Gómez, Madero's running mate, began to temporize in the face of Porfirian threats, and even indicated a willingness to allow another Díaz term if Corral was replaced as vice-president. Vázquez Gómez would gradually distance himself from the increasingly combative Maderista movement. After the unsurprising Díaz victory, Madero, released from prison, jumped bail and fled to the United States. He was now convinced that armed revolution was the only way to bring an end to the Porfiriato, and he made his way to San Antonio, Texas, to plan the uprising.[2]

San Antonio proved a comfortable temporary venue for the Maderista movement. The town had a sizeable Mexican population, and the Madero family had strong social and business ties with the local community. From this exile, Madero and a small circle of supporters that included brothers Julio, Raúl, and Alfonso issued the Plan of San Luis Potosí, refusing to recognize the new Díaz administration, designating Madero as provisional president, and calling for revolution. The Plan repeated Madero's commitment to the political principle of effective suffrage and no re-election, and focused on the issue of political change. Like the earlier Anti-re-elecionist platform, it reflected Madero's own background as a landowner and member of the elite, although Madero lent extremely cautious support to agrarian reform.[3] That support was both influenced and tempered by the Coahuilan context. While the large-scale displacement of a traditional peasantry had not occurred in Porfirian Coahuila, many smallholders and former military colonists, particularly in northern Coahuila, had experienced the effects of land concentration. A tradition of agrarian rebellion, moreover, had developed in the Laguna. Madero's own experience, however, was with a modern agrarian workforce consisting of landless, salaried workers, most with few traditional ties to Coahuila.

On the eve of Madero's revolution political division also characterized the state of Coahuila. The cliquish political competition among elites that was the rule throughout the Porfiriato was still a divisive force. The opposition movement, too, consisted of separate groups, often at odds with one another. Many Reyistas, including Venustiano Carranza, were reluctant and belated allies of the Maderista cause, and Madero's recent withdrawal of support from the PLM had generated some animosity, particularly in northern Coahuila and the border region. The Maderista movement itself stood on uncertain ground. Although many of its members were dedicated reformers from the middle class, in his coordination of the state-wide movement Madero seemed to rely more on the efforts of a small group of wealthy friends and relatives, so that his actions mirrored *camarilla* politics rather than suggesting a new style of more inclusive leadership. Porfirian persecution of Anti-re-electionist groups also hampered the movement's success and resulted in the disbanding of some groups. The November 1910 call for revolt, for example, found the Anti-re-electionist club of Ciudad Porfirio Díaz broken by persecution and its president exiled in Texas.[4]

While working-class support for Madero did exist in some areas of the state, the economic crisis that caused jobless workers in the thousands to wander about Coahuila and into Texas in search of work was hardly conducive to the co-ordination of a revolt. Yet this same factor would ultimately provide the recruits needed for a Maderista victory in Coahuila. The result was a largely spontaneous popular revolt, heavily tinged with elements of banditry, which, while responding to the opportunity created by Madero's call for revolution, would outlast any political victory.

Call to Revolution

After the publication of the Plan of San Luis Potosí, rumours surfaced of a planned rebellion in several areas of Coahuila, including Torreón, Saltillo, and the border region. When Madero approached the border for the planned November revolt, he anticipated a force of three hundred led by Catarino Benavides. Instead, he was greeted by only ten poorly armed men and was forced to retreat. A later attempt to cross into Coahuila likewise met with disappointment, and Madero turned his attention to the neighbouring state of Chihuahua, which promised more success.

Despite their reputation for rebelliousness and defiance of central authority, residents of northern Coahuila did not respond to Madero's call. As local officials combed the border zone they found no rebel activity, and noted only that several Maderistas had apparently crossed into Texas. The southeast was quiet as well. Rebels briefly captured Gómez Palacio, in the neighbouring state of Durango, and guerrilla attacks on the railroads unsettled the Laguna. No coordinated revolt occurred in Coahuila's Laguna region, however, and by the end of November Matamoros authorities reported that several thefts of corn had been the only result of the 1910 revolution. Only in central Coahuila did significant rebel activity occur in 1910.

The Maderista uprising in this region centred on the *hacienda* La Merced in the municipality of Ocampo, which contained several other properties owned by the Madero family. The revolt began a few days before the planned November revolution and was led by Cayetano Trejo, *hacienda* administrator and president of the Ocampo Anti-re-electionist club. Trejo, along with some fifty rebels, apprehended Ocampo municipal president and ranchero Pedro Martínez and two of his relatives. Insulted by the rebels and unceremoniously removed from his political office,

Martínez was pressed for a loan by the insurgents, who then fled to their base at La Merced. In nearby Cuatro Ciénegas, meanwhile, local police stood watch in anticipation of a similar attack. As 150 military troops led by Major Alberto Rezago marched to the defense of Cuatro Ciénegas, the municipal president joined other townsmen in passing a watchful night on the roof of a house. Rezago's arrival the next day, postponed by the destruction of a railroad bridge, ended the immediate threat to Cuatro Ciénegas, and the rebels stationed on the outskirts of the town dispersed after a brief skirmish with Federal soldiers. Rebel activity continued in the Ocampo-Cuatro Ciénegas area into December, and a few men were captured and imprisoned. Using La Merced as their base, small groups ventured out to commit isolated acts of banditry, burning bridges and destroying railroad tracks. A few additional skirmishes occurred between Federal troops and a larger group of rebels led by ex-Federal officer Manuel Escudero.[5] Few casualties were reported.

The rebels of central Coahuila consisted of a true cross-section of Coahuilan society. They included *hacienda* workers from La Merced and from the neighbouring *hacienda* of San Francisco. Labourers from the neighbouring mining community of La Mula also participated, but so did several small businessmen and a few professionals from Ocampo and Cuatro Ciénegas. The rebel profile included Cesáreo Castro, owner of a small transportation business and president of the Anti-re-electionist club of Cuatro Ciénegas; Vicente Flores, former professor and administrator of a Cuatro Ciénegas school (who had been dismissed in 1908); a tailor; an Ocampo farmer; an ex-Army officer; a day labourer; a contractor for the mines of La Mula; and a blacksmith. Several workers from the Madero family property Australia and the guayule factory of the same name also took part in the revolt. Ernesto Treviño, administrator of the guayule factory, was identified as a ringleader. His ranks included Apolinar Sánchez, an office teller for the guayule factory; Francisco de Anda, factory worker; and Toribio de los Santos, a cowboy from the Australia property.[6]

By the end of November, with Madero back in San Antonio and only isolated rebel activity occurring in Coahuila, officials reported the end of the Madero revolution. American consular agent Luther Ellsworth attributed Madero's failed incursion into

Coahuila to the heightened vigilance of U.S. and Mexican officials in the border region. Del Rio Mexican agent Manuel Cuesta offered the interesting explanation that Madero had advance warning of government attempts to suffocate his rebellion, because the Maderista sympathizers of Lorenzo González Treviño's cattle company (located in central Coahuila) had tapped the telegraph wires of the border area and were providing Madero with official information. González Treviño was Evaristo Madero's son-in-law, and had business ties with the Madero family.[7]

Madero's inability to generate more support for a revolution in 1910, while partly the product of official persecution of the Anti-re-electionist movement, was also due to the hesitancy of several leading figures, including Venustiano Carranza. Carranza had visited Madero in his San Luis Potosí jail cell and promised to join his struggle, but he did not respond to Madero's call for a November uprising. Most likely, Carranza wanted to achieve better organization before taking action and was reluctant to act alone in Coahuila, with Madero still in San Antonio. In January 1911 Carranza would join Madero in Texas. Yet while he helped in recruitment and preparation for the next phase of the rebellion, Carranza hedged on taking a more active role in the revolution that eventually succeeded in ousting Díaz.[8]

The Maderista Revolt of 1911

The revolution that eventually gained momentum in 1911 and that took Madero as its leader was a combination of organized revolt and spontaneous popular rebellion. The capture of specific towns in Coahuila and the drive to gain control of the state was accompanied by, and in many cases dependent on, the more localized outbursts that struck at the symbols of Porfirian control and abuse. The Maderista victory was followed by local demands for political change. Many Coahuilans petitioned for the redress of grievances and inequities that had accompanied the process of economic modernization and that were encouraged by Porfirian policies. Multi-faceted and lacking a single unifying theme or purpose, this unruly rebellion was inherited by both Madero and Carranza.

Central Coahuila

The main focus of Maderista revolt in 1910, central Coahuila experienced significant rebel activity in 1911 as well. In January Pablo González, a native of Nuevo León, a former Magonista, and a salesman for American companies in Coahuila and Chihuahua, rose in arms with some sixty men, including store clerk Gregorio Osuna. Venustiano Carranza directed González' revolt, and would soon count him among his most important generals. At the urging of Venustiano Carranza, brother Jesús Carranza and nephew Fernando Peraldi Carranza also revolted. They were joined by the son of a prosperous Nadadores family, Lucio Blanco. Maderista rebels in the northernmost municipality of Múzquiz were led by brothers and former Reyistas Luis Alberto and Evaristo Guajardo, who incorporated into their ranks Cayetano Ramos Falcón (son-in-law of former governor Miguel Cárdenas) and his small contingency of miners and *hacienda* cowboys from Lampacitos. With the co-ordinated efforts of these leaders, Cuatro Ciénegas and Monclova were in Maderista hands by May. Finally, in a pattern that likely repeated itself in central and northern Coahuila, the Madero rebellion gained unexpected adherents from within the Porfirian army when a small group of Federal soldiers revolted in Monclova under the leadership of Lieutenant Julio Escobar. Escobar began his rebellion by freeing fourteen men from the local jail and providing each one with a weapon. Soldiers and former prisoners moved on to the Monclova railroad station, where they robbed the station's strongbox and left town, meeting only a half-hearted resistance from loyal government troops.[9]

Co-ordinated rebel advances were also accompanied by more isolated incidents of banditry and guerrilla warfare. Small groups of Maderista insurgents attacked local *haciendas*, enlisting workers and appropriating guns, horses, and other goods. Local officials usually recognized the leaders of these bands, who often left receipts, promising indemnity after the revolution. In March a small group of rebels appeared in central Coahuila. Led by Apolinar Sánchez Fuentes, the band appropriated guns and horses from the Hacienda la Chata, and managed to enlist two of its workers into its ranks with the promise of payment for their services. Sánchez then moved on the neighbouring Hacienda del Sago, carrying away additional arms and other goods, including clothing, food, and soap. This time, he left a detailed list of what he had taken, promising to repay the rightful owners after the revolution and signing the promissory note with the words "Death to Porfirio Díaz."[10]

For local officials the Maderista revolt brought not only the danger of rebel attacks from without, but also the threat of rebellion from local residents. In March the municipal president and other local officials of Monclova were attacked by a small group of farmers from the independent agricultural community of Castaños. In a spontaneous display of hostility towards the municipal government, several Monclova residents joined the rebels, opening fire on the officials. The lands of Castaños had likely been encroached upon during the Porfiriato, since survey companies were especially active in the Monclova District.[11]

In central Coahuila and throughout the state, Maderistas challenged the symbols of Porfirian authority and *caciquismo* (boss rule). In Múzquiz, the heart of the economic and political empire of the Garza Galán family, thirty-five rebels led by Evaristo Guajardo apprehended Juan Garza Galán (one of José María's numerous kinsmen) and took the local *cacique,* bound and gagged, to the mining community of Palau. A hastily assembled group of eight Federal soldiers, joined by security forces from Múzquiz, followed in pursuit, arriving just in time to prevent the rebels from sacking the commissary of the local mining company. In a brief shootout that left two rebels and one Federal soldier dead, a bullet killed the insurgent who was guarding Garza Galán. A local official praised the success of soldiers and security personnel in freeing "one of the staunchest supporters" of the Díaz regime.[12]

The Southeast

By early 1911 a coordinated Maderista revolt was also taking shape in southeastern Coahuila. In February Dr. Rafael Cepeda published an act of rebellion in Saltillo, which found adherents in Serapio Aguirre and other members of the local Maderista club. Schoolteacher Gertrudis Sánchez rallied *hacienda* workers in the vicinity of Saltillo. Francisco Coss, who had worked in the mines of southeastern Coahuila and whose rebel credentials included participation in the 1906 PLM raid on Las Vacas, joined the ranks. The forces of Cepeda also included Luis and Eulalio Gutiérrez, brothers of a modest background. Eulalio Gutiérrez, like Coss, had worked as a miner and was a member of the PLM.

In 1908 he participated in the raids on Viesca and Las Vacas, and in 1910 he was part of a small revolt in southern Coahuila.[13]

Using the surrounding hills as a refuge, the Maderista rebels staged frequent guerrilla attacks, cutting the lines of communication, raiding for arms, and gaining recruits. Men left Saltillo . constantly to join the small bands of revolutionists operating in the surrounding hills. Rebel activity in the vicinity of Saltillo, which continued into May, underscored the widespread sympathy of Saltillo residents for the Maderistas. There was also a common feeling of animosity towards the town's large foreign population, which included Americans, Germans, and British. American consul Thomas Voetter remarked that a latent xenophobia had existed in Saltillo for many years, but he also emphasized the strong sentiment of the people that they "have been deprived of some of their rights in the matter of local self-government." Resentment over the 1909 overthrow of Miguel Cárdenas still lingered, as did animosity towards the Científicos. For Saltillans, remarked Voetter, the revolution was "favored as a means to bring about ... increased self government" and to end the domination of the Científicos.[14]

On April 16 miner Enrique Adame Macías led an assault on the town of Parras. In anticipation of the attack, and with a Federal garrison numbering only eighty soldiers, local officials had solicited and obtained arms and munitions from area businessmen and *hacendados*, including the Madero family. With the arrival of the Maderistas, however, several residents left the plaza to join the rebels, who approached the town with a force of some three hundred men. After they pounded Parras with gunfire and dynamite for nearly twelve hours, a group of townspeople raised a flag of truce, compelling the municipal president to surrender.

In the ensuing confusion Parras residents, including several workers from the local businesses of the Madero family, joined rebels in destroying local archives (including tax and property records), setting fire to government buildings, freeing prisoners, and looting. Threatening to apprehend the municipal president and sacking his private residence, the townspeople forced him to take refuge in the house of Salvador Madero. Prominent locals helped to negotiate a truce that allowed foreigners to leave. Fighting continued in the area of Parras into early May, as Federal forces tried to recapture the town. Exiled municipal judge Graciano Patino commented that Parras was "in the most complete anarchy," and an American official in Saltillo reported that some two hundred bodies remained unburied, strewn about the town's streets. These were the first significant casualties in a revolution that had thus far consisted primarily of guerrilla raids and brief skirmishes. Finally, on May 3 Federal troops ended their offensive in Parras and retreated.[15]

The Laguna

Beginning with the raid on Gómez Palacio in November 1910, the Laguna region of Coahuila and Durango was the site of a significant popular movement influenced not only by Maderistas, but also by Reyistas and the PLM. The region's popular movement was largely a product of the economic crisis that had produced large numbers of jobless workers. As in other areas of the state, rebel activity included attacks on the symbols and representatives of central authority. While largely spontaneous in nature, the 1910–11 revolution in the Laguna was also an expression of the long-standing problems facing the region's free agricultural settlements. Matamoros and Viesca, with a history of agrarian revolt and social banditry, and most recently affected by land and resource disputes that multiplied with Porfirian development, were centres of popular rebellion throughout the revolution.[16]

Despite the unorganized nature of rebel activity in the Laguna, by the spring of 1911 insurgent forces were co-ordinated under several prominent leaders, paving the way for the capture of San Pedro and Torreón. In late April some five hundred rebels led by Sixto Ugalde (a native of Matamoros), Gregorio García, Francisco Palacios, Orestes Pereyra, and others occupied a *hacienda* on the outskirts of San Pedro. Defended by only 140 Federal troops, the town itself had been fortified with cotton bales and sacks of dirt. *Hacendado* and staunch Porfirista Carlos Herrera sustained a volunteer force, and several residents had armed themselves in anticipation of the attack. On April 26 Captain Luis M. Rivera ventured out to the rebel base with a small force of Federal soldiers. Realizing the extent of the opposition forces, Rivera hastily retreated, but upon entering San Pedro was suprised by a group of hostile residents who loudly expressed their support for Madero. While Emilio Madero (another of Francisco's brothers) gave refuge to the Federal troops and town officials in his nearby house, Ugalde and the rebels occupied the town.

In an agreement reached between Emilio Madero and the rebel leaders, Federal troops were promised safe passage out of San Pedro. As they left, however, a mob attacked the men and stripped them of their guns and clothing, leaving many in their underwear. Taking refuge in a local *hacienda*, the humiliated soldiers finally made their way to Monterrey. With local officials deposed, several residents of San Pedro met to name their own leaders. A Torreón newspaper likened the capture of San Pedro to a "barbaric Indian attack" and warned that with this strategic town in Maderista hands, Torreón would soon fall.[17]

With Viesca and Matamoros also in rebel hands and the railroad connecting the Laguna to Saltillo and Monterrey destroyed, eight hundred Federal troops led by General Emilio Lojero clung tenaciously to Torreón. May 9 brought a rebel attack by over four thousand men, representing the coordinated forces of Sixto Ugalde, José Agustín Castro, Benjamín Argumedo, and other rebel leaders. After several days of fighting Lojero and his troops evacuated, leaving Torreón in rebel hands. Joined by local residents, the insurgents began sacking local stores, offices, and banks. One businessman noted that "to give an excuse to plunder a certain store containing desirable goods, somebody had only to cry that shots had been fired from the roof, and immediately the mob would break in the door and plunder."[18] The riot that ensued generated one of the first and most significant acts of anti-foreign violence of the Mexican Revolution: the massacre of over two hundred Chinese residents of Torreón.

Relative newcomers to the Laguna, the Chinese residents of Torreón numbered around six hundred. By 1910 they had become one of the region's most prosperous foreign groups, with interests in banking, restaurants, laundries, and other businesses as well as a virtual monopoly over the local sale of foodstuffs. Their success, exclusivity, and distinct culture, often identified with the use of opium, caused strong resentment among many Mexican residents of Torreón. Open expressions of anti-Chinese sentiment were common, and in a speech preceding the capture of Torreón, Maderista leader Jesús Flores had urged the extermination of the Chinese, claiming that they were "dangerous competitors for the common people of Mexico." During the attack on the town several members of the Chinese community had armed themselves at the urging, and perhaps with the help, of General Lojero. As the Maderistas entered the town they found several armed Chinese guarding the Chinese bank, some of whom fired on rebel troops.

With the arrival of Emilio Madero order was finally restored in Torreón. A special headquarters was established to hear the complaints of the remaining Chinese residents, and the national government began an investigation, which resulted in the promise of indemnity by the Mexican government—a promise that was lost in the continuing revolution.[19] Indeed, anti-Chinese sentiment persisted in the Laguna well beyond the Revolution. In 1934 Torreón residents established the Anti-Chinese Committee of Torreón, which adopted as its motto "For the Country and for the Race." The committee campaigned for the permanent departure of the Chinese from the Laguna, as well as from other areas of Mexico, in order to achieve the "cleansing of commerce and of the [Mexican] race."[20] The Chinese massacre, while certainly the most notable anti-foreign incident in Coahuila, was not the last. The next victims would be the Spaniards of the Laguna, who would incur the wrath of Pancho Villa.

The rebel groups that achieved a victory in the Laguna by May 1911 were composed primarily of members of the popular and middle classes. They included Benjamín Argumedo, a Durango native who had worked as a farmer and tailor, and Toribio V. de los Santos, a worker from San Pedro. Among the more educated rebels was Francisco L. Urquizo Benavides, another San Pedro native. Urquizo's father owned a small cotton *hacienda* and had managed to provide his son with an education that included business studies in Mexico City. Urquizo later became a general for Venustiano Carranza's revolutionary movement. He was also a prolific writer, producing several works of fiction and history. Argumedo, de los Santos, and Urquizo were representative of rebel ranks, which included men of many occupations: agricultural and industrial workers, artisans, small landowners, and teachers. Members of the elite, still divided by the cliquish political competition that characterized the entire state, were largely absent from the Laguna rebellion of 1911.[21]

Northern Coahuila

After Madero's abortive incursion into Coahuila and through the spring of 1911, when Madero achieved a national victory, the northern region remained an area of only sporadic rebel activity. Calixto Guerra, a participant in the 1908 Las Vacas revolt caused perhaps the biggest stir when, at the end of 1910, he began to recruit revolutionaries in the border zone. Guerra's efforts began in early December, when he appeared on the patio of the *Hacienda* San Graciano, property of Vicente Bartoni. Accompanied by twenty five armed and mounted rebels, each sporting a hat ribbon with the Mexican national colors of red, white, and green, Guerra enlisted six *hacienda* workers before passing on to the neighbouring *Rancho* San Antonio. There, fourteen more men, including cowboys from the *rancho*, joined the ranks. Guerra continued his efforts to recruit men and gather supplies until early the next year, appropriating arms, cattle, and other goods from *haciendas* and *ranchos*. Federal forces and the *Rurales* apparently did little to halt Guerra, and it was only through the efforts of property owners and local police that a fifty-five-man security force was assembled and given the task of capturing him. After ten days of active pursuit, however, the revolutionaries proved elusive. Hampered by the international border, which the rebels freely crossed in search of refuge, the security force, and the Federal soldiers who joined the chase, had to admit at least a temporary defeat.[22]

PLM activity, perhaps connected to the Maderista movement, continued in northern Coahuila as well. The immense Hacienda La Babia of General Gerónimo Treviño, centred in Múzquiz, was seized and converted into a centre of rebel operations, and guerrilla attacks frequently occurred from an insurgent base in the Burro Mountains. American consul Ellsworth reported rumours of an arms ring linking San Antonio and Comstock, Texas, to the Burro Mountain rebels.[23]

Although rebel activity in northern Coahuila remained sporadic during the 1910-11 Maderista revolt, the border zone continued to be a volatile area. Mexican and American officials confronted the problems of arms smuggling and rebel recruitment, and their efforts to prosecute revolutionary activities were hampered by the widespread sympathies rebel groups enjoyed in the Texas border towns. León Gómez, Mexican consular agent in Del Rio, reported that nearly universal hostility towards the Mexican government existed among the town's Mexican population, and that American residents were sympathetic to the rebel cause. Many Texas county authorities also displayed sympathy for the Maderistas, and local prosecution of neutrality violations by Mexican rebels was less than rigorous.[24]

The sympathies of the Texas and Mexican border population increased with reports of the sometimes brutal persecution of captured Maderista rebels. Suprised by Federal troops near the

northern town of Rosales, a small group of rebels was apprehended and executed in the town schoolyard before an audi-
ence of children. The outraged community of Mexican exiles in
Eagle Pass issued a public protest against the crime.[25]

Just as the Texas border towns had provided a refuge for the
economic and political exiles of the Porfiriato, so did the Texas-
Coahuila border provide an avenue of escape for the residents of
Mexican border towns. People passed as easily as guns across the
usually dry river bed separating Ciudad Porfirio Díaz from Eagle
Pass, and rumours of an impending rebel attack could generate a
mass exodus to Texas of residents and local Mexican officials.[26]

Resistance and Victory

The success of the Maderista revolt of 1910–11 was due not only
to the spontaneous and often overwhelming display of popular
support in many areas of Coahuila, but also to the failure of local
defence against the rebels. Federal soldiers, as well as the *Rurales*
consistently struggled to assert themselves against the insurgents.
The Federal Army that did battle with Maderista rebels represented a fighting force that by 1910 had been significantly curtailed. In the interest of Porfirian centralization and control,
individual states such as Coahuila were left with a handful
of regiments based in important towns such as Monclova and
Torreón, and dependent on the railway lines for their mobility.
The Porfirian military, moreover, was an unreliable fighting
force, consisting of many unenthusiastic draftees. The *Rurales*
too, were a less than impressive security force, known more for
corruption than for military capability.[27]

The limitations of government defence forces were readily
apparent during the first phase of the revolution, when army
garrisons were frequently outnumbered, and Federal troops and
the *Rurales*, hedged on pursuing rebel groups. As well, the hit-
and-run tactics of the insurgents, including the destruction of
railroad tracks and bridges, hampered soldiers' mobility and dis-
couraged any coordinated counter-offensive. Particularly in the
border area, where rebels freely crossed the international line,
rumours flew that the Mexican government could do little
to stop the Maderistas. Such rumours only intensified when
the municipal president of Ciudad Porfirio Díaz was forced to
buy arms in Eagle Pass to supply Federal troops. Frustrated in
their attempts to combat the insurgents, several Federal soldiers

stationed in northern Coahuila turned their attention to apprehending and imprisoning migrant labourers who attempted to
enter the state from Texas. In the Laguna, soldiers likewise occupied themselves with the detention of unemployed workers.[28]

As revolutionary activity increased in 1911, and as Federal
troops and the *Rurales* struggled to respond, local officials scrambled to organize their own security forces. Despite the willingness of many elites to lend support, several areas had difficulty
in recruiting and retaining volunteer soldiers. The municipal
president of Sierra Mojada reported that the offer of money and
horses did little to retain volunteers, and that the security force
changed personnel every other day. Even when the promise of
monetary reward succeeded in attracting volunteers, they were
often of dubious loyalty.[29]

Local demands for defence strained the state treasury. By May
1911 municipal governments from all corners of the state were
requesting additional money to cover the ever-increasing cost of
local security. On May 2, local officials in Matamoros left the
town since they lacked the means to repel an imminent rebel
attack. In other areas, government personnel simply resigned or
abandoned their posts when it became apparent that they could
do little to defend their jurisdictions.[30] Meanwhile, Governor
del Valle was compelled to use the revenues of coal companies in
central and northern Coahuila to provide an auxiliary force for
guarding the state's railroad lines. In response to the Maderista
revolt del Valle also revived the hated institution of the *jefatura
política* in central Coahuila and the Laguna region.[31]

Governor del Valle's efforts to persecute the Maderista rebels
were accompanied by the Díaz regime's renewed efforts to
punish the entire Madero family. Few of Francisco's relatives
were enthusiastic supporters of his political activities, and after
his grandson issued his revolutionary plan, Evaristo Madero sent
his sons to Mexico City to prove his own loyalty. When revolution broke out, however, Díaz and the Científicos began to
destroy the family's fortune, while the Maderos took refuge in
San Antonio. By early 1911 American ambassador Henry Lane
Wilson reported that the family's credit had been cancelled and
its loans called in.[32] Official persecution of the Madero family
did little to halt the popular movement that gave definitive
expression to Maderismo in Coahuila. By the end of May 1911
a combination of co-ordinated rebel attacks and more spontaneous outbursts had resulted in the capture of several important

towns, the deposition of many local officials, and the disruption of communications within the state.

Coahuila was but one state in which Madero's call to arms was answered, hesitantly at first and with greater resolve by 1911. Several small-scale uprisings occurred in 1910 in other parts of Mexico, including Puebla, Tlaxcala, and Veracruz. By 1911 Morelos, Sonora, the Yucatán, and Baja California were the scenes of additional and significant rebel activity. In Chihuahua, a strategically important northern state that shared borders with Coahuila and Texas, Abraham González (who would soon become the state's governor) equipped and encouraged Pascual Orozco Jr. and Pancho Villa. Orozco, a mule skinner with experience working in the fields and for foreign-owned mining companies, was motivated by a healthy dislike of Chihuahua's wealthiest and most powerful group, the Terrazas-Creel family. Villa, a native of Durango who had early on established his reputation as a bandit, tried his hand at a variety of trades. In 1905 he settled in Chihuahua where he became a cattle dealer and rustler.[33] In 1910 Villa and Orozco staged several successful raids within Chihuahua, and they became key players in Madero's campaign to overthrow Díaz. For as revolutionary activity sputtered in his home state, Madero shifted his attention and his base from San Antonio to El Paso, which lay across the international border from the Chihuahua city of Ciudad Juárez. Centrally located along the U.S.-Mexico border and of great economic importance, Ciudad Juárez quickly became the prize most coveted by the Maderistas. Its capture would allow ready access to arms and materiel.[34]

As rebel activity intensified in Chihuahua, and as rebels in other Mexican states succeeded in combating Federal troops, the Porfiriato entered its last days. In March U.S. troops were deployed along the Chihuahua border to help protect American lives and interests, an indication that Díaz was losing his ability to control the country. In May Ciudad Juárez fell into the hands of Maderista rebels, including Villa and Orozco. With the Treaty of Ciudad Juárez, Díaz and Corral resigned. Francisco León de la Barra, a diplomat and former ambassador to Washington, assumed control of a provisional government that would preside until democratic elections were held.[35]

The battlefield triumph of Maderismo seemed to endorse the popular victories that gave momentum to the rebel movement in Coahuila and elsewhere. In reality, however, the success of Madero's revolt was limited. The Treaty of Ciudad Juárez removed only Díaz, Corral, and a few state governors, leaving virtually intact the Porfirian army and bureaucracy. Still convinced that the democratic process would eventually prevail, Madero failed to sanction the complete dismantling of the old regime. This presented immediate problems on the local level. In Coahuila, popular triumphs were marred by the perpetuation of a Porfirian system; and the continuation of the economic crisis, exacerbated by the dislocations of revolution, ensured the persistence of popular unrest.

Official persecution of the Anti-re-electionist movement, the dislocations of a major economic crisis, elite political division, and the reluctance of several leading political figures to answer Madero's call for an uprising hampered the development of a co-ordinated revolt in 1910. By 1911, however, Madero's rebellion had finally gained momentum. In character and tone it was largely a popular revolt, although the support of workers and other groups was more a reflection of the immediate economic situation than an informed expression of support for the moderate principles championed by Madero. The localized outbursts that existed side by side with the more co-ordinated campaigns of Maderista groups responded to the opportunity created by Madero's movement. Through such outbursts popular expression against *caciquismo* and the loss of political autonomy, the effects of land concentration, and even the dominance of foreigners in some sectors of the economy worked their way into the revolution. These outbursts also helped create an unruly rebellion with no unifying theme or purpose—a rebellion that would outlast Madero's national victory.

General Porfirio Díaz, dictator of Mexico from 1876 to 1911.

Centre for Southwest Research, General Library, University of New Mexico, 997-005-0001.

Francisco I. Madero (center left) and his father Francisco Sr. in El Paso, Texas during the early phase of the Mexican Revolution.

Photo Collection, El Paso County Historical Society.

A photo of rebels in Torreón who joined Madero's revolt in 1911. The caption reads, "Maderistas who made off with my guns." This photo was probably taken by Frederick Wulff, an American merchant who lived in Torreón.

Frederick Wulff Collection, C.L. Sonnichsen Special Collections Department, University of Texas–El Paso.

*Francisco Madero flanked by revolutionary leaders Pascual Orozco (left),
Guiseppe Garibaldi, and brother Raúl Madero, 1911.*

Dr. H.E. Stevens' Scrapbook, El Paso County Historical Society.

Forces of General Lucio Blanco along the Rio Grande, c. 1911 or 1912.
Blanco, a native of Coahuila, served as a military officer in both the
Maderista and the Carrancista movements.

Dr. H.E. Stevens' Scrapbook, El Paso County Historical Society.

Francisco Madero and General Bernardo Reyes at inauguration of
Francisco León de la Barra, Mexico's interim president after
the overthrow of Porfirio Díaz, 1911.

Center for Southwest Research, General Library, University of New Mexico, 997-005-0088.

4

Madero, Carranza and Coahuila

The Dual Administration

O n June 3, 1911, a victorious Madero arrived in Ciudad Porfirio Díaz (a town that would soon reclaim its traditional name of Piedras Negras) enroute to Mexico City. In an open car he crossed into Mexico over the International Bridge that had been decked in palms and flowers. Americans and Mexicans greeted Madero with wild enthusiasm, and Mexican consul Francisco Villasana noted a restored sense of confidence among the border population. Venustiano Carranza had been received with equal enthusiasm in northern Coahuila a few days earlier, accompanied by 150 armed Maderista soldiers. Despite his reluctant participation in the Madero revolt, Carranza was designated Coahuila's interim governor, a concession to a man who, in the words of an American official, was "one of the most universally popular men in the state of Coahuila."[1]

The Maderista victory seemed to augur well for Coahuila's popular movement. From 1911 until the tragic end of the Madero presidency in 1913, both Madero and Carranza were confronted with numerous demands for concrete change and for the elimination of the Porfirian system. At the same time, however, Coahuila continued to experience unrest, economic dislocation, and political factionalism. Refusing to effect significant reforms, Madero quickly lost support in his native state. Governor Carranza, meanwhile, began to lay the foundations for his own Constitutionalist movement.

Carranza and the Popular Voice

As Madero began his campaign for the presidency and Carranza prepared for the November 1911 gubernatorial election that he would easily win, the popular revolt that had resulted in the victory of Maderismo in Coahuila continued to find expression in demands for local political and economic change. Madero's victory revived many Maderista clubs (the victims of Porfirian persecution) and encouraged the creation of others. With a new sense of confidence Coahuilans of all classes campaigned for Madero and Carranza, as they protested against local officials who had not been immediately removed by the revolution and asserted their right to choose their own local leaders.

The capture of Coahuilan towns by Maderista forces was often accompanied by the deposition and replacement of local authorities, usually by members of local Anti-re-electionist clubs. After the capture of Torreón Manuel Oviedo, a school-teacher and president of the local Anti-re-electionist club, was installed as municipal president. In San Pedro townsmen held a meeting that replaced newly exiled officials with Maderista sym-pathizers.[2] Popular protest after Madero's victory also resulted in the replacement of Porfirians. In Ciudad Porfirio Díaz Maderistas pressed for the resignation of municipal leaders, including customs officials; Rafael Múzquiz, an officer of the local Maderista club, became municipal president.[3] In central Coahuila complaints against the Garza Galán family—the "old *caciques*" of Múzquiz who were clearly identified with the Porfiriato in the popular mind—were frequent.[4]

Petitions to rectify the abuses of the Porfirian economic system accompanied political demands. Ranchers in northern Coahuila requested the re-opening of an old road used to trans-fer cattle to a local railroad station. The road had been closed off by a wealthy family that had been granted a special con-cession during the era of Governor Cárdenas. Smallholders given lands during the nineteenth-century liberal administration of Victoriano Cepeda and deprived of those lands during the Porfiriato also petitioned for the return of their independent holdings. In the Rio Grande District, demands for land targeted foreigners favoured by Díaz, and members of the military who had served General Bernardo Reyes and received economic favours in return.[5]

Demands for the restitution of communal lands and of the

properties of independent farmers also issued from the vast central region, which had witnessed dramatic economic growth with the development of mining. Governor Carranza received a request for the redistribution of communal lands in Abasolo, where expropriation during the Porfiriato had forced displaced smallholders to work as day labourers.[6] Several additional requests for land involved smallholders whose claims dated from the era of liberal reform during the mid-nineteenth century, and who included in their petitions pleas for the scarce water that was crucial to the farmers of central Coahuila. For instance, San Juan de Sabinas, established as a municipality of independent farmers by Benito Juárez, saw much of its land and water engulfed by the new municipality of Sabinas, created by a decree of Miguel Cárdenas. The municipality had been carved out to accommodate foreign mines and survey companies, depriving the older community of both resources and an adequate tax base with which to support its local government. In 1912 the residents of San Juan de Sabinas petitioned Carranza for a redrawing of the old municipal boundaries.[7] From various points in central Coahuila, Carranza also received petitions for the opening of blocked roads, cut off by barbed wire as prominent foreign and Mexican entrepreneurs enclosed their lands.[8]

Independent farmers of the Laguna also sought redress of Porfirian abuses. The local government of Matamoros petitioned Carranza for the return of lands separated from the municipality and annexed to the neighbouring community of Viesca. This change had been the earlier work of prominent landowners Manuel de la Fuente and Miguel Cárdenas. It effectively deprived smallholders of the use of these lands, and exempted the properties from further taxes.[9]

Although it is difficult to document the extent to which Carranza sided with those petitioning for land and water, he did respond favourably to several of their requests. In particular, he ordered *hacendados* to share water with smallholders and communal landowners, and he designated agents, such as Pablo González, to oversee this. Yet Carranza, himself a landowner, did not take significant steps towards true agrarian reform in his native state. Furthermore, his rulings were not always obeyed by wealthy landowners, and the privileged members of the Coahuilan legislature tried to block decrees that threatened *hacienda* lands.[10] Frustrated with the slow pace of change, many Coahuilans were quick to rectify Porfirian abuses themselves. This was particularly true in central Coahuila, where smallholders had developed a tradition of barbed wire cutting and other methods of frontier justice during the Porfiriato. Carranza responded to such activities at the end of 1911 by sending Andrés García to investigate and attempt the resolution of various water and land disputes. García's efforts were only partially successful.[11]

Particularly in the Laguna, demands for change had a decidedly anti-foreign tone. In Torreón, the Maderista victory created panic among the sizable foreign population. The large Spanish community, which consisted of several prominent *hacendados*, was especially threatened. On a *rancho* near Torreón, peons rounded up and beat several Spanish employees, killing two of them. Leaflets and other anonymous publications circulated, encouraging Mexicans to kill and rob foreigners. With the approach of the Mexican Independence Day celebration of 1911, Torreón residents were urged to kill all Spaniards. Attacks on Chinese businesses in the city also continued. Despite the reassurances of Maderista leaders, foreigners began to leave the Laguna in large numbers. They were joined by many wealthy Mexican families.[12]

While Carranza could do little to stem anti-foreign sentiment (and showed little inclination to do so), he did take steps to ensure that foreign concessions were negotiated with greater regard for Mexico's welfare, including the welfare of its workers. The state government retained a large degree of control over all new foreign concessions, and insisted that foreign companies open more employment opportunities (particularly in management) to Mexicans. Carranza also acted to eliminate tax exemptions and special privileges granted during the Porfiriato to both foreign and Mexican entrepreneurs. Porfirian tax breaks for foreign businessmen were especially resented, and had left many municipal governments strapped for funds. As part of a broader plan to equalize taxes and to promote fiscal independence, Carranza allowed municipalities to collect taxes from *hacendados* and others previously enjoying exemptions. In this way, Carranza fulfilled his campaign promise to restore a degree of autonomy to Coahuila's municipalities.[13] Like Madero, Carranza recognized the importance of the *municipio libre*, and acknowledged the degree to which Porfirian economic policies had undermined that ideal. But tax breaks for the wealthy were not simply a Porfirian phenomenon. They were also a function of the state's *camarilla* system, which often secured such economic favours for its members. Hence Carranza's concession to local government contained within it an implicit challenge to the traditions of elite privilege, although that challenge was certainly limited in its scope and intention.

The Maderista revolution also provided added impetus to the workers' movement in Coahuila. Industrial and agricultural workers, many already politicized by their exposure to the radicalism of the PLM and of American unions, organized in large numbers and became increasingly vocal. The Unión de Mineros Mexicanos (UMM) was established in central Coahuila in July of 1911, and several branches were founded throughout the state. Other workers' organizations were created as well, including a union of railroad workers in Monclova, which urged its members to participate actively in elections and work for the "Mexicanization" of the railroads.[14] While lacking the institutional base of industrial workers, agricultural labourers in some areas of Coahuila also became more vocal after Madero's victory. In central Coahuila the municipal president of Sacramento complained that since Díaz' removal day labourers refused to work, and demanded their own land and water as well as the dismissal of their debts.[15]

1911 and 1912 were years of great labour agitation in Coahuila, much of it centred in the mining communities. Accustomed not only to generous economic concessions but also to a large degree of control over the mining communities and their workers, mine owners and administrators found their power disputed by an increasingly politicized workforce. Miners complained of the arbitrary acts of mining company administrators, owners, and company police. Because of the prevalence of foreigners in the mining industry, worker protest often had a strongly anti-foreign tone. At the Fenix coal mines in northern Coahuila, workers struck against the monopoly Americans held over the management of the mines. The exclusive control mining companies held over all commerce within the mining camps and the artificially high prices that this caused were additional sources of complaint, as were wages and living conditions.[16] Union recognition was an issue as well, with many companies refusing to recognize the UMM and threatening to dismiss union members.[17]

Disputes within some mining communities extended into the political arena. Elections for local officials in central Coahuila polarized the Rosita mining camp into two parties, one including managers and high-level employees of the Companía

Carbonífera de Sabinas and the other formed by workers. The miners of Rosita, many of whom attended classes on "History and Socialism" sponsored by the UMM, described the situation in terms of a class struggle, revealing the influence of anarcho-syndicalist and socialist ideas: the town was split between a "propertied" class and other "supporters of the old regime," and the "proletariat." Workers appealed to Carranza for justice against the "inhuman foreigner." When work was suspended they complained that foreign companies were practicing "extortion" on workers, "cynically ignoring the laws that regulate the fight between capital and labour." Mining companies were notably concerned about socialist propaganda, as were Maderista officers who feared that some workers might be in contact with the Magonistas of the PLM.[18]

Faced with increasing unrest among Coahuila's miners, Carranza attempted to address some of their complaints. In response to a petition of labourers and merchants against a foreign investor who had closed his mining camp in central Coahuila to all outside commerce, forcing all workers to buy at the company store, Carranza ordered the opening of the camp to all local merchants. He also supported local efforts to force mining companies to pay property taxes, and encouraged the peaceful settlement of mining strikes. Carranza's efforts helped establish better conditions for many Coahuilan workers; and in 1913 Coahuila enacted one of Mexico's first worker protection laws. Carranza's efforts to help the workers of Coahuila's mining communities and to break the Porfirian system of foreign privilege, however, were often met with defiance, and even Carranza's support of unionism was accompanied by a desire to discourage strikes. In 1911 Carranza ordered local officials to punish those initiating strikes among workers of the mines, *ranchos*, *haciendas*, and factories, and those impeding others who wished to work.[19]

Carranza's reforms, while not always far reaching or successful, helped the governor develop an important personal base of support, particularly among the state's workers. Carranza also appealed to Coahuilans of all classes with his campaigns for better health and an improved educational system and a crusade against vice. Efforts to promote better sanitation included the clean-up and regulation of food industries and provision of vaccinations. Educational improvements consisted of financial help for rural schools, prompt and adequate payment of teachers, and modernization of the curriculum. Convinced that education was the key to progress, Carranza sought to improve and extend the state's educational system and, as in the case of his fiscal policy, he saw greater municipal control over school-related issues as a prerequisite for success. A tax on alcohol, prohibition of gambling, and regulation of prostitution were among Carranza's anti-vice measures.[20] In Torreón the Chinese community frequently requested permission to smoke opium, which was imported through several commercial houses in the city and sold by Chinese dealers. Although the municipal president suggested that this "ugly vice" be allowed as long as it did not spread to the Mexican population, Carranza refused permission, claiming that opium caused depression.[21]

Although Carranza emphasized democracy and municipal autonomy, his administration was in reality highly centralized. The continuing unrest in Coahuila and the need to pacify the state compelled Carranza to continue the time-worn practices of rigging elections and punishing opponents. His own electoral victory in 1911 was ensured through the manipulation of municipal officials. While Carranza passed a law that promised autonomy in the election of local officials, he also used the *jefatura política*, which had been revived during the Maderista revolution, to help gain control over the municipalities. In the Laguna, for example, Carranza decreed the creation of a temporary *jefatura* in 1912, then extended its existence into 1913.[22]

Carranza's efforts to gain political mastery over Coahuila often encountered resistance. As interim governor he acted quickly to remove local Porfirians, but his designated replacements did not always meet with approval. In the wealthy mining region of Sierra Mojada, Carranza's designation of nephew Fernando Peraldi as municipal president generated popular protest. Led by Maderista army leader Juan B. Silva, residents of local mining communities presented a petition at a municipal meeting protesting the imposition of Peraldi and asking for the right to choose local officials through a popular vote. Assuring the petitioners of his support for Maderismo, Peraldi publicly announced that he would not assume his post unless it met with the people's approval. Carranza promptly negotiated a replacement, but was also quick to find Peraldi another post in Sierra Mojada. Eventually, however, local Maderista clubs petitioned again for the removal of Carranza's imposed officials. The governor's efforts to control the political life of this mining region would soon ignite a local rebellion.[23]

Popular attempts to force the renunciation of other officials imposed by Carranza or fraudulently elected occurred in other municipalities as well. In Juárez protests against the newly elected municipal president raised fears that members of the defeated opposition would stage a coup against local authorities, as they had done in 1887. Abasolo residents blocked the installation of newly elected officials with the impassioned appeal "No more tyranny, no more *caciques*."[24]

Obstacles to Peace and Centralization

As Carranza struggled to impose order and assert his authority in his native state, Madero faced immediate challenges as he attempted to convert military victory into national leadership. The Maderista movement brought together a host of rebels with a variety of ideas for transforming Mexican society. Many of those ideas, most notably Emiliano Zapata's demand for land reform, ran counter to Madero's own focus on moderate and predominantly political reform. The Maderista capture of Ciudad Juárez in 1911 gave an early indication that rebel goals and personalities would hamper Madero's attempts to assert control: Orozco and Villa, whose efforts were instrumental in the revolutionary movement in Chihuahua, unilaterally pursued the attack on Ciudad Juárez even while Madero was attempting an armistice with Porfirian forces. More significantly, they clashed with Madero over the composition of his cabinet. Orozco, who anticipated a position as minister of war, was snubbed, and both Orozco and Villa were critical of the Coahuilan's decision to use family and *camarilla* ties as he formed his leadership circle. Finally, the two Chihuahuans bristled over Madero's refusal to execute Porfirian general Juan Navarro after the rebel capture of Ciudad Juárez.[25]

Madero's crafting of a cabinet, specifically his choice for vice president, generated additional opposition from within the Maderista ranks. At the party convention that officially endorsed Madero's candidacy (and that renamed the Anti-re-electionist party the Progressive Constitutional Party), José María Pino Suárez, a journalist from Yucatán, was selected as Madero's running mate. Pino Suárez' selection was a snub to Francisco Vázquez Gómez, the vice-presidential choice in 1910. At the convention supporters of Francisco, including his brother Emilio Vázquez Gómez, tried to block Madero's vice-presidential choice. Their efforts were unsuccessful. Lingering resentment over the choice of Pino Suárez would soon provide yet another obstacle to Madero's attempts to govern Mexico.[26]

As he campaigned for the presidency, however, Madero's main challenge came not from the rebel or Anti-re-electionist ranks but from Bernardo Reyes, the Porfirian strongman of northeastern Mexico. Returning home from his European exile as the Díaz regime faltered, Reyes arrived in Mexico after the Treaty of Ciudad Juárez had sealed Madero's victory. The general pledged support for Madero's candidacy, but he quickly became the hope of wealthier and more conservative elements, as well as many in the middle class who sought a stable regime that would quickly end the violence in Mexico. His candidacy was particularly attractive in cities that had experienced significant unrest during the 1910-11 Maderista rebellion, including the city of Torreón. In August Reyes accepted the presidential candidacy proposed by several Reyista clubs, but he was unable to generate the momentum needed for a victory. Pressure tactics of Maderista groups as well as Reyes' declining popularity soon caused him to abandon the campaign. By the end of September he had left Mexico for San Antonio, Texas, where he plotted revolt. One month later, Madero and Pino Suárez were chosen in elections most notable for their tranquility and for lack of participation among workers and peasants.[27]

Reyes' candidacy revived several Reyista groups within Coahuila. But Maderista clubs, apparently aided by local and national officials, continually harassed the Reyista opposition. In the Laguna, formerly a strong base of support for Reyes, Madero supporters imprisoned officers of Reyista clubs and used armed force to prevent Reyista gatherings. In Torreón the mere announcement of a public demonstration for Reyes brought Maderistas into the streets, brandishing guns and shouting "Death to Reyes!" Hoping for protection, several Reyista clubs petitioned Carranza for help. The governor, himself a former adherent of Reyismo, did little to ensure the Reyistas a fair electoral fight.[28]

Still, although not as well organized as before the Madero revolt, Reyismo was a force of some significance in Coahuila during the political campaigns of 1911. When he realized that Carranza was no longer a political ally, Reyes promoted Manuel Garza Aldape, a prominent Laguna businessman, for the governorship of Coahuila. From his self-imposed exile in Texas,

Reyes continued to show an interest in Coahuilan politics, and throughout the summer of 1911 Reyista groups in many areas of the state campaigned for Garza Aldape.[29]

Calling for the nullification of the elections of Madero and José María Pino Suárez, and advancing his own revolutionary plan, Reyes finally entered Coahuila in revolt on December 7, 1911. At the border he was joined by some six hundred men, but despite the initial show of support Reyes failed to enlist additional followers, and surrendered later that month. He remained in a Mexico City prison for over a year.[30]

Although ultimately unsuccessful, Reyes' revolt of December 1911 again called attention to the fading Reyista movement in Coahuila. The insurrection was aided by Colonel Fructuoso García, Reyes' former strongman in northern Coahuila and past municipal president of Ciudad Porfirio Díaz. From the border town of Las Vacas, García prepared for the revolt by smuggling arms and provisions across the border with the help of a customs officer.[31] Officials also anxiously monitored the activities of Reyista clubs, particularly in Saltillo, the Laguna, and northern Coahuila.[32]

Madero's electoral victory did little to calm the various factions born of the 1910-11 rebellion, and even less to discourage the growth of opposition. Madero tried to assert his authority, in particular by ordering the demobilization of rebel groups led by the likes of Pascual Orozco and Emiliano Zapata. But his failure to respond effectively to the various demands arising out of his own revolution, especially the demands of the popular classes, ensured that resistance and unrest would continue. Among the first to challenge Madero's claim to national authority was Zapata, who issued the Plan of Ayala in November 1911. Underscoring his experience in the south-central state of Morelos, where Porfirian growth and economic policies had occurred at the expense of peasants and small landowners, Zapata demanded land reform, including the return of lands stolen by *hacienda* owners and the expropriation of one third of all *hacienda* properties.[33]

In northern Mexico, the most serious challenge to the Madero regime was the revolt of Orozco, whose break with Madero was apparent by the end of 1911 and who issued a formal revolutionary plan in March 1912. Orozco endorsed familiar political themes, including municipal autonomy, and embraced Zapata's call for land reform. But his plan also insisted on workers' rights, including improved wages and working conditions, and it advocated the nationalization of Mexico's railways. From his base in Chihuahua, Orozco generated support from a broad cross-section of local society. In addition to the popular classes and members of the middle class disgruntled with the slow and limited nature of change under Madero, many Chihuahuan elites cast their lot with Orozco. Elite support, ironic but with a logic of its own, sought to resist any significant reforms (including tax reform) that might be pursued by the progressive Maderista governor, Abraham González. Elites also looked to Orozco as the only popular leader who could help control the masses and restore order.[34]

Orozco's leadership appealed to Coahuilans, primarily workers, who were increasingly disaffected by the moderation of the Madero movement. Even before the publication of Orozco's plan, several adopting the banner of Orozquismo rebelled in the Laguna region. Former Maderista leader Benjamín Argumedo invaded the town of Matamoros, then retreated before the advance of Maderista troops led by Sixto Ugalde. Argumedo's forces also staged an unsuccessful attack on San Pedro. Orozquismo found echoes in central Coahuila as well. In May 1912 José Inés Salazar led over one thousand men in the capture of Sierra Mojada and Cuatro Ciénegas. In Sierra Mojada rebels gained the support of several miners' unions; mine workers and insurgents joined together to loot the houses of local officials that Carranza had imposed.[35] Failing in their attack on Monclova, Salazar and his men abandoned Coahuila. Federal troops, Maderista soldiers, and various volunteer groups organized by Carranza continued to battle small bands of Orozco rebels in northern and western Coahuila. As Orozco and his followers were beat back in Chihuahua by Victoriano Huerta, a general in the old Porfirian army, Coahuilan troops gave chase to the rebel forces of Marcelo Caraveo, who had entered the state through the western sierras. By early October, Caraveo was defeated and his troops dispersed, many returning to Chihuahua or fleeing into Texas.[36]

In his efforts to pacify Coahuila Carranza also confronted the ambitious Garza Galán clique led by brothers José María, Juan, and Andrés, all of whom had actively opposed the Maderista revolution. During Madero's electoral campaign of 1911, Galanista groups were active in northern Coahuila and in Texas, where they were identified with the broader revolt of Emilio Vázquez Gómez, who protested his exclusion from the 1911 elections by calling for Madero's removal. Andrés Garza Galán was a member of the International Club in San Antonio, identified as a centre of anti-Maderista activity. Along with his brothers, he was active in fomenting rebellion in Coahuila's border region.[37]

In addition to centres of organization in San Antonio and along the Texas-Coahuila border, Galanistas also had a base in the northern municipality of Guerrero. There Gabriel Celvera, a local *cacique* whose fortunes had waxed and waned according to those of the Garza Galán faction, led a Galanista party. After the victory of the Maderistas in 1911, Celvera and others attempted to manipulate local elections in order to restore the power of the Galanista clique.[38]

In the border region too, Galanismo and Vazquismo were sometimes identified with the continuing Magonista movement.[39] Although many members of the PLM both within Coahuila and in its border region aided the Madero revolution, Magonistas were quickly disappointed with the new regime, and they continued to sustain a separate movement. Almost immediately after the victory of the 1910 revolution, Maderistas were skirmishing with Magonista rebels in the border area. Clinging to their base in the Burro Mountains of northern Coahuila, Magonistas staged periodic attacks on *ranchos* and *haciendas*. An active propaganda campaign gained many adherents among border communities. Magonistas often distributed part of the spoils of their raids to workers, while assuring them that their employers had no right to own more than they. Promising land to those who would join in a struggle of the poor against the rich, the Magonistas succeeded in swelling their ranks with Mexicans from both sides of the border.[40]

Del Río remained an active centre of PLM activity throughout Madero's presidency. There, too, Magonistas planned raids into Coahuila and engaged in arms smuggling. Late in 1912 Primitivo Gutiérrez, Magonista and leader of the "Colorado" political faction of Del Río (so-called because of the black and red flag adopted by the Magonistas), led an attack on the ranch of Enrique del Castillo, a prominent resident of Las Vacas, Coahuila.[41] As with Galanismo and Vazquismo, the activities of the PLM often meshed with those of other rebel groups. Mexican consular agent Rafael Múzquiz noted that Magonista rebels would adhere to whichever party or group gave them funds, and members of the Galanista clique provided several donations.[42]

In attempting to prosecute the various rebel groups operating in northern Coahuila and the border area, Madero and Carranza faced not only an unpredictable system of alliances among these groups, but also the uncertainty that border officials were actually working in support of the Madero administration. Galanista plotting was of special concern to Madero, who suspected that it was gaining adherents among federal officials (former agents of the Díaz regime) who continued to operate in an official capacity along the border.[43] The pursuit of Magonista bands in the Las Vacas-Del Rio area was hampered by the rebel sympathies of Ildefonso Vázquez and Calixto Guerra, members of the local Maderista security forces, and ex-Magonistas.[44]

In addition to the rebellions that plagued northern Coahuila and the border region, Madero and Carranza faced a special challenge in the Laguna. Here the popular movement that had been instrumental to the Madero revolution had begun to fragment, while rebel discontent with the new regime was expressed by defiance among Maderista troops and ultimately by new revolts and a wave of banditry. By the summer of 1911 the still-armed Maderista forces of the Laguna had begun openly to express their dissatisfaction with Madero. Disciplining Maderista soldiers proved especially difficult in an area crowded with *Rurales*, Federals (mostly members of the old Porfirian army), and Maderistas, and in which confusion reigned over who was in charge. In June Maderista leader Inés Sosa apprehended and imprisoned a former Porfirian official in San Pedro, without official orders. When Emilio Madero, leader of Maderista forces, compelled Sosa to leave town local residents blocked his departure, yelling their support for the rebellious soldier and expressing their own disgust with old Porfirian officials.[45]

The conflict between *Rurales*, Federals, Maderistas, and local police forces exploded again in October, when Sixto Ugalde and Benjamín Argumedo led Maderista soldiers in attacking the Torreón police station and assaulting Federal forces. The instigators of the attack were discharged, and several other participants deserted. Argumedo soon became a notorious bandit in the Laguna, destroying property, burning railroad bridges, and causing other disruptions while Federal and volunteer forces followed in hot pursuit.[46]

Argumedo's actions were by no means isolated. In the aftermath of the Madero revolt the Laguna experienced a wave of banditry, including numerous attacks on *haciendas*. Many *hacendados* began to arm their workers for protection; Maderista troops often refused to pursue bandits.[47] In response to the demands of Laguna landowners and businessmen, Madero sent additional Federal troops to Torreón and finally demobilized the rebel army. In doing so he unwittingly gave added encouragement to the popular unrest that would plague the Laguna throughout his administration and after his death.[48]

Madero's refusal to deal with the Laguna's popular movement was characteristic of his approach to the entire state. As president, he received frequent warnings from Coahuilans that he must bring about some reform or risk losing all support in his native state. Laguna resident Antonio Farías wrote a series of letters to Madero in 1912 warning him that only land reform would bring about peace, and urging him to make his revolution more than simply a political movement.[49] That the land issue was important to many Coahuilans was evident in the several petitions Madero received from different areas of the state. Maderista leader Cesáreo Castro informed Madero of a plan to create an agricultural colony for several families in central Coahuila as a means to calm tensions and prove to Madero's enemies that the president was a committed reformer. Expatriate Mexicans in Texas petitioned for the acquisition of abandoned *hacienda* lands in northern Coahuila, and Madero received a similar petition from residents of Matamoros.[50] Such requests frequently went unanswered, and Madero often showed his preference for elite landowners, both Mexican and foreign. In 1912, for instance, he ordered Carranza to protect the interests of Patricio Milmo, whose *hacienda* in central Coahuila had been appropriated by several men, divided into separate plots, and prepared for planting.[51]

Coahuilans also complained of the nepotism of the Madero administration, even as appeals for employment based on family ties to the Madero family were frequent. A San Pedro widow accused Madero of offering federal posts to friends and relatives. She also chastised him for refusing to take steps against several members of his family who had initiated legal proceedings to appropriate water from the Nazas River, to the detriment of other landowners.[52] Despite the urgings of his own supporters and to the chagrin of the sizable Reyista opposition, Madero condoned the electoral fraud that installed Eugenio Aguirre Benavides, a close friend of the Madero family, as municipal president of Torreón.[53] Madero also intervened to assure a relative of a legislative post, forcing the withdrawal of another candidate who enjoyed the support of workers and ranchers.[54]

The continuation of popular unrest in Coahuila, as well as local manifestations of rebellions led by such as Bernardo Reyes and Pascual Orozco, hampered Carranza's attempts to calm unrest in his native state, just as they underscored Madero's inability to assert his authority on a national level. Animosity towards Madero and his plan for change surfaced almost immediately after (and in some cases before) his electoral victory. Indeed, it was an ill-defined anti-Maderismo that caused many Coahuilans to support the rebellions of Reyes and Pascual Orozco, rather than a commitment to the leaders or ideas of these two revolts. As in the neighbouring state of Chihuahua, sentiment against Madero took many forms, crossed class lines, and made for strange bedfellows. The Reyes' revolt, for example, found supporters in the unlikely pair of Amado Gutiérrez (Del Rio journalist, PLM adherent, and former Maderista) and brothers José María and Andrés Garza Galán, who sought to restore their own authority in the aftermath of the Porfiriato's collapse.[55] While much of the animosity towards Madero was a product of unfounded hopes and ignorance of the truly moderate nature of Madero's Plan of San Luis Potosí, in his home state Madero succeeded in angering many and pleasing few. By late 1912 a fellow spiritist wrote the president from Saltillo, predicting a revolt by Madero's own supporters that would result in the president's execution.[56] In Coahuila, Madero hastened his own demise by alienating Carranza.

The Uneasy Alliance

The alliance between Madero and Carranza was above all one of convenience, and the personal differences between the two leaders were always significant. Although both men were part of Coahuila's privileged class, Carranza's fortune was more modest than that of Madero. The age difference between the two men was also significant, and the younger Madero, much to Carranza's dismay, displayed many of the paternalistic qualities of a wealthy and foreign-educated *hacendado*. Carranza, whose six-foot frame cut a more impressive figure than that of the shorter and considerably slighter Madero, proved the more charismatic of the two men. This fact was not lost on Madero, who fretted about the considerable popularity of his fellow Coahuilan. The products of two traditionally rival political factions in Coahuila, Madero and Carranza provided only lukewarm support to each other's political campaigns: Madero was half-hearted in his commitment to Carranza's 1909 bid for the governorship, and Carranza hedged on providing support for Madero's revolution of 1910–11.[57]

The differences between Carranza and Madero surfaced immediately with the negotiations that ended the 1910–11 revolution. Carranza urged Madero to take a much stronger stand against Díaz, erasing all vestiges of the old regime instead of compromising with its various elements. He also criticized Madero's emphasis on political reform and questioned the younger Coahuilan's commitment to meaningful change. In turn, although Madero designated Carranza for the post of Coahuilan governor after the rebel victory and rewarded him with the post of minister of war and marine, he remained distrustful of the latter's motivations and feared his great prestige.[58] With reason: as governor, Carranza displayed both a marked degree of independence from the central government and a tendency to defy Madero's own wishes.

The mutual animosity of the two leaders encouraged the development of a dual administration in Coahuila. Madero's friends and relatives, rather than Carranza, became the president's main source of information on events in the state, and Madero attempted to manipulate political and military events through them. This was especially true in the Laguna, where Madero's brother Emilio commanded Maderista troops and co-ordinated many activities, including arms acquisition. Emilio worked in conjunction with other Madero friends and relatives in the border region, and acted independently of Carranza. In an especially telling letter of late 1911 Emilio Madero wrote to Catarino Benavides, now the commander of a small band of men in northern Coahuila, ordering him to send the entire contents of an expected arms shipment to him and none to Carranza.[59]

Madero's attempted manipulation of Coahuilan politics through his friends and relatives understandably angered Carranza. To the suggestion of Adrián Aguirre Benavides, Madero family lawyer and close friend, that a certain military leader was politically dangerous and should be moved, Carranza replied that Aguirre Benavides' warning stemmed from political inexperience and jealousy. Carranza insisted that as governor and actual resident of Coahuila he was better able to judge the character of local leaders.[60] Carranza also bristled at orders from the centre. Occupied with repairing revolutionary destruction and protecting the state from banditry and rebellion, Carranza was particularly indignant at orders to perform monthly audits of the state treasury. Scolded for not complying with this duty, Carranza retorted that he lacked the time for such things, and that the request was an insult to the dignity of his office. Madero fired back with the suggestion that another official without Carranza's "scruples" should perform the task.[61]

The issue that most affected the relationship between President Madero and Governor Carranza was the dispute over Coahuila's irregular forces. Carranza organized these volunteer forces in an effort to combat Orozquismo and to bring peace to the state in the aftermath of Madero's revolution. Unlike the Federals and *Rurales*, the Coahuilan irregulars answered directly to the governor. Not surprisingly, Madero and the Federal commanders stationed in Coahuila, bickered with Carranza over who should control these troops. Madero was determined to assert his authority over them, and by the end of 1912, he had ordered the auxiliary soldiers commanded by Pablo González placed under Federal control and assigned to operations in Chihuahua and Durango. Another, and much smaller contingency of irregulars led by Francisco Coss, remained at Carranza's disposal in Coahuila. This was not a clear victory for Madero, however. For even as he grudgingly acceded to the president, Carranza took independent action, partially dissolving Coahuila's irregulars so that they would not be fully absorbed into the regular army, and most importantly, making a pact with Pablo González that ensured Carranza the personal support of González and his men.[62] With these actions Carranza maneuvered to retain the independent military force necessary to protect Coahuila from the continuing rebellions that the Federals seemed helpless to prevent. This same force would provide a basis for the nascent Carrancista movement that began to emerge just as the Madero regime was showing signs of atrophy.

Carranza's staunchly independent stance in Coahuila was in many ways a product of his tense relationship with Madero. It was also largely governed by conditions within Coahuila, which contributed to the continuation of popular unrest. From Carranza's rise to the governorship in 1911 and beyond, Coahuila's economy continued to feel the effects of the pre-revolutionary crisis, while experiencing the added economic stagnation and physical destruction brought by the revolution itself.

In general, unemployment was a significant impetus to the 1910-11 rebellion, and economic stagnation a key to the persistence of popular unrest beyond Madero's victory. But a particularly explosive situation developed in the mining region of central Coahuila. Already beset by the increasing demands of unionized workers and struggling to avoid strikes, mining companies were forced to curtail or halt production due to lack of demand as well as revolutionary unrest. In the coal mines of Río Escondido, mine owners were compelled to suspend and then completely halt operations. These actions forced hundreds of miners out of work. When anti-Maderista activities escalated in 1912, disrupting railroad service and cutting Coahuilan mines off from their markets, another nine thousand workers faced unemployment. With justification, American consular official Luther Ellsworth remarked that "at the mines we are living on the crest of a volcano that is likely to burst forth at any time. At the least provocation, the miners will break forth in rebellion."[63]

Unrest among agricultural workers also flourished, and in many areas of the state *haciendas* and farms were completely abandoned. As rebel raids and banditry increased, many *hacendados* turned their lands over to caretakers and left for the greater safety of towns and cities, sometimes putting hundreds out of work and providing ready recruits for insurgent bands. In the Saltillo area businesses stagnated and food was scarce. By late 1912 popular sentiment was overwhelmingly against Madero, and rumours flew that the entire army would soon turn against him.[64]

In the Laguna, with its particularly large industrial and agricultural workforce, the Madero revolution brought many businesses to a virtual standstill. Mines in the region lacked the currency needed to pay workers, and in Torreón families rushed to stock up on increasingly scarce supplies of food.[65] The crisis continued after Madero's victory. By late 1911 the Laguna was experiencing a wave of strikes by agricultural and industrial workers. American consular agent Theodore Hamm estimated that a strike of industrial workers in Torreón included almost ten thousand men.[66] Madero and Carranza sent troops to stop worker protests, so that most of these strikes were unsuccessful. Nonetheless, worker unrest continued into 1913.

As anti-Maderista rebellion escalated in 1912, a severe food shortage threatened to set off a new wave of banditry in the Laguna. Agricultural labourers as well as textile and railway workers were affected by the continuing economic crisis and revolutionary unrest. In San Pedro several residents asked Carranza to order *hacendados* to resume working their lands or to distribute the fallow land to idle workers. To discourage banditry Federal troops distributed free food and seeds to those without work. Carranza also sent some relief to Torreón.[67]

The Madero revolution ended, as it began, in Coahuila—with the continuation of popular revolt and unrest. Madero refused to address local demands for change, and his administration within the state faced numerous political challenges. Tensions between Madero and Carranza as well as the exigencies of the continuing revolution ultimately encouraged the development of a dual administration in Coahuila.

As governor, Carranza did not succeed in quieting the popular rebellion. Nor did his policies respond to some of the deeper social and economic problems that were a product of the broader transformation of the state, and that intensified with the Porfiriato. Yet Carranza's popularity and his attempt to address some of the state's specific needs, particularly those of the working class, won him valuable support, while his moderate political tack prevented his administration from alienating important sectors of the elite. In the end Carranza's success lay in channeling popular unrest into the new movement of Carrancismo, or Constitutionalism. Crucial to the success of this new movement was Carranza's establishment of a revolutionary army with a broad base of support.

5

Mobilizing Discontent

The popular revolt and unrest that continued to plague Coahuila, and the escalation of anti-Maderismo in many areas of Mexico, served only to strengthen Carranza's already independent stance. A private meeting with Madero in early January 1913, at which Carranza requested the post of minister of government and urged Madero to make fundamental political changes, yielded no results. A disgruntled Carranza returned to Saltillo and called for a meeting of several northern governors whose future support would be important to Carranza's emerging movement: Rafael Cepeda of San Luis Potosí, Abraham González of Chihuahua, Alberto Fuentes of Aguascalientes, and José María Maytorena of Sonora. Under the pretext of a hunting trip, Governor Cepeda and representatives of the other state leaders gathered in Arteaga, just east of Saltillo, to discuss the future of Madero's faltering government and to plan for the anticipated civil war that would likely follow its demise.[1]

While lobbying the leaders of neighbouring states, Carranza, with the endorsement of the Coahuilan legislature, assumed extraordinary powers and began to gather revenue for the anticipated conflict. He also re-asserted his hold over Coahuila's irregular forces. These now included troops stationed in the environs of Mexico City, as well as those under the command of Pablo González, which had been sent to combat Orozco in Chihuahua. Just eleven days before the fall of the Madero regime Carranza notified the president that Pablo González and Gregorio Osuna (a native of Tamaulipas who had joined the Maderista rebellion in central Coahuila and then become an officer in Carranza's irregular forces) had requested discharges from the Federal Army, into which they had been incorporated at Madero's insistence. He asked that Madero allow them to return to Coahuila with the forces under their commands.[2]

Carranza's dissatisfaction with Madero's leadership and his anticipation of continued conflict were unsurprising. The moderate nature of Madero's plans for change, his failure to recognize and respond to the demands inherent in popular unrest, and the survival of conservative and Porfirian elements in the government and the army all contributed to the president's difficulties. Within his fifteen months in office Madero had little time in which to act, and his initiatives on behalf of peasants and workers could not begin to satisfy rebel leaders like Zapata, who determined to carry on his personal struggle for land reform. As such disaffection grew, conservative forces, whose voices were heard in Congress, the press, and even the president's cabinet, assailed Madero from the other direction. Amid popular revolts and more conservative plots, the Madero regime was on increasingly shaky ground. Complicating things further was the attitude of the American ambassador, Henry Lane Wilson. As President William Howard Taft's representative in Mexico, Wilson early developed a personal aversion to Madero, and became convinced that the Coahuilan could not protect the significant American interests in the country. Wilson was unabashedly vocal in his criticism of the Madero government, and his actions would directly contribute to the end of Madero's presidency.[3]

By the beginning of 1913 Mexican conservatives, including members of Porfirio Díaz' Científico clique as well as supporters of Bernardo Reyes, had devised a scheme that would seal Madero's fate. At the beginning of February and under the initiative of conservative forces in the army, Bernardo Reyes (cooling his shoes in a Mexico City prison after his abortive revolt at the end of 1911) was released. At the same time Félix Díaz, nephew of Porfirio, was sprung from the prison where he was being punished for an equally unsuccessful rebellion that had unraveled in 1912. As they and their supporters approached the National Palace to effect a coup, forces loyal to the Madero government opened fire, immediately killing Reyes. Díaz and the insurgents retreated to another point in the city and dug in for a fight against Madero loyalists. The ensuing artillery barrage, which occurred in the heart of Mexico City for over a week, is recorded in Mexican history as the Tragic Ten Days.

The confrontation between government and insurgent forces provided Ambassador Wilson with the opportunity to shape the future of the Mexican Revolution. Ignoring the rules of diplomatic protocol, Wilson attempted to arrange a truce that would include Madero's resignation. He met regularly with Félix Díaz and with Victoriano Huerta, a general in the old Porfirian army who was in charge of defending Madero and the National Palace. Clearly biding his time and seeking a suitable personal outcome, Huerta soon betrayed the president with Wilson's blessing. On February 18 Huerta ordered Madero and his vice-president Pino Suárez arrested. Under duress, their resignations were extracted, and Huerta assumed the presidency, contriving a transfer of power that would allow him to claim constitutional legitimacy.

In the aftermath of the resignations, relatives and friends scrambled to protect the lives of Madero and Pino Suárez. Fresh in their minds was the arrest and brutal murder, just days earlier, of Gustavo Madero, Francisco's brother and a member of his cabinet. Ambassador Wilson turned a deaf ear on pleas for protection for the two men, and on February 22 they were shot (most likely on Huerta's orders) while being transferred to a federal prison. With the coup complete, Madero's widow, his parents, and other family members fled the country. The family's persecution, which had begun at the hands of Porfirio Díaz, had finally resulted in exile.[4]

Huerta versus Carranza

Carranza's independent course in Coahuila, which began before the machinations of Reyes, Díaz, and Wilson, was quickly transformed into rebellion when Victoriano Huerta replaced Madero. Carranza and the state congress immediately denounced Huerta, and several contingents of Coahuilan irregulars based in Mexico City and Chihuahua just as swiftly marched for Saltillo, effectively deserting the Federal Army. Carranza issued a public announcement of his opposition from the balcony of the government palace in Saltillo, and Huerta's Federals were sent to attack Coahuila.[5]

As Coahuila braced for the impending civil war, Carranza established the first headquarters of his rebel army in Arteaga, just east of Saltillo. As Carranza refused the requests of Mexican and U.S. officials that he end his rebellion, the Coahuilan legislature left Saltillo for the relative safety of the northern border.

The congressmen settled in Piedras Negras and named Gabriel Calzada military commander of that town. In early March the Carrancistas joined in their first battles with the Federals. A small force led by Roberto Rivas succeeded in briefly capturing the Laguna town of San Pedro, occupying the municipal president's office and extracting a forced loan. At the same time the Carrancistas suffered a defeat at Anhelo, near rebel army headquarters. The most spectacular of the early clashes between Federals and Constitutionalists occurred later that month, when Carrancistas, reportedly numbering almost one thousand, staged an attack on Saltillo. Forty hours of combat resulted in over two hundred fatalities, as some eight hundred Federal troops overpowered the rebels.[6]

After defeats at Anhelo and Saltillo, Carranza retreated north to Monclova. At the Hacienda de Guadalupe, Carranza's revolt was formalized with the Plan of Guadalupe. Issued on March 26 and quickly endorsed by Gabriel Calzada, the Coahuilan congress, and military leaders throughout the state, the resolution denounced the Huerta government and named Carranza First Chief of the new Constitutionalist movement, which aimed to restore legal and constitutional government to the country. The plan also designated Carranza as Mexico's interim president and called on the governors of other states to join the rebellion against Huerta. Carranza's proclamation garnered the immediate support of insurgent leaders in northern Mexico, including Pancho Villa and Pablo González. The Plan of Guadalupe also earned the endorsement of several large landowners. In Sonora Alvaro Obregón, the son of *hacendados*, mustered his troops to the Constitutionalist cause, and soon became one of Carranza's most important generals. Fellow Sonoran Plutarco Elías Calles, a primary school teacher who had been born into a poor family, joined Obregón and became one of his loyal supporters.[7] In the south, Emiliano Zapata hedged on formally endorsing Carranza, but nonetheless mustered his troops for the defeat of Huerta.

By April 1913 Carranza's movement was headquartered in Piedras Negras and the Constitutionalists appeared to dominate a large area in central and northern Coahuila. Huerta's attempts to negotiate with Carranza were futile. An envoy sent to the Constitutionalist camp was imprisoned, and the First Chief warned that all peace commissioners would be so treated. Despite Carranza's intransigence in the political arena and on the battlefield, Federal troops began to challenge the Carrancistas by the summer of 1913, encouraging Carranza to move his base of operations to Sonora. Federal occupations of Monclova and Piedras Negras robbed the Constitutionalists of strategic railroad lines that provided valuable daily income, and by the end of 1913 Federal forces claimed to control the entire state.[8] Military predominance, however, was temporary, and did not translate into political mastery. The Huerta regime would continue to struggle against a growing and increasingly vigorous Carrancista movement.

Immediately after Carranza's initial denunciation of the new regime, Huerta named Saltillo physician Dr. Ignacio Alcocer as provisional governor of Coahuila. Alcocer was one of four Huertista governors who, along with Federal generals Joaquín Maass and José Refugio Velasco as well as Práxedis de la Peña (the Laguna landowner who had been imposed as an interim governor by Porforio Díaz and who had rigged the election of 1909 so that Venustiano Carranza would lose his bid to govern Coahuila), served until the Carrancistas again seized control of Coahuila's capital in May 1914. In addition to confronting a strong Carrancista opposition, Huerta's governors inherited an economy in shambles, a state still torn by Porfirian factionalism, and a countryside still alive with banditry.

Alcocer's first task was to crush the Carrancista's armed movement. Yet from the start the Huertista military strategy floundered. Huerta's attempts to increase the size of the Federal Army throughout Mexico forced his military governors to resort to the hated *leva,* or draft, which had been utilized throughout the Porfiriato. In Coahuila Huertista officials tried to press bandits into military service, and sometimes resorted to imprisoning and then drafting *hacienda* workers.[9] The result throughout Mexico was a reluctant fighting force with little discipline and a corrupt officer corps.

In Coahuila, moreover, the Federals frequently lacked adequate troops and supplies to combat the Carrancistas. Governor Alcocer constantly begged for Federal reinforcements to battle the rebels, and remarked that the lack of Federal troops in Coahuila was causing local uprisings. As the *Carrancistas* tried to capture Torreón in the summer of 1913 local officials, desperate for manpower, organized a force of soldiers made up of criminals from the local jail to aid in the defence of the town. Not surprisingly, Federal desertions were also common, and *Rurales* sometimes defected to Carranza's side. During another pitched battle for Torreón men deserted the Federal Army in large numbers while officers scrambled to fill the void by drafting people on the merest pretext. As Carrancista attacks escalated in Coahuila throughout the spring of 1913, Federal troops were frequently without adequate arms and supplies. On May 3 rebel troops captured Matamoros after the Federal forces defending the town ran out of ammunition.[10]

Financing the Huerta regime and the Federal Army in Coahuila was always problematic, particularly since economic activity, already interrupted by the Maderista revolt, virtually ground to a halt during the Carrancista rebellion. Instability slowed production in agriculture, mining, and industry. The destruction of railway lines or the appropriation of coal, coke, and guayule by Constitutionalist rebels was enough to paralyze local foundries and smelters and halt rubber production. Ranching declined as rebel groups appropriated cattle in massive numbers, then sold them to the United States to obtain arms or used them to feed troops. Carrancista commandeering of horses from Coahuilan *haciendas* was so extensive that a decree requiring *hacendados* to contribute horses to the Federal Army met with replies that few or none were left. On one *hacienda* cowboys were forced to use mules to conduct vigilance work.

Indeed, the contest between Constitutionalists and Federals was largely a battle to control Coahuila's increasingly scarce but valuable resources. Control sometimes meant the destruction of such resources. In July 1913, as Federals worked their way into central Coahuila's rich mining region, rebels began burning coal reserves in local mining towns.[11] Weeks later, with Carrancista rebels still threatening Saltillo (now closely guarded and its streets barricaded with barbed wire), American consul John R. Silliman reported that the rebels had stripped the surrounding country of crops and animals. Fields were abandoned and remained unharvested, and basic staples were scarce. In August 1913 Carrancistas attacked and destroyed the Bella Unión textile factory. Although not operating at the time of the attack, Bella Unión was one of the principal industrial plants in the Saltillo area.[12]

The local economic crisis was exacerbated by the rebel strategy of destroying railway lines and bridges, especially those linking Saltillo and the Laguna region to points farther south. This not only disrupted communication between Federal troops but also, and more significantly for Coahuilans, contributed to the shortages of basic goods such as coffee, sugar, rice, and petroleum, while driving up their prices. Huerta's officials restricted the sale of these items outside of Saltillo, forcing residents of surrounding *haciendas* and *ranchos* to do without. Within the capital an anonymous flyer circulated blaming local merchants for inflated prices and accusing them of being Carrancista sympathizers. To prevent further rebel attacks on the railroads, a harried General Joaquín Maass threatened to transport the relatives of rebel leaders in pilot railroad cars. Federal troops threatened to seize three of Carranza's sisters for this purpose.[13] Railroad lines that connected Coahuila's coal mining region were likewise a source of intense competition between Federals and Constitutionalists. In Piedras Negras Rómulo Zertuche led a special corps of *"dinamiteros"* entrusted with blowing up railroad bridges from Sabinas to Monclova as Federal soldiers worked their way into northern Coahuila.[14]

The situation in the Laguna region was likewise discouraging. By May 1913 all railroad communication had been cut and businesses were at a standstill. Without fuel and other necessary materials, factories in Torreón shut down, leaving thousands without work. American official J.D. Carothers feared that, as during the Maderista revolt, these unemployed labourers would join the Carrancistas, and he noted that the lower classes tended to favour the rebels. The interruption of railroad traffic from Torreón to other areas of Mexico had economic ramifications that extended beyond Coahuila. Since the Laguna was a major source of cotton for Mexico's textile factories, workers in Puebla and other states faced the prospect of unemployment. One Huerta official recommended that cotton be purchased from the United States to supply the textile factories until communications with Torreón were restored. The owner of a textile factory in Coahuila made a similar request, and nervously noted that three hundred of his workers were idle.[15]

Carrancista banditry and general instability not only contributed to the sorry state of the Coahuilan economy, but also made tax collection by the local Huerta regime difficult if not impossible. Ravaging of *haciendas* and *ranchos* drastically devalued some properties, and many were forced to ask for exclusion from taxes. In 1914 León de la Garza asked Governor Maass for an end to taxes on the cattle once owned by his father in northern Coahuila. De la Garza's petition noted that all of the cattle had either been sold in the U.S. or consumed by Constitutionalist forces. In central and northern Coahuila a genuine revenue crisis developed when many property owners fled to the U.S., leaving their holdings without legal representation and making tax collection impossible. Throughout the state, banditry made the establishment of local police and security forces difficult, since property owners and businessmen victimized by such activity could not contribute to security maintenance.[16]

While the general economic decline made revenue difficult to obtain, Coahuilans themselves were angered at the often unrealistic tax demands of Huerta's governors. Requests for exemptions were especially prevalent in northern Coahuila, where the Carrancistas, who dominated the area for several months in 1913, had imposed their own taxes. After the revolutionaries departed, Huerta's officials tried to exact taxes retroactively, causing an outcry by locals. San Pedro's residents also bristled under Huertista demands for money. For nearly six months this town was left without troops as Federal forces went to the defence of the neighbouring town of Torreón. Townsmen insisted that they were not responsible for contributing to the Huerta regime and wryly suggested that *they* should be paid for the time they remained abandoned and at the mercy of the "Carrancista horde." For all Coahuilans the ultimate indignity was the extraordinary war tax declared in April 1914. This was to be paid by all taxpayers within eight days and was the equivalent of two years' worth of ordinary taxes.[17]

In addition to the increase in state taxes, on the national level Huerta ordered the printing of new paper currency. In Saltillo, however, a currency problem surfaced immediately when foreign-owned banks and town businesses refused to accept bills issued by banks in rebel territory. A local decree by the military commander ordering banks to accept all bills was ignored, and local merchants used the opportunity to unload unwanted currency on the Huerta government by buying post office money orders. Local officials also resorted to forced loans and other measures to raise revenue. In the Laguna the sale of cotton became a means to pay Federal troops. Huerta's officials also attempted to encourage gambling throughout the state, hoping that the proceeds would help finance the anti-Carrancista campaign.[18]

The use of repressive political measures furthered fueled the Huerta regime's unpopularity among Coahuilans. With Huerta prevailing against Carranza, local military officials designated *juntas de gobierno* to take over the task of municipal governance in Coahuila. Governor Alcocer also began to designate new local officials.[19] The increased use of the *jefatura política* and the manipulation of local elections became additional hallmarks of the local Huerta regime.

Under Alcocer three *jefaturas* were established: one for the Viesca District, including the Laguna region; one for central Coahuila, or the Monclova District; and one for the northern Rio Grande District. While Carranza had also revived the hated institution of the *jefatura política* during his governorship, the Huertista use of the office suggested, in some respects, the re-emergence of Porfirian patterns. Prior to the formal establishment of a *jefatura* for the Viesca District, Alcocer named Luis García de Letona *jefe* for Torreón. García de Letona had served in the Garza Galán administration, worked against the election of Miguel Cárdenas, and was named municipal president of Torreón in 1909 as Díaz and Reyes intensified their efforts to gain control over Coahuila. Alcocer's designate for Viesca was Miguel Garza Aldape, whose brother Manuel held several posts in the Huerta government and had supported the re-election of Díaz in 1910. For his part, Miguel had been a member of a Reyista club in his native town of Múzquiz.

Luis Alberto Guajardo, a former *jefe* during the Porfiriato, assumed the post in the Rio Grande District. Although Guajardo had established a Reyista club in Múzquiz, joined the Madero revolt, and been designated a *jefe político* during the Carranza administration, he ultimately supported the Huerta regime. Finally, Alcocer named Melquiades Ballesteros, a prominent cattleman, *jefe político* for the Monclova District.[20]

Alcocer's *jefes* openly meddled in local politics, selecting appropriate municipal officials. In his district, Ballesteros simply assumed the post of municipal president in the important town of Monclova. Guajardo (who also appears to have used his post to grab lands abandoned by those fleeing the revolution) personally named new local officials for the Rio Grande District rather than bother with scheduled elections. He noted that all suitable candidates had been forced to emigrate because of revolutionary violence, so that an open vote might result in the selection of those not supporting Huerta. Indeed, municipal and national contests held during the Huerta regime were an acknowledged farce. Coahuilans approached the national elections of October 1913 with complete apathy, and election day found Saltillo completely quiet, like a "deserted city."[21]

Although rigged elections and the rule of *jefes* were nothing new, and although the Carrancista revolt focused attention away from political reform, at least some Coahuilans recognized Huertista policies as a backward step. When Governor Maass made his selection for *jefe político* of the Viesca District several Torreón residents protested, arguing that the naming of a *jefe* would halt the progress that had been made in the political administration of the town since the Madero revolt. The return of old Porfirians and Porfirian practices under Huerta prompted one observer to remark that in Coahuila "'things are back to the same old state as in the time of the rule of Sr. Garza Galán,.. all the old crowd is back.'"[22]

The impositions of the Huerta regime also included police brutality and hyper-vigilance over the populace. As the Carrancista rebellion escalated, Coahuilans were arbitrarily apprehended and interrogated. Federal soldiers could also be ruthless in their treatment of entire populations. The town of Candela, considered a main focus of Carrancismo, was virtually destroyed when one of Huerta's officers ordered the burning of one hundred houses and caused six hundred families to flee into the surrounding mountains. Huerta's officials also showed little concern for local needs and appeared determined to erase the reforms of the Carranza administration. Governors Alcocer and Maass, for example, completely overturned Carranza's educational reforms, returning control of the state's public schools to the governor, thereby further eroding the municipal autonomy that seemed to be at least partially championed by Carranza.[23]

Despite the general unpopularity of the Huerta regime, the continued banditry and revolutionary violence encouraged some members of Coahuila's elite to cast their lot with the new president and contribute to the campaign against Carrancismo. Although Huerta and his officials frequently browbeat the locals into providing money and manpower for security, some propertied residents voluntarily contributed to the regime. After the failed Constitutionalist assault on Saltillo in March 1913, local merchants donated money to express their gratitude to the Federal Army for its defense of the town. *Hacendados* in the Laguna region willingly answered the call to form a rural police corps, and even agreed to higher taxes if it meant guarantees against rebel depredations. In central Coahuila owners of *haciendas*, *ranchos*, and factories likewise contributed voluntarily to the establishment of a rural police force. Fear of further rebel attacks sometimes made strange bedfellows: in the Monclova District Miguel Cárdenas, Jesús del Valle, and Práxedis de la Peña (each a former governor and representative of the three rival political factions in Coahuila during the Porfiriato) joined together to establish a *junta patriótica* for protection.[24]

Many Coahuilan elites also co-operated in the establishment of Defensas Sociales. These urban volunteer groups first developed during the Madero revolt to provide defence against banditry. For some members they also became a means of persecuting any suspected rebels or rebel sympathizers. Several such groups, including those of Torreón and Monclova, became auxiliary forces for the Federal Army and pledged their support for Huerta. Yet with few exceptions these defense forces had little effect. Their success depended on that of Huerta's struggling Federal Army, and Defensa members, clearly composed of the wealthiest and most conservative elements, bore the brunt of local animosity against the Huerta regime.[25]

Nor was elite support for the Huerta regime unqualified and persistent. U.S. consul John R. Silliman indicated that the endorsement of Miguel Cárdenas, a boyhood friend of Carranza, was half-hearted at best. Cárdenas had initially attempted to help Carranza and Huerta reach a negotiated settlement. When that attempt failed, and wary of further revolutionary violence, Cárdenas simply chose what he perceived to be the lesser of two evils. By 1914, with support for Huertismo in general decline, Cárdenas was questioning the wisdom of his choice and was soon suspected by Huerta's agents of being a Carrancista sympathizer.[26]

Even as Huerta failed to garner the definitive support of Cárdenas and other members of Coahuila's traditional political factions, he confronted the plotting of the Garza Galán clique. Active members of the anti-Maderista movement in Texas and the border region, the Garza Galán brothers had rejected affiliation with either Huerta or Carranza. As early as February 1913 Andrés and Juan Garza Galán were rumoured to be organizing a coup that would take control of Nuevo Laredo and proclaim army veteran and Porfirista general Gerónimo Treviño president of Mexico. The Galanista plot reportedly included several old Porfirians, including General Francisco Naranjo and even Pascual Orozco Sr.[27]

The Treviñista movement briefly bore fruit on February 15 when Gerónimo Villarreal seized control of Nuevo Laredo, deposed customs officials, announced a discount on importation fees, and declared Treviño president of Mexico. By August Huerta's officials had discovered a similar plot aimed at establishing the presidency of either Carranza or General Treviño. They suggested that this was a grab for power by the faltering Carrancista movement, as well as a product of General Treviño's anger at being detained twice by Huerta's men on suspicion of being a Constitutionalist sympathizer. In fact, Carranza had approached the aging general seeking support for his rebellion. In Coahuila Lorenzo González Treviño (who had marriage ties to the Madero family) was linked to the plot. The properties of his cattle company, which had reportedly been used to help the Maderista movement, were now identified as gathering places for arms and munitions.[28]

The Growth of Constitutionalism

Although Huerta's regime was destined to fail in Coahuila and to give added impetus to the growth of Constitutionalism, a string of Federal military victories in 1913 forced the First Chief to carry his rival government to Sonora. There, Carranza co-ordinated the revolt against Huerta, and Carrancismo took shape as a national phenomenon. Like its Maderista cousin, Constitutionalism rejected radical social reform in favour of a moderate liberalism. Within Coahuila, however, Carranza's movement had a distinctly populist tone. Successful in garnering and maintaining the support of the state's popular and middle classes, Carranza was able to prevent his movement from going the way of Maderismo. Particularly among workers, Carranza succeeded in building both a political and military foundation that would help defeat Huertismo and effect the destruction of the old regime. At the same time, however, Carranza's success in recruiting Coahuila's popular classes for the battle against Huerta was not the product of any pledge to significant social change. Rather, it was a product of the state's ongoing economic and political crisis—itself an expression of the broader transformations and dislocations that had provided the earlier momentum for Madero's movement.

As governor, Carranza had already learned the importance of Coahuila's workers, responding to their needs with specific legislation and reforms. His efforts were rewarded even before the Huerta coup, as workers began to enlist in and establish the local forces that would soon be incorporated into a Carrancista army. The state's mining region was a significant source of support, and as revolutionary violence forced the closure of many mines, workers enlisted in Coahuila's irregular forces. Juan Hernández García, president of the Unión de Mineros Mexicanos in Coahuila's coal-mining region, organized some two thousand miners and *campesinos* to help Governor Carranza in his fight against Orozquismo. These unionists would later form part of the Constitutionalist forces, in which Hernández García had by 1914 assumed the rank of colonel.[29]

In the Laguna economic stagnation provided the backdrop to the establishment of additional military forces that would become part of a broader fighting force after Huerta's coup. And while Huerta was in power, the continuing economic crisis simply provided more recruits for Carrancismo. In the months following Huerta's ascension to power and with Carranza and his followers still in control of central and northern Coahuila, jobless workers flocked to the Constitutionalist ranks. In Piedras Negras many worked in the railroad shops, making dynamite and manufacturing cannons. Unemployed railroad workers were ready recruits, and those still employed were often rumoured to be aiding the Carrancista cause. Ricardo Castillo, a long-time railroad employee who claimed to be a victim of the Garza Galán regime, wrote to Carranza from his exile in New Mexico to offer his services. Carranza replied with the request that Castillo join the Constitutionalist forces in Chihuahua. Idle *hacienda* workers also volunteered or were recruited by the Constitutionalists. Even after Huerta's soldiers had gained military control over most of Coahuila, Carrancistas continued to recruit the employees of Lorenzo González Treviño's vast properties in the centre and north. These properties were reportedly full of Madero sympathizers during the 1910-11 revolt. Federals scrambled to recruit the same workers or to find work for those unemployed.[30]

Carrancista recruitment was especially successful in Coahuila's mining communities, where the First Chief continued his careful cultivation of worker support. Carranza maintained close contact with his military leaders in the mining region, ordering them to do everything they could to help unemployed miners and their families. Constitutionalist commander Ildefonso Castro played a significant role among the members of the miners' union, finding them food, lobbying mining companies to resume work, and briefing idle workers on the Carrancista movement and its commitment to the working class. Carranza himself ventured into the fray between workers and mining companies. In one incident he ordered Fernando Benito, the Spanish manager of the Sabinas Coal Company, to advance unemployed workers a month's salary and to pay for their passage out of the mining community.[31]

Carranza's commitment to the state's miners also garnered him more spontaneous support as the Federals advanced northward. The latter soon discovered that the closing of additional mines meant not only the loss of valuable resources, but also the certainty that the newly unemployed would take up arms for the Constitutionalist movement.[32] In Coahuila's mining region Carranza channeled worker support into military strength.

Carranza's aggressive and sometimes ruthless persecution of his enemies, and especially of representatives of the Porfirian system, also inspired the confidence of many Coahuilans, just as it lent credence to the view that Constitutionalism was dedicated to the destruction of the old order. Carranza personally ordered the imprisonment or execution of those suspected of disloyalty. Several deserters from the Constitutionalist forces, including the brother of Huertista *jefe político* Luis Alberto Guajardo, were pursued and shot. In the town of Nadadores eleven Porfirian *caciques* were apprehended, and Carranza ordered them judged according to a nineteenth-century decree that would permit their execution. Constitutionalist troops transported the prisoners to Múzquiz, where they were kept in horrible conditions. Nothing could prepare the men, however, for the next phase of their journey. Strapped to railroad cars that carried dynamite and powder and threatened to explode at the slightest bump, the prisoners were transferred to Sabinas. There Pablo González, perhaps out of sympathy for the frightened and exhausted captives, set them free.[33]

That Coahuila's popular and middle classes tended to place their confidence in Carranza may be seen in the numerous petitions sent by individual Coahuilans to the First Chief, even as Constitutionalist troops began to waver before the advancing Federals. A small-scale merchant in the mining community of Palau asked Carranza's help for the workers there, who could not afford meat, continued to be paid in coupons valid only at the company store, and were lured by the games of chance that became more appealing as work at the mines dwindled. Railroad workers left unemployed after the Constitutionalist withdrawal from Coahuila requested work with Carranza's forces in Chihuahua. A more humble request came from María E. Castañeda, who received the eleven pesos needed for her school in the mining town of Agujita.[34]

Even without the active recruitment of Carranza and his leaders, many Coahuilans established armed groups of their own and pledged their support for the rebel movement. Carranza received notice of the formation of several such groups and channeled many of the new troops into already existing forces. With Huerta's Federals temporarily triumphant in Coahuila, Carranza also received statements of loyalty and offers of support from state officials who had served during his governorship and fled the state rather than submit to the new regime.[35]

The Coahuilan irregular forces established during Carranza's governorship, and augmented to combat Huertismo, included members of many social classes. In addition to the miners that joined Carranza in large numbers, among the rebel troops could be found local judges, teachers, cattlemen, merchants, farmers, tailors, *hacienda* and railroad workers, and cowboys. Although many had Maderista antecedents, having joined rebel ranks in 1910 and 1911, several (such as UMM president Juan Hernández García) were mobilized for the first time only on Governor Carranza's initiative. A few, such as Cesáreo Castro Villarreal, Francisco Coss Ramos, Lucio Blanco, and Eulalio Gutiérrez Ortiz, had Magonista antecedents. Finally, Constitutionalist ranks included at least a few career military men, including Colonel Juan Vela Leal and Colonel Luis G. Garfías, who had served in the Porfirian army.[36]

While Carranza succeeded in organizing a viable fighting force within his native state, here as elsewhere Constitutionalist forces faced the problems of supplying troops and keeping officer rivalry in check. Huerta's officials sometimes noted the demoralization of Carrancista soldiers, who hedged on fighting, and the desertions from rebel ranks because of lack of food and basic necessities. Tensions between rebel officers Pablo González and Jesús Carranza were apparently also a source of concern. The latter actually ordered González apprehended in October 1913 because of a recent military defeat and in light of rumours that González was attempting to desert. Nor could Carranza and his officers always draw independent rebel groups into the rebel army. The Laguna region, the site of so much banditry during the Madero revolt, continued to be an unruly area. Carranza's nephew Sebastián reported the existence of numerous small bands that wandered the area, robbing and plundering under the banner of the revolution, while refusing to be incorporated into the rebel army.[37] Despite such obstacles, by 1914 Constitutionalist forces began to gain the upper hand in Coahuila. In this they were aided by the national failure of the Huerta regime, as well as the continued American attempts to shape the Mexican Revolution.

Carranza Ascendant

Despite the initial victories of Federal troops in Coahuila and elsewhere, Huerta's attempts to control the revolutionary forces earlier unleashed by Francisco Madero had little success. The core of Huerta's support always came from the wealthier elements of Mexican society, and it involved the same nostalgia for the strong-armed Porfiriato that had infected many of Bernardo Reyes' supporters. Huerta, a grizzled army veteran with a fondness for alcohol, had little incentive or inclination to listen to the popular voice. And although he enacted a very limited agrarian reform, and he respected the hard-won rights (including the right to strike) of Mexican workers, his support never reached beyond the elites. The practical effect of the Huerta regime was to exacerbate the social polarization of Mexican society, and to contribute to the country's armed struggle. As Zapata, Villa, and Carranza struck at the Federal Army, Huerta struggled to find the material and moral means to stem the revolutionary tide. Not surprisingly, his rule was increasingly heavy-handed, extending to the assassination and imprisonment of legislators and ultimately to the closing of the national Congress.[38]

The nature and limitations of the Huerta regime ensured that the new dictator's enemies would only add to their ranks. Unfortunately for Huerta, those ranks included the United States government. Under President Woodrow Wilson (who had succeeded Taft), Huerta failed to gain the diplomatic recognition that would have legitimized his regime. In February 1914 Wilson tightened the screws, lifting an American arms embargo and allowing the Constitutionalists access to arms and supplies from the United States. Two months later, Huerta sustained an additional blow when Federal troops in the port city of Tampico briefly detained a group of American sailors who had gone ashore for gasoline. Seizing upon this additional opportunity to embarrass and weaken Huerta, Wilson sent American troops to occupy Veracruz. And while Carranza and his followers denounced the American interventionism, they were the ultimate beneficiaries. As Obregón, Villa, Jesús Carranza, and Pablo González successfully battled the Mexican Federals and then worked their way toward Mexico City (already being pressured from the south by Zapata's forces), Huerta tendered his resignation and headed into a brief exile in Spain. In August, one month after Huerta's abdication, Obregón presided over the Treaties of Teoloyucán, which called for the disarmament and demobilization of the Federal Army, finally dismantling an important cornerstone of the Porfiriato. On Obregón's heels came Carranza, who victoriously occupied Mexico City in the name of the Constitutionalist movement.[39]

As Huerta's regime wobbled and Constitutionalism assumed national significance, Carrancista supporters in Coahuila battled for control of the First Chief's native state. Particularly in the Laguna, Constitutionalist troops began to work with the large and growing forces of Chihuahua's rebel leader Pancho Villa. Villa's campaign to capture the strategically important Laguna region began in March. The assault on the coveted railway centre of Torreón started at the end of the month and continued until Villa entered the town in triumph on April 3. Federal generals Velasco and Maass were pursued by Villistas and Carrancistas as they retreated to the nearby town of San Pedro. There, a disagreement over command between the two Federal officers further weakened the Huertista resistance. American consular agent Theodore C. Hamm reported from Durango that Velasco split the ranks, retreating to Saltillo and leaving Maass and his men to provide a "half-hearted resistance" to Villa's assault. Maass received little help from the Federal forces led by Benjamín Argumedo, who were described by another Federal as "disorganized" and "drunk." With the victory of rebel forces imminent, San Pedro residents opened fire on the Federal troops, who began to desert the ranks and finally retreated. The line of retreat, reported Hamm, "was heavily strewn with abandoned guns, ammunition, and clothing and everything which might serve to identify a man with the Federal Army."[40]

Villa's occupation of Torreón set off the persecution of the Laguna region's significant Spanish population, who were predominantly members of the wealthy, land-owning elite. Even as the Constitutionalist movement began, Carrancista rebels were openly declaring their displeasure with these foreign residents, and they echoed Villa's vilification of the Spaniards for their role in the betrayal of Madero. Indeed, most Spanish residents in Chihuahua and Torreón had supported the Huerta regime. Villa had first captured Torreón in 1913, and his victory was followed by the execution of several Spaniards and by Villa's exhortation that others leave the area. In 1914, after Villa had expelled the Spanish population of his own state of Chihuahua, Torreón's remaining Spaniards braced for his assault on the town. Representatives of several foreign governments tried to convince Villa that rumours of the Spaniards' support of Huerta's Federals were false. In response to foreign pressure, Villa finally agreed to respect the foreign residents of Torreón, but he urged them to take shelter in a few designated buildings. Although the frightened Spaniards followed his instructions, with the rebel capture of the town Villa harangued them for morally and materially aiding the Federal forces. He suggested that the Spaniards should be executed, but instead decreed their expulsion from Mexico.[41]

Almost immediately, train cars carried the harassed Spaniards and their families to Ciudad Juárez. Then, despite Carranza's orders to the contrary, Villa began seizing Spanish stores and other properties in Torreón and the surrounding area.[42] Villa's independent stance with regard to the Laguna's foreign population and his defiance of Carranza hinted at a rift between the two leaders that, by the summer, would widen dangerously.

With the Laguna in the hands of Villa and the Constitutionalists, Pablo González and Francisco Murguía began a campaign that, by the end of May, would seize control of central and northern Coahuila. On April 29 the Carrancistas occupied Piedras Negras, ending a prolonged fight for that strategic border town and precipitating additional desertions from the Federal ranks. One assault on Piedras Negras resulted in the Carrancista capture of enemy soldiers, several of whom joined the rebels on the promise that they would be elevated two ranks within the Constitutionalist army. Adding to the already complex border situation during the rebel assault on Piedras Negras was the U.S. invasion and occupation of Veracruz. U.S. and Texas officials placed additional troops along the border to prevent retaliatory action from the other side, and Texas governor Oscar B. Colquitt suggested the seizure of several border towns, including Piedras Negras. Rumours of a possible U.S. invasion prompted some Coahuilans to begin seizing livestock belonging to Americans in northern Coahuila.[43]

For U.S. consul William P. Blocker, however, the greater concern was that Federal soldiers and Carranza's troops would unite forces in response to American actions in Veracruz and along the border. Blocker reported that as the rebel troops of General Murguía approached Piedras Negras they were met by Federalist General Guajardo, who urged them to join Huerta's ranks and help resist a U.S. invasion. A suspicious Murguía declined the invitation and proceeded to occupy the border town. Blocker claimed that most of Guajardo's troops then chose to join the Constitutionalists.[44] In May, the rebels completed their campaign with the capture of Monclova and Saltillo. The next month Carranza returned to his native state, establishing Constitutionalist headquarters in the capital.

Coahuila's Constitutionalist rebellion of 1913–14 was a product of the same conditions that had produced Maderismo: economic crisis, dislocation, and political repression. Just as the earlier revolt added to the state's economic quandary, so the unfulfilled expectations generated by Madero's movement contributed to the climate of unrest. In the Huerta regime, moreover, Coahuilans confronted a renascent Porfirismo that rewarded and reassured some traditional elites while alienating the popular classes. For most, the new Mexican government brought increased taxes and repressive political measures.

Although many wealthier residents cast their lot with Huerta, Carranza's rebellion did not simply split the state along class lines. Constitutionalists garnered the support of several propertied Coahuilans, while Porfirian elites such as the Garza Galáns took an independent stance. Support for Huerta, moreover, was often absent support. While claiming a pro–Huerta orientation, many *hacendados* and businessmen simply fled the state to escape the inevitable depredations that accompanied the continuing revolution.

Even before his rebellion against Huerta, Carranza had begun to build his own military force. As governor, his policy of deliberate but careful reform won him the support of the state's popular classes. Carranza's rebellion also gave added definition to Carrancismo while demonstrating its success among those classes. At the same time, continued unrest and economic crisis meant that for the First Chief the challenge of the situation lay not in formulating a program of social revolution that would attract support, but in drawing the local population into a viable fighting force. Already the beneficiary of his own populist policies, Carranza largely accomplished the latter task. In the end Carrancismo triumphed in Coahuila because its leader succeeded in mobilizing discontent.

Winning recruits was not the only key to rebel victory, however. The ability to bankroll the movement was also important. And here the critical factor was control of the vast Coahuila–Texas border.

6

Cattle, Contraband, and Customs

Financing the Constitutionalist Movement

As the Federal troops of General Maass advanced towards the Coahuila-Texas border in the summer of 1913, Constitutionalist leaders Pablo González, Jesús Carranza, and Gabriel Calzada gathered in Piedras Negras to discuss the problem of paying and providing for their own soldiers. Although Venustiano Carranza's rebellion continued to attract recruits throughout Coahuila, it often struggled to retain them for lack of revenue and resources. Huerta's officials reported the demoralization of ill-equipped rebels, and observed that some troops suspected their principal officers of appropriating scarce funds for their own use. In the mining town of Sabinas all but two soldiers deserted the ranks when Constitutionalist authorities announced that a financial crisis would limit payment of wages to fifty centavos every other day. On alternate days the men would be given a ration of flour, meat, and corn.[1]

To finance the campaign against Huerta, Carranza had already begun to issue paper money. A decree of April 1913 ordered the "forced" circulation of five million pesos worth of currency to help support the Constitutionalist army. Carranza's generals, including Alvaro Obregón, Pancho Villa, and Pablo González also issued their own paper money, so that several currencies competed, side by side, with that of Huerta. Public confidence in these monies was understandably lacking, and depreciation and inflation were perpetual problems.[2]

Rebel leaders, like Huerta's officers, also resorted to forced loans. Just after the declaration of rebellion, Carranza demanded and received a forced loan from Saltillo banks and merchants. Another decree authorized such loans, and Constitutionalist leaders in several areas of Coahuila began to act upon it. In some cases Carranza's officers left receipts for extracted money and merchandise, but more often than not they simply seized funds and other items, so that their activities were more akin to banditry. Some rebels attacked post offices, appropriating money and stamps. Finally, the Constitutionalists targeted some mining communities for forced loans and pillaged their company stores.[3]

The appropriation of the state's natural resources, most notably cotton and guayule, was another means used to bankroll the rebellion. In 1914 Pancho Villa and other rebel leaders attempted to sell cotton stolen from Torreón. The profits were to be deposited in an El Paso bank in order to guarantee the circulation at high value of Constitutionalist currency. The plan apparently failed, and generated protest among El Paso's community of Spaniards, recently banished from the Laguna region by Villa himself. Most of these foreigners were participants in the Laguna cotton economy. In central Coahuila Constitutionalists seized a guayule factory owned by the Madero family; a German company processed the guayule confiscated by rebels and shipped it for sale to Hamburg.[4]

Although efforts to finance Carranza's movement affected the entire state of Coahuila, it was in the northern Rio Grande District and the border region that those efforts were most developed and of most consequence. Indeed, events in Coahuila from the eve of Francisco Madero's revolt of 1910 through the triumph of Carrancismo provide an excellent illustration of the importance of the international border to the Mexican Revolution in the northern states.

Never a true dividing line, the border between Coahuila and Texas more often served as a point of connection: it was a meeting place for rebel factions, a safety valve for local residents, and an economic opportunity for all concerned. Coahuila's international border was especially important to the financing of the revolution. Border towns, most notably Piedras Negras, supplied the customs revenues coveted by rival factions. Control of territory in the border region could also provide rebel groups with the resources (principally cattle) needed to establish a contraband trade, providing arms and revenue while bolstering the individual fortunes of an opportunistic few.

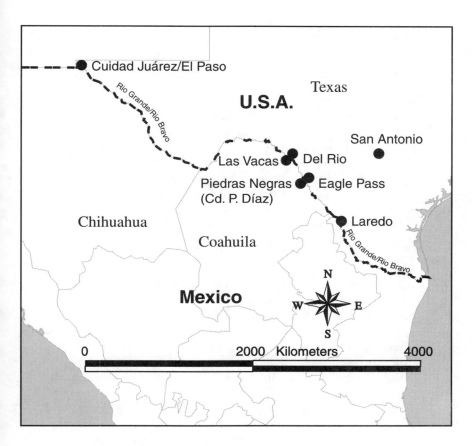

Coahuila–Texas Border Region

Although Madero's call for revolt against the Díaz regime in November 1910 received little immediate response in northern Coahuila, the movement that gained momentum by 1911 ultimately benefited from the situation in the border zone. Texas border towns were a traditional refuge for economic and political exiles of the Porfiriato, and throughout the Revolution people passed easily across the usually dry river bed separating Piedras Negras from Eagle Pass. During Madero's revolt, some Mexican officials claimed that "at least nine-tenths" of the revolutionary forces were made up of Mexicans crossing into Coahuila from Texas. Open demonstrations of support for Madero occurred in Texas border towns, sometimes with the goal of collecting money and arms for the revolt.[5]

Even before the rebellion authorities complained that border area merchants freely sold arms and munitions to "all comers." A major smuggling point was the Indian Ranch, a property in Texas that stretched along the international line for some fifty miles and was owned by a personal friend of Madero.[6] While Madero the rebel benefitted from the border situation, Madero the president faced many of the same problems as his predecessor in trying to pacify the region. For Madero and Governor Carranza, the porous nature of the border presented frequent problems. It encouraged the organization of opposition groups and helped support occasional uprisings. The abortive revolt of Bernardo Reyes, plotting by the Garza Galán faction in Coahuila, and the continuing activities of the PLM all sprang from the border zone and demonstrated the difficulties of monitoring that area.

Huerta's coup against Madero ushered in a new era of revolutionary activity and factionalist competition in the Texas-Coahuila border area. The international frontier served as a supply line for various factions, while the border region, with its resources and customs houses, tempted soldiers, local officials, and would-be entrepreneurs with the promise of revenue.

All revolutionary and counter-revolutionary groups coveted Coahuila's northern border, especially the town and customs house of Piedras Negras. To control Piedras Negras was to control the major railway lines that linked Coahuila to Texas and the rest of Mexico and provided access to fuel from Coahuila's rich coal-mining region. The customs house itself was a major source of revenue, and by placing high taxes on imports and exports, rebel leaders like Carranza could pay and supply their troops. From 1913 to 1915, Piedras Negras changed hands five times among Carranza's Constitutionalists, the Federals of Victoriano Huerta, and the forces of Pancho Villa. The course of the revolution in Coahuila was often determined by who controlled this strategic border town. From 1913 to 1915 it was the Constitutionalists who most often held sway, and in September 1915 they captured Piedras Negras for the last time, establishing definitive control over the border area.

Battle for the Border

With Carranza's revolt against Huerta and the temporary withdrawal of most Federal troops to Monterrey, northern Coahuila
was left in the control of forces loyal to the new Constitutionalist
movement. On February 24 Jesús Carranza led four hundred
men in the occupation of Piedras Negras. All federal employees
in the town reportedly fled across the international border,
and Carranza designated new local authorities. Constitutionalist
troops immediately occupied the customs house, posting the
sign "Palace of the Government" above its doors. In April, after
the announcement of the Plan of Guadalupe, Carranza himself
followed the Coahuilan legislature to Piedras Negras, where he
established temporary headquarters.[7]

Huerta's authority in the Coahuilan border region was never
established, and with Constitutionalist control of Piedras Negras
and Las Vacas, the loyalty of federal border officials was immediately called into question. With the rebel occupation of both
towns, customs employees and customs guards crossed into
Eagle Pass and Del Rio. Several were then recruited to the rebel
cause. Meanwhile, the Huerta government scrambled to prevent
more defections by relocating fiscal agents away from the volatile Texas-Coahuila border. U.S. officials responded favourably
to a petition from Huerta's representatives that these agents be
allowed to relocate to the safer environs of Laredo.[8]

Faced with the challenge of raising and equipping a large
army to battle Huerta's forces, Constitutionalist leaders took
immediate advantage of their control of Piedras Negras and the
border zone. Many residents of northern Coahuila experienced
forced loans, special taxes, and rebel appropriations of goods.
Mexican consul Ricardo S. Bravo claimed that all property
owners and men of means had left Coahuila rather than
"contribute to an enterprise that everyone disapproves of and
that all consider crazy." Federal agent J.A. Fernández reported
that Carranza was depositing large amounts of money in Eagle
Pass banks. He suggested that complaints of forced loans and
other plunderings be documented, so that the Mexican government could attempt legal confiscation of that money.[9]

The Piedras Negras customs house and the international
bridge connecting that town with its Texas sister city of
Eagle Pass provided special opportunities for revenue. Sebastián
Carranza led Coahuilan troops in raising money by selling

merchandise contained in the customs house and destined for the interior of Mexico. Rebel fundraising efforts also affected the Mexican National Railroad. When the railroad company refused to pay import fees already extracted before Carranza's revolt, the new Constitutionalist customs chief began to sell sugar, coffee, and other items owned by the company. Gabriel Calzada, the newly designated chief commander of Piedras Negras, extracted "heavy ransoms" on hides and other exports to the United States. Calzada also presided over the extraction of fees from those wishing to cross the international bridge. It cost thirty-five centavos to cross the bridge, and another fifty centavos to get Calzada's permission to do so. In some cases, residents of Piedras Negras were forced to stay in Eagle Pass, unable to pay the duty needed to return to their country.[10]

Calzada's actions as chief commander of Piedras Negras sometimes reached despotic proportions. When Felicitas de Trueba, wife of a local Spanish merchant, crossed into the town and then attempted to return to Texas, Calzada refused to let her pass. The woman's complaints simply resulted in her detention until her husband bought her freedom. Calzada's actions towards Trueba may have been the result of anti–Spanish sentiment that existed among some of Carranza's officers. (Indeed, upon assuming control of Piedras Negras, Jesús Carranza reportedly singled out Spaniards for forced loans.) Like several other rebel officials, Calzada quickly crossed the fine line between revolutionary financing and personal profit. After he had been only a month at his post, Carranza replaced Calzada, whom he suspected of embezzlement, with former federal customs official Raymundo Navarro, a recent recruit to Constitutionalism. Calzada was moved to a safer position away from the border zone.[11]

Carranza's control of the border area extended across the international bridge and into Texas. At the end of April 1913, Constitutionalists established a "rebel consulate" on the main street in Eagle Pass. The consulate, which openly flew the Mexican flag, served as the office of Carranza's commercial agent for Eagle Pass, Luis Mesa Gutiérrez, who oversaw the collection of money for legalizing commercial documents. Huerta's complaints of neutrality violations in Eagle Pass brought no results, as Carranza sympathizers were in the majority and included Eagle Pass mayor E.H. Schmidt. U.S. consul Luther T. Ellsworth noted that his attempts to abolish the rebel consulate were futile, and that the people of Eagle Pass laughed at his efforts to do so. Ricardo Bravo was convinced that even the Texas Rangers patrolling the border were in sympathy with the Constitutionalists.[12]

In Del Rio, too, Carranza established a consular agency. He named José Martínez Garza to review and inform about any commercial activity between Del Rio and Las Vacas, and to examine all documents relating to the introduction of goods into Coahuila. Martínez Garza served in other capacities, recruiting Del Rio residents for the Constitutionalist army and, after the Federals had recaptured Las Vacas, providing information on their movements to rebel leaders. For Huerta, the Las Vacas–Del Rio area was as difficult to secure as the Piedras Negras zone. In both, local sentiment was so overwhelmingly Carrancista that neutrality violations were rarely prosecuted. The rebels continued to recruit openly in Texas, using Del Rio as a gathering point for new soldiers. Even defeated Federal troops who had crossed the border provided ready recruits to Constitutionalism when faced with the prospect of returning to the unpopular and poorly paid ranks of Huerta's army.[13]

During the summer of 1913, the Federal troops of General Maass regained control of central Coahuila and slowly worked their way to the border. News of their approach prompted Carrancista rebels and local residents of northern Coahuila to flee across the border to the relative safety of Texas. Consul Bravo estimated that some ten thousand people from Piedras Negras and surrounding towns fled into Eagle Pass. Carranza's officers tried to halt the flow by raising the price of crossing the international bridge, but were forced to reconsider when confronted with the desperate threats of irate refugees. Two days before the Federal capture of Piedras Negras, large numbers of people continued to arrive in Eagle Pass. Mexican consular inspector Arturo M. Elías reported that "thousands" were camped in the plazas and streets of the Texas border town, enduring a persistent rainfall. Constitutionalist troops, meanwhile, worked quickly to mine railroad bridges and tracks and the international bridge.[14]

Only a few shops remained opened in Piedras Negras when Generals Maass and Luis Alberto Guajardo peacefully captured the town on October 7. The reception they received from those residents still in the town was noticeably cold, and Huerta's control of Piedras Negras was tenuous from the start. Threatened by pro-Carranza sympathizers on both sides of the border, the

Federal troops were also poorly clothed and equipped, and slow payment of Federal soldiers only added to the danger of desertion. Guajardo, a former Porfirian *jefe,* once again assumed the post of *jefe político* and helped designate other officials to fill local posts. Despite the semblance of order and despite Maass' assurances that they would not be drafted into the army, most inhabitants of Piedras Negras remained in Eagle Pass. That Federal officers abused their authority and harassed local residents did little to increase the popularity of the Huerta regime.[15]

The capture of Las Vacas now became crucial, since it was the last important border outpost of the rebels. From their base in the sister city of Del Rio, Carranza's rebels recruited men and passed arms into Mexico, often with the help of PLM leaders such as Calixto Guerra. They easily obtained arms and supplies from the merchants of Del Rio and Eagle Pass, and one of Huerta's agents acknowledged that any Federal attempt to get arms from the same merchants would surely fail, since all were open supporters of the Constitutionalists.[16]

The Federal approach on Las Vacas generated another exodus of Constitutionalist troops and local residents, to the relative safety of Del Rio. By the end of November, after three brief encounters with the rebel troops of Roberto Rivas, government forces captured the town. Before themselves fleeing across the international line, Rivas' men burned all public buildings as well as the properties of Huertista sympathizers. *Jefe político* Guajardo and the Del Rio Mexican consul named new officials for the captured town, and the area from Piedras Negras to Las Vacas was declared "free of bandits."[17]

This initial optimism was short lived. Carranza's special agents continued to operate in south Texas, recruiting, securing arms and supplies, and helping to co-ordinate the financing of the Constitutionalist movement. Early 1914 saw Guillermo M. Seguín acting as Carranza's commercial agent in Eagle Pass. Seguín provided a variety of services, including recruitment and arms smuggling, and he received funds for his expenses from Carranza's accounts in the First National Bank of Eagle Pass. In March Seguín was arrested for violation of neutrality laws; U.S. Commissioner F.A. Bonnet, an ardent supporter of the rebels, quickly exonerated Seguín.[18]

Constitutionalists continued to harry Federal troops with persistent military pressure along the border. Las Vacas was the main focus of conflict, and by March 1914 eight-hundred rebel troops at the command of Sebastián and Jesús Carranza were threatening the town. A see-saw battle for Las Vacas began, with the rebels gaining control of the town on several occasions. Federal troops could never claim a complete victory; insurgents freely crossed into Texas at the first sign of danger and, from bases in Del Rio and Langtry, prepared for the next attack.[19] Even without control of the crucial towns of Piedras Negras and Las Vacas, the Carrancista's *de facto* mastery of the border area continued, bolstered by the continuing support of border residents. Central to Constitutionalist dominance of the Texas-Coahuila border was an active arms trade.

The Border Arms Trade

During the Madero revolt, U.S. neutrality laws were interpreted and enforced in an inconsistent manner, so that Madero and his supporters were able to buy arms in Texas and send them to Mexico. Even before November 1910, Mexican officials reported numerous cases of rebels gathering arms in Texas, and noted that Texas merchants were doing a brisk business in munitions, which were probably smuggled to insurgents in Mexico. Boquillas, Texas, with its sister city of the same name in Coahuila, was an especially active smuggling point, as was the Indian Ranch.[20] Madero apparently also utilized the services of his grandfather's old trading partners in Texas to obtain and transport arms.

Even as President Madero struggled with the problem of contraband, Governor Carranza and his followers began to work the border to their advantage. Although Carranza did obtain arms from the U.S. with the permission of the Madero regime, importation of munitions was often hampered by diplomatic wrangles and by the reluctance of some U.S. authorities to grant the permission needed. Thus, in 1912 Madero received complaints of an intriguing contraband arrangement in the Eagle Pass–Piedras Negras area. A hardware store owner identified only as Cobo hired men to cross the international bridge with munitions concealed in specially constructed underclothes. It was unclear for whom the munitions were destined, and an investigation suggested that local officials and supporters of Governor Carranza had little inclination to stop the contraband.[21] In light of the always tense relationship between Madero and Carranza, the latter's lack of faith in Madero's ability to lead the country, and their insistence on following separate paths in the organization and support of pacification efforts in Coahuila, it seems likely that Carranza was involved in his own unauthorized arms trade.

One of the local officials who hedged on pursuing contraband was Rafael E. Múzquiz, who had helped found the Antire-electionist club of Piedras Negras and who had served as Eagle Pass consul for the Madero government. By 1912 Múzquiz had emerged as a key arms agent for Carranza's state government. He would continue to perform this function after Huerta's coup, and Carranza soon entrusted him with the creation of a rebel consular service. [22]

In the aftermath of the Huerta coup, Carranza's followers struggled against a U.S. arms embargo that now applied to all factions. Only in February 1914 was the embargo partially lifted to allow the Constitutionalists to import arms, and yet another embargo, imposed as a result of the U.S. occupation of Veracruz, hampered Carrancistas through the summer of the same year.[23] As U.S. policy wavered, Múzquiz exchanged his official stripes as consul for those of a master contrabandista. He routinely smuggled munitions, often disguised as cases of beer, through Piedras Negras.[24] Other members of the Constitutionalist revolution also smuggled arms into Coahuila. Hardware stores in Texas border towns, particularly Eagle Pass, were the usual sources of munitions, which were disguised in sacks of coffee and flour, barrels of beer and lard, and even in women's dresses. In San Antonio, Constitutionalists had reportedly rented a church building and were employing Mexicans to pack arms and disguise them as perishable items that would easily pass customs inspection.[25] At least some of Carranza's agents were also engaged in creating the diversions that allowed contraband to pass. A Las Vacas bullfight staged to raise money for the rebel cause attracted people from both sides of the border and generated well-founded suspicions among Huerta's officials that the event was a cover for contraband activity.[26] The insurgents also made the most of the Mexican exile population of Eagle Pass. There, female refugees from the revolutionary violence were employed in a makeshift clothing factory, sewing uniforms for Constitutionalist troops.[27]

Among the agents and sympathizers aiding in the acquisition and transport of arms was Ernesto Meade Fierro, a journalist from Parras who had joined the Madero revolt and, as a state congressman in 1913, seconded Carranza's rebellion. In the border region, Meade was editor of the pro-Carranza newspaper *El Demócrata,* and he engaged in the clandestine transportation of munitions from San Antonio to Piedras Negras. Briefly imprisoned for arms smuggling and neutrality violations in July 1913, Meade caused a stir when, accompanied by Constitutionalist commercial agent Luis Mesa Gutiérrez, he addressed a crowd of hundreds of Mexicans in front of the American consulate in Piedras Negras. The rebel journalist eulogized the United States and argued that Carranza's revolution sought to win for Mexicans the same liberties enjoyed by their neighbours on the other side of the border. Meade's smuggling activities resulted in at least one additional arrest on U.S. soil, but he continued to serve the First Chief in various capacities.[28] In other interesting and effective arrangements, the Constitutionalists utilized the services of some veteran *contrabandistas.* Salomé Arce, a long-time resident of the border region and former participant in the rebellions of Catarino Garza during the 1890s, lent his knowledge of the terrain and the smuggling trade to Carranza for a handsome price.[29]

Revolution on the Hoof

For the Constitutionalists in Coahuila, the availablility of cattle and other items, and the proximity and permeability of the border, proved crucial to the purchase of arms and supplies needed to support a viable fighting force. Huerta scrambled unsuccessfully to secure the Coahuila-Texas border against the smuggling of stolen cattle, wool, and istle. Guayule was an especially popular item that was cut and sometimes stockpiled by rebel officers who arranged its sale to companies in Texas. Most often, however, the Constitutionalists relied on revenues generated from the sale of stolen cattle obtained in northern and central Coahuila. The Carrancistas had numerous agents along the border involved in helping to pass cattle into Texas for sale. The Huerta government even blamed the Madero family for selling cattle in Texas to help finance the revolution. More likely, the Maderos were selling their own cattle and depositing the money in Texas banks for safekeeping during the Revolution.

Constitutionalist smuggling efforts received significant support from an agricultural company located in northern Coahuila. Owned by nineteenth-century army veteran General Lorenzo González Treviño (who by marriage was an uncle of the late

Francisco Madero), the Compañía Agrícola y Ganadera del
Rio de San Diego had property and offices in Las Vacas and
Jiménez, Coahuila, as well as Del Rio. The company's Hacienda
San Carlos, located in the Las Vacas area, served not only as
a recruitment centre, with many *hacienda* workers joining the
Constitutionalists, but also as a finance hub. Here, stolen cattle
were gathered to be smuggled into the U.S. Some cattle were
immediately slaughtered and the hides sold to buy munitions.

The Hacienda San Carlos had also been a focal point of
Maderista activity during the 1910–11 revolt, serving as a headquarters for rebel leaders. Marcos Hernández, the *hacienda*'s
administrator and another Madero family relative, played a
role in co-ordinating revolutionary activities. He supported
the Constitutionalist movement as well, and helped organize
demonstrations against the Huerta regime. Huerta's agents also
implicated Lorenzo González Treviño himself in revolutionary
activities, claiming that he donated his own money to the rebellion and allowed his agricultural company to be used for smuggling and other activities. González Treviño also had more
formal business dealings with Carranza, including a contract
to make infantry uniforms for Carranza's troops. He regulary
crossed the border between Del Rio and Las Vacas, often stay-
ing in a Del Rio house owned by Marcos Hernández. The
Hacienda San Carlos was a gathering point for Constitutionalist
leaders and sympathizers from Texas, especially from Del Rio.
The Huerta regime claimed that the company was crucial to
the success of Carrancismo in northern Coahuila and the border
region, as all revolutionaries of Las Vacas and Del Rio were
somehow connected to it.[30]

Coahuila's cattle industry provided other opportunities for
revenue. Unrest and rebel plundering threatened to destroy
many a Porfirian fortune, so that cattlemen attempted to sell
their herds, converting their investment into currency and
depositing the money for safekeeping in Texas banks. In anticipation of Carranza's revolt against Huerta, Lorenzo González
Treviño was among those who transported a large portion of his
cattle to Texas early in 1913. As ranchers drove their herds to the
border, Constitutionalist officials extracted ever-higher export
fees. Complaints and attempts to evade the export tax were frequent; Rafael Múzquiz co-ordinated efforts to impede the passage of Coahuilan cattle to Texas through Laredo, where no tax
was charged.[31]

Even when Carranza's rebels were not in control of Coahuila's important border towns, they could still count on strong connections in the border region to obtain revenue and munitions through the cattle trade. In early 1914, Federals controlled the port of entry at Las Vacas and were themselves collecting an export tax on cattle crossing into Texas. Not to be outdone, Carranza's men camped on the other side of the border, where they met the cattle coming across and extracted another fee. When cattlemen balked at paying a double duty, the Constitutionalists threatened them with confiscation of their properties in Coahuila.[32]

In Del Rio, Dr. Fred Ross, George Miers, and a local merchant family named McLymont provided valuable assistance to Carranza's revolt. In addition to helping with Carrancista propaganda, these men sold munitions to the Constitutionalists in exchange for stolen cattle. They constructed a special bridge to pass cattle over the Rio Grande, and even crossed into Mexico to import cattle that the Constitutionalists themselves could not get across the border. That such traffic was significant became apparent early in 1914 when Ross was briefly apprehended in the Las Vacas area and Federal troops led by Major Génaro Rodríguez confiscated 3,800 head of cattle.[33]

With the prevalence of contraband trade and smuggling along the Texas-Coahuila border, and the volatile political situation, it was perhaps inevitable that some enterprising revolutionaries would seek personal profit. In many cases, personal opportunism was a means of survival, particularly in the early stage of the Constitutionalist movement, when payment of salaries to troops was never certain. Huerta's officials often commented on the disorganized and demoralized state of insurgent troops in the border area, and lamented the general state of unrest that this caused. The situation must have seemed a throwback to Coahuila's wilder days as an Indian frontier to Ricardo Bravo, who noted that along the border "there is no discipline and no respect, everyone is a commander, and since there is no money to pay salaries, every [soldier] dedicates himself to the robbery of cattle and sacking of local businesses, spending the acquired proceeds on drunken brawls and other scandals."[34]

The extent to which the border provided an economic opportunity for individual Constitutionalist officials became especially apparent in 1914, with Carranza's troops in control of Piedras Negras. Although the partial lifting of the U.S. embargo would soon make arms more readily available to the Constitutionalists, cattle thieving and contraband increased at an alarming rate. In response, Huertista governor Práxedis de la Peña desperately attempted to protect Coahuila's already scarce supply of cattle by decreeing a tax on all cattle destined for export.[35] It was in this context that Huerta's officials uncovered a well-entrenched cattle ring led by the ubiquitous Rafael Múzquiz, now serving as Carranza's local treasury official. With the help of friends and family members, Múzquiz established a group of men charged with recovering stolen cattle, mules, and horses. Known as the "Cuerpo de Reateros," this group periodically appeared at the border, where Múzquiz' relatives received their booty, which then "disappeared" across the international line. Only a few of the recovered animals passed legally through customs at Piedras Negras and Las Vacas.

The 39th Regiment stationed along the Rio Grande and entrusted with patrolling the banks of the river for illicit activity actively supported Múzquiz' cattle ring. Composed primarily of local Coahuilans, many of whom were related to one another, the regiment routinely neglected its official duty, and just as routinely participated in the smuggling. Indeed, Major Ramón Múzquiz (a nephew of Rafael) had his own business selling cattle in Eagle Pass, apparently with the support of the local Texas sheriff.[36] Cattle thieving and contraband trading by Constitutionalists in Coahuila's border region became so common that one border official warned that if the situation continued, cattle would quickly become extinct and the entire border population would be forced into vegetarianism.[37]

The threat of vegetarianism was more imagined than real, but the continued prevalence of contraband and cattle smuggling indicated the extent to which Carranza's followers had become entrenched along the Coahuilan border. That the area would continue to provide an economic opportunity for rebel troops and officers was clear to American consul William Blocker. In early 1915 he reported over eight hundred soldiers in Piedras Negras "riding about the city contentedly as if the border was the ideal place for happiness and a sure chance of getting away with their proceeds from the revolution." In 1916 Blocker related the arrival of Constitutionalist general Francisco Murguía at the border town, then under the command of Coronel Fernando Peraldi, Carranza's nephew. Accompanied by General Alfredo Ricaut, Murguía intended a display of force that would put him in control of Piedras Negras, and facilitate his personal business in exporting products appropriated from the areas under his command. The general, reported Blocker, had engaged in a "rich graft in hides and skins" while stationed in Durango. Residents of Piedras Negras remarked that one could always tell where Murguía was "by just noticing the carts [that] go up main street loaded with hides and skins, known as Murguía's share of the revolution."[38]

The stories of Múzquiz and Murguía are not unique in the history of the Mexican Revolution. Such opportunism would be replicated in many areas of Mexico. Nor was profiteering a new phenomenon in Coahuila's border region, which since the late nineteenth century had provided a safe haven for rebels and contraband traders. Yet for the Constitutionalist movement, this extensive international frontier had broader significance.

Although both Huerta and Carranza struggled to support their campaigns through forced loans, the appropriation and sale of local goods, and the printing of currency, Coahuila's northern border presented the First Chief with other opportunities for supporting his movement. President Huerta, meanwhile, quickly learned the necessity, and the difficulties, of controlling this volatile area. Thus the border remained the object of heated competition throughout the Constitutionalist rebellion.

The town and customs house of Piedras Negras were at the centre of much of this competition, but Las Vacas and other border towns were also of strategic and economic importance. With a base of support that extended into Texas border towns such as Eagle Pass and Del Río, the Constitutionalists succeeded in preserving their mastery over the border zone. Even when Huerta could claim military control over Piedras Negras and Las Vacas, Carranza continued to use the international frontier to secure arms and supplies, recruit soldiers, and finance his rebellion. In the final analysis, the border was crucial to the support of Carranza's movement in Coahuila. Like Madero before them, the Constitutionalists inherited a porous and volatile international frontier. They took full advantage of it.

7

Villismo in Coahuila

In June 1914 Venustiano Carranza returned to Saltillo after a string of Constitutionalist victories succeeded in recapturing his native state from Huerta's Federal forces. President Huerta's resignation, the treaties of Teoloyucán, and the triumphal entry of Obregón's troops into Mexico City soon followed. As the tide turned in Coahuila, many Mexican Federals stationed in the border area took refuge in the United States. Constitutionalists along Coahuila's frontier were remarkably successful in recruiting these soldiers. An office established in Piedras Negras attracted large numbers of men, and many Federal refugees repatriated by the United States were persuaded to join Carranza's army.[1]

Exiled Huerta supporters were also numerous, however, and by the end of 1914 they were plotting against the Constitutionalists. In December ex Federal officers Blas Opinal and Ramón Chimuela led a group of twenty-five men into Mexico, crossing from Texas in the vicinity of Eagle Pass. Anticipating the help of Carranza's soldiers stationed in Piedras Negras, many of whom had received money to join the conspiracy, Opinal and Chimuela instead walked into a trap set by officers Rafael Rodríguez and Cesáreo Castro. Opinal and Chimuela, along with several members of the Piedras Negras garrison implicated in the scheme, were immediately executed. Their bodies were displayed in the city hall as a warning to other conspirators.[2]

The plot of Opinal and Chimuela was indicative of the still-volatile situation in Coahuila's border region. By the summer of 1915 the Plan of San Diego had found adherents in the area as well. This scheme, which called for the unification of south Texas and Mexico, was primarily the work of the Mexican-American population of the Texas border zone and reflected that group's response to Anglo discrimination. It built upon the discontent of Mexican workers in both south Texas and northeastern Mexico who, since the nineteenth century, had seen their social and economic position deteriorate. Particularly in south Texas, Mexican-American landowners had seen a rapid reversal of their fortunes as Anglo land speculation converted many into labourers. Improved technology encouraged such speculation and made possible the diversion of water from the Rio Grande, to the detriment of farmers in Mexico's northeast.

Drafted in a Monterrey prison in January 1915, the Plan of San Diego began as a call for the armed reclamation of all Mexican land that had been lost to the United States, and promised to exact revenge against the Anglos, who were seen as responsible for the oppression of Mexicans and other minority groups. As the movement unfolded, it embraced the idea of a social revolution that would bring economic justice to the border region. The San Diego plan echoed the earlier program of Ricardo Flores Magón and the PLM, which had gained adherents in Coahuila's border region and in the Laguna at the turn of the century. It attracted PLM supporters such as Aniceto Pizaño and Luis de la Rosa, Texas residents who became prominent figures in the San Diego rebellion.[3]

The San Diego revolt began in the summer of 1915 with raids on irrigation works along the Rio Grande and assaults on Anglos in south Texas. American border officials worried that the raids were being aided by former Huerta soldiers and exiled Huerta supporters, now left without a leader or cause. Huerta himself returned from his European exile to lead a plot against the Constitutionalists in the summer of 1915. U.S. officials quickly arrested him, however, and the movement ended. Pascual Orozco, the Chihuahuan rebel leader who had risen against Madero and then declared his loyalty to Huerta, was also a casualty of the old general's plot. Orozco was hunted down and shot in Texas, where he had fled after Huerta's fall. The Plan of San Diego remained alive through July 1916, generating raids along the Texas-Mexico border. Active recruiting for the Plan occurred in the Eagle Pass–Piedras Negras area, and at least one municipal official of Piedras Negras participated in publicizing the Plan and gathering support for it.

The San Diego movement also garnered the not always discreet support of Carranza, who held out his ability to control the raiding as a means of winning the U.S. government's recognition as Mexico's next legitimate leader. American fears of the rebellion were justified, particularly when rumours flew that the Japanese and Germans might be supporting the San Diego rebels in an attempt to prevent the United States from entering World War I. Reportedly, Carranza's commanders, including Pablo González, held back on apprehending the San Diego rebels until Carranza received *de facto* U.S. recognition in October 1915. Then Carranza's forces moved against the leaders of the rebellion. At the same time, the United States took a final crack at the PLM, jailing Ricardo Flores Magón, who would die in a U.S. prison in 1922.[4]

The Plan of San Diego was significant in adding to the already volatile border situation and in strengthening American resolve to shape the Mexican Revolution. Within Coahuila, however, the main challenge to the Constitutionalists came not from San Diego rebels, nor from ex-Federals and Huertista exiles, but from Pancho Villa, who quickly proved that his loyalty to the First Chief was dubious at best. The alliance between the two leaders that had succeeded in defeating the Huerta regime quickly unraveled. The result was another round of violence that would last over a year. Villismo appeared in Coahuila primarily as an agency of further destruction. At the same time, however, Villa's governors did attempt to gain a more solid political footing within the state, while Villa himself won the support of at least a few Coahuilans who welcomed the Chihuahuan leader in anticipation of significant agrarian reform.

Inconvenient Alliance

Pancho Villa had already established himself as a significant force in northern Mexico during the Madero revolt and in its immediate aftermath. Villa remained loyal to Madero, helping to combat the forces of Pascual Orozco and pursuing those sympathetic to the cause championed by Ricardo Flores Magón. His importance continued to be acknowledged after Huerta's coup, and in September 1913 revolutionary leaders designated Villa

General of the Division of the North. It was these troops that scored a significant Constitutionalist victory with the capture of Torreón one month later. As a centre of railroad communication, Torreón was a key to supplying revolutionary troops, and this victory bolstered Villa's reputation, particularly since Carranza himself had earlier failed to capture the town. And although Torreón was soon recaptured by Huerta's Federals, the Division of the North repeated its success in May 1914, clearing the Federal troops of Refugio Velasco from the Laguna's strategic centre and from southwestern Coahuila.[5]

In Chihuahua, Villa translated his military successes into political power, becoming governor of that state in December 1913. Although he held the post only briefly, tendering his resignation in January 1914, Villa's brief governorship gave a clear indication of his intention to stretch the limits of the moderate reformism that had characterized the Madero regime and that had also come to characterize Carranza's approach. Most significantly, Villa promised land reform and the division of the lands of Chihuahua's oligarchs. Revenue from the confiscation of such lands was to be used not only to pay Villa's army, but also to support the widows and orphans of revolutionary soldiers. Villa's plans for agrarian reform never came to fruition but, particularly in the minds of the more moderate Carranza, they caused concern.[6]

Tensions between Carranza and Villa appeared even before the second and decisive capture of Torreón in 1914. The younger Villa only grudgingly accepted the leadership of the First Chief, while Carranza was increasingly wary of Villa's growing popularity. Carranza ordered Villa not to pursue radical reforms in Chihuahua, and he pushed for Villa's resignation as governor. With Villa replaced by Manuel Chao, another military leader who the First Chief hoped would be more pliant, Carranza sought to bring the Chihuahan rebel to heel. But Villa continued to test the limits of his authority as commander of the Division of the North, even after Carranza had temporarily transferred his rebel government to Ciudad Juárez, Chihuahua.[7] Carranza's determination to check Villa primarily took the form of attempts to prevent him from reaching Mexico City before the First Chief's most trusted general, Alvaro Obregón. After his second capture of Torreón, Villa naturally looked to the neighbouring state of Zacatecas, which would pave the way to Mexico City and a decisive victory against Huerta. Carranza, however, ordered Villa to focus his efforts in the other direction and to recapture Saltillo for the Constitutionalists. Still hoping for some kind of reconciliation with Carranza, whose fortunes seemed to be growing, Villa consented and the Division of the North captured Saltillo in May. The next month, Carranza returned to his native state, establishing his government anew in its capital city.

Despite this significant concession to the First Chief, tensions between Villa and Carranza did not abate. The situation was complicated by the United States occupation of Veracruz. Although Carranza staunchly opposed such interventionism on nationalist grounds, Villa was less adamant, and he remained mindful of the need to cultivate U.S. support, most immediately for the purpose of keeping a steady stream of arms flowing to his troops. As Villa steered an independent diplomatic course, Carranza's continued efforts to halt the march of the Division of the North faltered. After the capture of Saltillo, Carranza ordered Villa to split his troops, sending only part of the force to help with the capture of Zacatecas under other Constitutionalist commanders. Correctly assuming the First Chief's goal of dissolving his army, Villa resigned. In protest, Villa's generals rallied to his defense. The Division of the North remained intact and played a central role in the successful battle for Zacatecas in June.[8]

In the aftermath of Zacatecas, George C. Carothers, an American mining engineer in northern Mexico with close ties to American officials, reported on the worsening relations between Villa and Carranza. Carothers was a strong supporter of Villa, who he believed would provide greater protection and support for American interests in Mexico than the more clearly nationalistic Carranza. Carothers insisted that Carranza was afraid of Villa. He described Carranza's efforts to paralyze the Division of the North by blocking its access to coal, a resource crucial to the movement by railroad of troops and supplies, and one concentrated in the rich mining region of Coahuila. Carranza also prohibited the shipment of munitions to Villa, who was already struggling with the U.S. arms embargo that was established in the aftermath of the Veracruz occupation. This embargo was modified to give Carranza's forces in the Veracruz region access to munitions through the port of Tampico, but it further hampered Villa's forces by blocking arms shipments (if only temporarily) across the U.S.-Mexico border. Without the means to move or steadily equip his forces, Villa was compelled to halt the advance of the Division of the North on Mexico City.[9]

In early July, just before Huerta tendered his resignation as president of Mexico, Constitutionalist general Pablo González made another effort to mend the breach at a conference with representatives of Villa's Division of the North. In the resulting Pact of Torreón, Villa and Carranza were to offer each other mutual recognition: Carranza as leader of the revolution and Villa as leader of the Division of the North. Carranza was to ensure Villa's forces were supplied with coal and munitions. The agreement also pledged Carranza to a revolutionary convention at which the interests of the military forces, including the Division of the North, were to be represented. The convention was to designate an interim president, who would convoke national and local elections. Finally, the Pact of Torreón endorsed social and economic change, including land reform and legislation for the benefit of Mexico's working class.[10]

Although both Carranza and Villa had endorsed the attendance of their supporters at the Torreón conference, neither felt bound by the resulting agreement. Carranza in particular wavered on the agenda for social and economic reform, and while both leaders endorsed the idea of a convention, they inevitably sought ways to shape its outcome in advance. Subsequent attempts to prevent a complete break between Carranza and Villa, including the efforts of Alvaro Obregón, only added to Villa's discontent and suspicion of the First Chief. Carranza in turn became all the more convinced of the need to crush his Chihuahuan rival. Indeed, Carranza never resumed shipments of coal and arms to Villa, and he used a confrontation between Villa and Obregón as an excuse to further isolate the Division of the North, ordering the destruction of railroad tracks so that Villa's forces would be further hampered in their attempt to reach Mexico City. Villa's response was predictable: by the end of September he had withdrawn his support of the First Chief and was in open rebellion.[11]

As he divorced himself from the Constitutionalist movement, Villa cultivated the support of Emiliano Zapata, the Morelos rebel whom Carranza had also come to see as a threat to his leadership. Zapata and Carranza distrusted each other, and several attempts by the First Chief to negotiate with the Morelos leader had run aground, as Zapata continued to insist on the centrality of agrarian reform in the revolutionary plan. As with Villa, the First Chief had taken steps to halt the Zapatista advance on Mexico City in the summer of 1914: the Treaties of Teoloyucán provided that soldiers from the soon to be defunct Federal Army would help to protect the city against the Zapatistas until Obregón's troops arrived. Aware of the importance of Zapata's movement, and of the possibilities of an alliance, Villa appealed to Zapata with a call to replace Carranza with a leader who would pursue land reform on behalf of the Mexican people.[12]

The official break between Villa and Carranza did not stop the followers of either camp from attempting a reconciliation. The strength of the Division of the North, and of Zapata's movement, foretold a hard time for Carranza unless a compromise could be reached. With the blessing of Obregón, and despite the clear reluctance of Carranza, a revolutionary convention of military leaders and representatives was convened in October 1914. The Convention of Aguascalientes became the forum in which Carrancista generals, Villistas, and representatives of Emiliano Zapata attempted to chart a future course for Mexico. Central to the Convention's deliberations was the question of leadership, an acknowledgement of the rivalry between Carranza and Villa that threatened to break apart the revolution. With Obregón's guidance, the Convention endorsed Eulalio Gutiérrez, the governor of San Luis Potosí who had ties to both the Villa and Carranza camps, as provisional president. And in a nod to Zapata, the Convention officially adopted the idea of sweeping agrarian reform. This move was engineered by Villista general Felipe Angeles, a veteran of the Porfirian army who had supported Madero and who encouraged many Federal officers to join the Division of the North after Madero's death. Angeles' efforts at the Aguascalientes meeting further solidified the alliance between Villa and Zapata.[13]

As the Villa-Zapata alliance was strengthened, the threat to Carranza, still in control of Mexico City, became increasingly clear. Not only had he been unceremoniously deposed as the leader of the revolution, but he also faced military pressures, as Villista troops rattled their sabres in the environs of Aguascalientes. Expecting the inevitable Villista advance on the capital, Carranza left the city, heading east. He remained adamant in his opposition to the Convention and its resolutions, and in Aguascalientes several Carrancista delegates quit the Convention. On November 10 Gutiérrez and the Convention declared the First Chief in rebellion and appointed Villa commander of the Convention forces that would now pursue

Carranza in the Mexican Revolution's last and bloodiest round of civil war. By December 1914 the combined forces of Villa and Zapata entered Mexico City in triumph. Meanwhile, Carranza, who had retained the support of Pablo González and, more importantly, Obregón, directed his own government and military campaign from the port city of Veracruz, which U.S. troops had only recently abandoned.[14]

A State Divided

Within Coahuila the break between Venustiano Carranza and Pancho Villa left the state divided into two zones, with Villistas controlling the Laguna region and the southeast and Constitutionalists dominating in the east, centre, and north. The two factions wrestled for control of the state until September 1915, when Villa abandoned Coahuila. Command of the state's coal reserves was the main object, as this was crucial to any military effort. Carranza's initial mastery of central and northern Coahuila provided him with an important strategic advantage, particularly since it included the municipality of Múzquiz, which supplied most of the coal used by the Constitutionalists. Control of the railroads in central and northern Coahuila provided additional leverage for Carranza's forces, since freight destined for Villa's troops in Torreón and Chihuahua could be blocked. As an added precaution, Constitutionalist authorities placed railroad engineers between Saltillo and Piedras Negras under military rule.[15]

Despite such strategic advantages, the national events of 1914 threatened to precipitate a split within Coahuila's Constitutionalist ranks. After Villa's formal withdrawal of recognition of the First Chief, American official William Blocker reported that Coahuilans were divided in their sympathies for the two leaders. While Carranza continued to enjoy support in Piedras Negras and the border region, Villa's popularity was growing among rural workers in several areas of Coahuila. Even in the border zone Rafael Múzquiz warned Carranza of a possible "coup" by Villa sympathizers in Las Vacas, Eagle Pass, and Laredo. In these areas the Villistas were reportedly expanding their forces with promises of rank and lands. Customs official Higinio de la Fuente also reported wavering support for Carrancismo in Piedras Negras.[16]

Many soldiers were in fact simply biding their time, awaiting the outcome of the Convention to decide their own futures. Villa's troops in the Laguna, moreover, were not immune to dissension. Villa's refusal to join Carranza in public condemnation of the U.S. invasion of Veracruz was a particular sticking point. In June Mexican diplomatic official Arturo M. Elías related numerous Villista desertions occurring from Torreón to Ciudad Juárez, precipitated by the discovery of compromising papers that reportedly indicated Villa's willingness to sell Mexican territory to the United States. In the Laguna alone, one thousand troops had reportedly left the ranks and were preparing to fight against Villa.[17]

The situation was no clearer by the end of 1914, after Carranza had formally broken with the Convention and established his own government in Veracruz. In Coahuila Carranza's designated successor, Jesús Acuña, continued to perform the duties of governor. Yet Acuña was also aware of the importance of the rupture between Carranza and the Convention. He lamented the relaxation in military discipline among the Constitutionalist forces of Coahuila and Nuevo León, suggesting that soldiers easily switched from one faction to the other.[18]

At the beginning of 1915 an enemy advance forced Acuña to flee to Piedras Negras, as General Raúl Madero occupied Saltillo and established Villa's control over all of southern Coahuila. The capture of Saltillo gave the Division of the North control of most of the railroad equipment used between the state capital and Piedras Negras. Train service between the two towns quickly halted, and the Villistas began a drive that by March would leave them in control of most of Coahuila. Constitutionalist forces scrambled to tear up the railroad and reinforce their own troops as Villa's men descended upon the coal region.[19]

Meeting little resistance, Rosalio Hernández took possession of Monclova on January 25. With only five hundred Constitutionalist troops patrolling the area from Monclova to Piedras Negras, the capture of the border town was imminent. Convention agents already operated in the area, working to designate their own local officials and to recruit Constitutionalists. Residents and Piedras Negras officials began to move their belongings to the American side of the frontier. Constitutionalist general Luis Gutiérrez, believing that his men feared Villa's troops and would desert rather than resist their advance, urged Governor Acuña to allow a complete evacuation of Piedras Negras and a retreat to Nuevo Laredo, another border town in the neighbouring state of Tamaulipas. On March 8 Gutiérrez and his men left the plaza in a pouring rain. Acuña, customs officials, and other residents soon fled to Eagle Pass, Texas.[20]

Rosalio Hernandez' occupation of Piedras Negras occurred without incident and was quickly followed by the capture of Las Vacas. With control over the coal region and completion of repairs on the railroad line south, Villa's forces began daily shipments of precious coal to other areas dominated by the Division of the North. The battle for Coahuila, however, continued. Operating in several areas south of Piedras Negras, and with control of Nuevo Laredo, the Constitutionalists harassed Villa's troops, attempting to cut the lines of communication and deprive the Division of the North of supplies. In these efforts the Carrancistas drew upon their still significant connections along the international frontier. From a base in the Burro Mountains they received supplies from the Las Vacas–Del Rio area. By May Villista fortunes began to reverse. Villa's men struggled to obtain enough ammunition, and their rivals succeeded in cutting railroad and telegraph communication with the interior.[21]

After a brief occupation of Saltillo during the summer of 1915, General Alvaro Obregón led the Constitutionalists in the definitive capture of that city. A steady advance into northern Coahuila soon recaptured Piedras Negras, where popular sentiment was still reported to be overwhelmingly pro-Carranza. An offer of amnesty issued by the First Chief encouraged many Mexicans to return to that border town from Eagle Pass. Constitutionalist control over Las Vacas was quickly re-established as well, aided by the defection of a number of Villa's troops. The eventual capture of Torreón, Monclova, and the railway centre of Paredón sealed the fate of the Villistas. William Blocker reported that the coal fields were now virtually useless to Villa's army, since Paredón and Torreón "are the keys to all points out of Coahuila and shipments of coal must necessarily pass through one of the two towns."[22]

Carranza returned to Saltillo in October. The victory in his native state mirrored Carranza's growing fortunes on the national level. Despite an initial optimism that stemmed in part from the greater strength of its military forces, the Convention government soon began to unravel. By 1915 Villa's insistence on waging a virtually autonomous war against Carranza, as well as disagreements between Villa and Eulalio Gutiérrez, had combined to destroy the Convention government. Meanwhile, the

Carrancistas, guided primarily by the capable Obregón, directly confronted the Division of the North, recapturing Mexico City and inflicting serious losses on Villa's troops at the pivotal battles of Celaya, north of the capital. To the south, Zapata's forces struggled unsuccessfully against the Carrancistas, and were reduced to guerrilla warfare against the growing enemy troops. Politically, the alliance between Villa and Zapata faltered, while Carranza continued to successfully consolidate his own popular support. In October (in the wake of the San Diego revolt that had heightened tensions along the border) the United States cast its lot with Carranza, recognizing him as Mexico's legitimate ruler. U.S. recognition provided Carranza with a crucial political advantage, just as it tightened the screws on the Convention by effectively blocking its ability to obtain arms and supplies from the United States. By the end of 1915 the Constitutionalists claimed military control over much of Mexico and the government of the Convention had disintegrated.

The Price of Revolution

The struggle between Constitutionalists and Conventionist forces contributed to the further deterioration of Coahuila's economy. As during the rebellion against Huerta, the circulation and devaluation of rival currencies was a central problem. Coahuila's workers shouldered most of the burden through the inevitable inflation in prices of basic goods. Miners in the community of Agujita threatened to rebel when they were paid in Villista bills, which were worth only half the value of the less prevalent Constitutionalist money. Merchants responded to the situation with a 50 per-cent rise in prices for those using Villa's currency. Local officials tried to punish such behaviour and warned that the workers might withdraw their support if more Constitutionalist money was not made available. The situation in Agujita became so serious that many workers were reportedly reduced to living off of pecans growing along the margins of the Sabinas River. Speculation and counterfeiting were rampant. As Villa gained the upper hand in the spring of 1915, the Eagle Pass Lumber Company and the M. Cirilo Company of Monterrey exchanged false bills for Villista currency.[23]

Villa's generals complicated the situation by prohibiting the circulation of Carrancista money in areas under their control. The Convention government took additional measures to raise the value of Villista bills and to discourage the dumping of cheap Villista fiat money on the managers of coal mines. Villa himself ordered the establishment in Torreón of an office to review bills and ensure their authenticity. Those involved in counterfeiting or circulating falsified bills were to be "militarily" punished. Two months after this order was issued, Laguna residents got a taste of Villista justice when Villa ordered the execution of seven persons charged with circulating counterfeit money. [24]

The currency crisis, the lootings committed by revolutionary factions, and the frequent interruptions in communication and transportation also created a food shortage in Coahuila. Rather than accept the unreliable currencies circulating in the interior of the state, and despite decrees forbidding the practice, some merchants and speculators began to export food supplies to Texas. Even Villa's officials in Piedras Negras eagerly exported corn, cattle, and beans in exchange for American gold. Despite the Red Cross's efforts to get corn to the interior of the state, unreliable transportation and unexplained losses of corn shipments (perhaps appropriated by Villa's men in Piedras Negras) sparked rumours that the people of Monclova and Saltillo had been reduced to eating cactus pears and donkey flesh. "The situation," lamented Blocker, "is deplorable. It has ceased to be one of patriotism and has turned to graft, robbery, and murder." [25]

Famine seemed imminent in the Laguna as Carranza's troops began to regain control of Coahuila in the summer of 1915. Corn supplies in the towns of Durango and Torreón were dangerously low, as most had been sent to feed Villa's army. Desperate women raided the local storehouses for their daily corn, and with no seed to plant and a lack of rain, agricultural workers organized into small bands for the purpose of plundering. In Torreón people began sacking the truck farms of Chinese residents. [26]

Coahuila's persistent economic crisis was the prominent concern of the four governors who represented the Villista regime from January to September 1915: Felipe Angeles (one of Villa's most trusted generals), Santiago Ramírez (a Coahuilan of humble origins who had risen to become a Villista general), Raúl Madero (younger brother of the assassinated president), and Orestes Pereyra (an early recruit to the Divison of the North from the state of Durango). For all of these men, the currency problem was a central issue and a constant source of aggravation. Some businesses insisted on payment in precious metals.

The local water company of Piedras Negras demanded payment in silver, exacted exorbitant prices, and cut off water supplies when payments were not made. The municipal president was compelled to suppress the town's water service for lack of funds. Many merchants also resisted Santiago Ramírez' attempts to prohibit the circulation of Carrancista bills, and the lack of Villista money in many areas exacerbated the situation, encouraging many merchants to simply close their doors.[27]

Payment of Coahuila's miners was especially problematic. Villa addressed the special needs of Mexico's mine workers by attempting to guarantee the worth of Villista money in areas under his control. To further protect miners from highly priced goods, he prohibited the existence of all company stores. Villa also ordered the re-initiation of work in Mexico's mines and supported the right of others to claim inactive mines. At least a few such claims were filed in Coahuila. Despite such efforts, however, Coahuila's mining industry continued to stagnate, and mining companies tended either to refuse Villista money or to accept it at an outrageously low rate.[28]

The attempts of Villa and his Coahuilan representatives to alleviate the currency crisis had little effect, and speculation and counterfeiting continued. Local merchants and businessmen, faced with economic ruin, ignored Villista decrees. Villa himself acknowledged the economic hardships created by the continuing revolution with a decree that suspended debts, interest, and mortage payments to banks. Ultimately, however, he was powerless to head off the decline of Coahuila's productive base. Saltillo provided a good example of such decline. Revolutionary violence destroyed or closed many of the city's factories, which had been established at the height of Coahuila's economic boom during the Porfiriato.[29]

Villa's governors were likewise hampered by the food shortages that continued to plague Coahuila. The scarcity of corn, beans, and other staples in Saltillo and Torreón compelled Santiago Ramírez to decree favourable terms and price guarantees for merchants introducing and selling such items in these two municipalities. The food shortage was especially acute in southern Coahuila, which suffered the most when railroad transportation was interrupted. Viesca's municipal president was compelled to buy corn for his municipality in neighbouring Zacatecas, and Santiago Ramírez allowed residents from Parras to extract wheat from confiscated properties in the neighbouring municipality of General Cepeda. In another attempt to address the worsening agricultural crisis in the Laguna, the Convention government sought people to work the region's ranches, offering any who would come a modest wage and passage to Gómez Palacio, Durango. Shortages of food affected other areas as well; Monclova's residents, for instance, depended on the import of corn and corn seed from the United States.[30]

Villista Support

During his brief period of control over Saltillo, the Laguna, and other areas of Coahuila (and even in the face of the immediate economic crisis), Villa did attempt to place his political stamp on the state and to create a semblance of formal government. Governor Santiago Ramírez presided over the first Villista elections in February 1915, in which Saltillo and San Pedro chose new municipal presidents. Elections, however, were the exception rather than the rule. As Villa's forces extended their control over other areas of Coahuila, municipal presidents were simply designated by Villa's governors. At the same time, Carranza's officials remained in power in several areas of the state, and Villa had difficulty finding local officials who would serve and support him. In Múzquiz Captain Josafat Ramón urged Santiago Ramírez to designate an outsider and a military man for the post of municipal president, since there were few locals who would prove loyal. Perhaps convinced that they lacked the support of the local populace, the Villista presidents of three northern municipalities abandoned their posts in fear. In an interesting attempt to retain Villista officials, and to prevent the graft that flourished in the midst of economic trouble, Governor Orestes Pereyra raised the salaries of all public employees.[31]

In the final analysis, Villa's political control of Coahuila was, like his military hold on the state, short lived and tenuous. Only for a brief period in 1915 did Villista military gains threaten the outcome of the Revolution in this part of Mexico. Villa's support in Coahuila was always limited, although it was not insignificant; it could not prevail against Carranza, but that support would help Villismo persist even beyond Carranza's national victory.

In his recent biography of Pancho Villa, Friedrich Katz analyzes Villa's popular appeal in Chihuahua. He argues that Villa appealed to Chihuahua's rural population through "Robin Hood–type acts of social justice," such as the occupation of one of the state's largest *haciendas* and the execution of its hated administrator. During his brief reign as governor, Villa made good (albeit with only temporary results) on promises of land reform, while giving material support to Chihuahua's poorest elements. In short, Villa cultivated an image as a protector of the poor.[32]

That Villa's popularity among the rural lower class could travel readily across state lines was noted by American official William Blocker, who in 1914 observed that (as in Chihuahua) Coahuila's cowboys and *hacienda* workers "idolize General Villa."[33] Not surprisingly, Villa appealed to Coahuila's rural poor; and particularly in the Laguna, peasant leaders such as Calixto Contreras supported Villa in the expectation of significant agrarian reform. At least in the short term, the hopes of Contreras and others were not frustrated. In the Laguna region of both Coahuila and Durango, expropriations of large estates did occur during the period of Villista control. These lands were administered by military officials and by the Comisión de Agricultura de la Laguna (Laguna Agricultural Commission). It is not clear, however, where revenue from the lands ultimately went. Many estates were rented directly to poor sharecroppers, and confiscated lands were often held by or in the name of revolutionary generals.[34]

Some of Villa's representatives also hinted at their desire to effect a more general agrarian reform in Coahuila, though their motives were unclear and they had neither the time nor the means to carry this out. Governor Santiago Ramírez and Major Cirilo Mendiola, commander of the rich mining community of Sierra Mojada, began to investigate the political antecedents of Sierra Mojada's landowners, who held the best agricultural land but had not "formally" purchased it.[35] At the same time, Villa's governors received from several Coahuilans petitions for the use of lands and waters owned by Huerta supporters and other "enemies," or abandoned because of the revolution. Las Vacas residents asked for the use of an abandoned plot in return for repairing it and bringing it under cultivation. In Piedras Negras, locals requested the use of lands and waters of Huerta sympathizers who had left Mexico. It is not clear if these petitions were favourably answered. In addition, the destruction of barbed wire and the more spontaneous grab for land and resources that occurred during the nineteenth century and again during Madero's revolt was still an option for some Coahuilans. In San Buenaventura, for example, local residents, with the apparent authorization of the municipal president, destroyed the barbed wire surrounding the *hacienda* of Pedro Cuéllar and carried away some of its products.[36]

Some Villa supporters also expressed interest in the properties of Carrancistas. Francisco Cárdenas, municipal president of Piedras Negras and a Villista, noted that many Carrancistas in northern Coahuila had left, with several taking refuge in Eagle Pass. While Cárdenas wished to make the properties of these exiles available to those in need, the owners refused to even rent their lands. Indeed, Rafael Múzquiz (Carranza's former consular official and master contraband agent) remained in the Piedras Negras area, representing and attempting to protect the interests of these owners.[37]

In the end, expectations of significant land reform in Coahuila were not met, and the issue received relatively little attention from Villa officials, who were consistently hampered by the broader economic crisis and whose authority was always on shaky ground. At the same time, Villa's own commitment to significant agrarian reform beyond Chihuahua was never clear. Only belatedly did Villa's governors establish an administrative structure for confiscated lands. A committee to supervise property confiscation in Saltillo, for example, was designated as late as April 1915. Villa's own national agrarian reform law, promising the division of large estates among peasants, appeared in May 1915 (after decisive losses on the battlefield) and was never implemented.[38]

Considered in its northern context, Villa's apparent hesitation on the issue of agrarian reform was not entirely surprising. Indeed, there was an important difference between northern states such as Chihuahua and Coahuila, and the central Mexican state of Morelos that had given birth to Zapata's struggle for land reform. In the latter case, an indigenous peasantry had been despoiled of its communal lands, and hence of a source of cultural identity. The struggle for land was thus central to Zapata's rebellion, and took the form of a collective, class-based resistance to economic change.[39] Coahuila (and many northern states), by contrast, did not have a large, indigenous peasantry with deep connections to communal lands. Nor were the popular classes united on agrarian issues. For this group also included elements with a limited interest in acquiring land, including a large population of miners and a mobile and often well-paid rural and urban workforce.

At the same time, Coahuila did have its fair share of smallholders, which often included the descendants of military colonists of the eighteenth and nineteenth centuries. Communal property, in the form of lands and waters used in common by smallholders, was also a part of the Coahuilan landscape. The Laguna, moreover, was home to a few independent towns (San Pedro and Matamoros) consisting of communal lands granted to small-scale farmers during the nineteenth century. Thus, the land concentration that affected Zapata and his people and that was encouraged by nineteenth-century economic growth was destined to have an impact on many Coahuilans as well. And while *latifundia* was certainly not a recent addition to the state's history, in the decades preceding the Revolution it was encouraged by national economic policies and by the broader forces of modernization. The disputes over rangeland and water that sprang up in various parts of the state underscored these developments, as did the numerous requests for lands and water that Coahuilans made to President Madero, Governor Carranza, and then to Villa's local representatives.

In Coahuila, then, agrarian issues were an important part of the Revolution, and for at least some smallholders and peasants Villismo held out hope for change. At the same time, and in the context of revolutionary violence and economic hardship, some Coahuilans embraced the image of Villa as a protector of the poor. Yet even had Villa acted more decisively on issues of social justice (including land reform), it is not clear that he would have found the popular support to defeat Constitutionalism. For Carranza appears to have been largely successful in maintaining the support that he had begun to cultivate earlier during his term as Coahuila's governor. This was particularly true in the case of workers (and particularly miners), who continued to endorse Carranza during his bitter war against the forces of the Convention.

One specific indication of Carranza's success in the face of Villa's challenge may be found in his ability to cultivate and retain the support of Coahuilan Maderistas (former supporters of Francisco Madero and his movement). Although the extent to which Maderistas later sided with Villa or Carranza is difficult to gauge, an examination of the Constitutionalist army in Coahuila after the Villa-Carranza split is instructive. There were no significant desertions of soldiers with Maderista antecedents.[40] Carranza seems to have been remarkably successful in maintaining the support of these soldiers, many of whom were part of the state's irregular forces prior to Madero's fall. Where they occurred, defections to Villa's army were most likely confined to the Laguna region, which remained under almost continuous control of the Division of the North from April 1914 to September 1915.

Likewise, and perhaps not surprisingly, Villa does not appear to have garnered the support of Coahuilan elites, who tended to share Carranza's reservations about this uncultured man whose actions resembled those of an outlaw. The one exception to this general rule was the Madero family, which included several of its members in Villa's ranks. Brothers Emilio and Raúl Madero were perhaps the most notable elites who sided with Villa. Both supported their brother's earlier call for revolution, aided in the fight against Orozco, and cast their lot with Villa after Francisco Madero's death. Both were recognized as members of Villa's inner circle, and Raúl had attended the Convention, where he voted against Carranza's leadership. Understandably, given the always-strained relationship between Francisco Madero and Carranza, no connection had been established between members of the late president's immediate family (most of whom had fled into exile after Francisco's death) and Carranza's movement. Any expectation that the Maderos would side with the Constitutionalist movement was quickly dispelled in the months after Carranza's rebellion against Huerta. More broadly, the Madero brothers represented an elite clique that had traditionally been in competition with the Carranza family.

Some Coahuilans readily embraced Villa's image as a champion of the poor and an advocate of land reform. In the end, however, Villa was unable to generate the more broad-based support that was needed to defeat Carranza. This inability was based on the short-term and transitory nature of Villismo. But it was also a function of Carranza's already strong base of support in his native state. Only in the Laguna was that support consistently challenged.

The Persistence of Villismo

Villismo continued beyond 1915 in the form of sporadic attacks and raids, and the Laguna continued to be the most problematic region. Local support for Villa still existed, and Villa's soldiers remained active. The Constitutionalists attempted to halt such activity by granting amnesty to Villa rebels, with limited success. In October 1916 a skirmish between

Constitutionalists and Villa's soldiers once again resulted in the destruction of railroads, leaving Torreón isolated. Already in the midst of a typhoid epidemic, the town's residents were also subjected to high taxes, which were rumoured to be lining the pockets of Carranza's officers. Late in the year another Villista advance into Coahuila's coal region began. Although Carranza's troops succeeded in defending the area, Villa's men soon moved towards the Laguna. Rumours of Villista atrocities in western Chihuahua and certain areas of the Laguna caused yet another exodus of Laguna residents to the Coahuila-Texas border zone. William Blocker reported that Villa's followers were murdering Arabs, Spaniards, and Japanese, and that enemy soldiers released from captivity were arriving in Piedras Negras "shorn of their ears."[41]

Fears of an impending attack on Torreón were well founded. On December 21 Villa's troops occupied the town, looted stores, extracted forced loans, and massacred Chinese, Arabs, and some eighty Carrancista sympathizers. Constitutionalist General Maclovio Herrera was among those executed; his body was hung out for display at the railroad station. Villa declared protection for all residents but the Americans and Chinese.[42]

The Villista occupation of Torreón was brief, and by January 1917 the Constitutionalists had regained control of the town. American consular official William Blocker reported only slight damage from the latest rebel attack, but a foreign resident insisted that "the city is now a real dirty hole ... [with] the bodies of soldiers and horses laying in the streets for four or five days." British vice-consul Patrick O'Hea, himself a Laguna businessman, confirmed this view, noting that the latest occupation had wasted Torreón, paralyzing all business and causing any merchants remaining in the town to sell out their stocks and leave. The latest violence also contributed to the lack of sanitation in Torreón: "the air reeks of decomposing flesh in shallow graves, there are no medicines and scarce any doctors...." Villa's soldiers added to the food shortage by loading trains with the town's meagre food stores and transporting them back to Chihuahua. "The Villistas," insisted O'Hea, "are predatory raiders, destroyers only... Villa professes nothing ... but a frenzied patriotism. His career is that of a dog in rabies,... a Malay running amock."[43]

The return of Carranza's troops, in the opinion of O'Hea, did little to help the situation. Themselves starving and unpaid,

Constitutionalists began looting Torreón stores, encouraging local residents to flee into the surrounding hills. To this Englishman the Carrancistas were no better than the bandits who had just left: "These hordes of locusts, these soldiers and their women, haggard, savage, starving, and reeking of filth and disease, are consuming and wasting everything. They complain they are not paid.... Whether their officers have pocketed their pay or not,... the result is the same."[44]

The continuing conflict between Villa and Carranza in the Laguna region mirrored the still volatile situation that confronted Carranza as he attempted to solidify his claim to national leadership. Although he was firmly entrenched in Mexico City by the end of 1915, and although the earlier granting of American recognition had underscored his legitimacy as Mexico's next leader, Carranza continued to find in Villa an irritating and sometimes formidable rival. For Villa, who had taken great care to cultivate U.S. support, American recognition of his rival was the ultimate affront. In the defiant and blustery style to which his followers and enemies had become accustomed, Villa retaliated in 1916, first with an attack on Santa Isabel, Chihuahua, and then with a raid on Columbus, New Mexico. American casualties, and Villa's invasion of American territory, brought a swift response from the United States. Ten thousand U.S. soldiers under the leadership of General John Pershing unsuccessfully pursued Villa, penetrating far into Mexican territory while Carranza protested against this violation of Mexico's sovereignty. Although the Pershing Expedition failed in its attempt to capture Villa, it refocused attention on the border area, where the Plan of San Diego was still alive.

In May raiders struck at Glen Springs and Boquillas, Texas, then retreated into the mountains of northern Coahuila. Expectations of another U.S. invasion brought panic and an exodus of residents from Piedras Negras. Placards appeared in that town urging Mexicans to take up arms and defend the nation. Blocker, meanwhile, claimed that local authorities, including Carranza's provisional governor Gustavo Espinosa Mireles, were encouraging anti–American activities such as the confiscation of horses and cattle from American ranches. Anti-American sentiment was reportedly strong in Saltillo as well.[45]

Border raids ended in July 1916 when the U.S. and Mexico agreed to settle their differences in a diplomatic forum. The Plan of San Diego subsequently sputtered out and the Pershing

Expedition ended early the next year. Espinosa Mireles trav-
elled to northern Coahuila to assure the border community
of his determination to keep the peace and protect American
interests. By 1917 Villa's activities were largely isolated to
Chihuahua. In the Laguna, Villista raids would continue until
1920, but they were limited in scope and easily rebuffed by
Constitutionalist forces.[46]

Most Coahuilans experienced the struggle between Villa and
Carranza through further violence and a worsening economy.
And while Carranza's officials reported that the last round of
violence caused loyalties to both revolutionary leaders to waver,
it was Villa who in the end found himself and his movement dis-
credited.[47] Villa's support in Coahuila was largely premised on
false hopes of significant social (and for some, agrarian) reform.
The persistence of that support depended upon the willingness
of the popular classes to tolerate further hardship and to turn
against a known quantity: Carranza. In the face of this reality,
Villa's charisma and populist image proved only somewhat por-
table. They faltered in the face of persistent military pressure
and especially in the face of worsening economic conditions.
Meanwhile Carranza, who had already begun the hard work of
cultivating popular support and whose appeal extended across
class lines, became the better and more secure answer for war-
weary Coahuilans.

8

Reconstruction and Reform

The Triumph of Constitutionalism

The Constitutionalist victory over Villa in 1915 signaled the end of the bloodiest fighting in Coahuila. But Carranza's was not simply a military victory. On both the national and local levels, he had succeeded in translating his success as a Coahuilan leader into a broader movement that was capable of crossing state boundaries and class lines. The substance of that movement emerged earlier during Carranza's stint as a Maderista governor. During that time, he had demonstrated his willingness to act on certain issues that had popular appeal. Thus he eliminated several tax exemptions and special economic privileges, and he courted labour through a worker protection law and efforts to end the company store. Official measures to improve public health and education as well as a campaign against vice also informed part of the populist image that Carranza carried with him into national politics. Finally, Carranza's insistence on more official supervision of economic concessions granted to foreigners, as well as his willingness to concede certain rights to local governments, gave an indication of the nationalist and federalist tendencies that would help Carranza win support for some of his national policies.

Particularly after Madero's death, and as he sought to form a national movement, Carranza became more aware of the need for a concrete plan of reform. Particularly in the midst of his struggle with Zapata and Villa, he was compelled to assume a stance that went beyond the more moderate reformism of Madero and the strictly political agenda of the Plan of Guadalupe.

One month before the Convention of Aguascalientes, Carranza convoked his own revolutionary meeting at which he indicated his willingness to address the issues of land and labour reform. Echoing his earlier work in Coahuila, he also pledged support for municipal autonomy and for a nationalist economic policy.[1]

After breaking with the Convention, Carranza continued to expand and publicize his support for reform. His most important efforts focused on helping Mexico's *campesinos* and workers. In January 1915 Carranza issued his own agrarian law, which promised to return communal lands that had been taken away by Porfirian concessions and other corrupt practices. Constitutionalist governors and generals were given temporary authority to divide estates and distribute the land, and the law established a National Agrarian Commission that would oversee confiscations and land grants. Although not as sweeping as Zapata's Plan of Ayala (which called for outright expropriation of *hacienda* lands), the 1915 agrarian law predated that of Villa, who waited until his forces had suffered decisive losses on the battlefield to issue a formal plan. From his headquarters in Veracruz, Carranza also appealed to workers by outlawing the company store and debt peonage, and by ordering an increase in wages. By early 1915 his efforts had garnered the crucial support of the Casa del Obrero Mundial, an anarchist workers group established as the Mexican Revolution was just beginning. Casa troops would aid in the military struggle against Villa and Zapata.[2]

In the final analysis, Carranza's approach to reform was measured, and no doubt tempered by his social background. As an owner of a good amount of property in Coahuila, and as a resident in a state where the agrarian question, while real, was not as sweeping as in Morelos, Carranza would never be as sympathetic as Zapata to the issue of land reform. Similarly, as a member of the local political elite who had (at least initially) been a successful participant in the Porfirian political game, Carranza would not share the outlook of Villa, whose own background and success had been based on more informal, and often extralegal, paths to power.

Carranza's willingness to embrace the issues of land and labour reform during his confrontation with the Convention probably entailed a bit of opportunism, in the same way that Villa's deference to the United States was calculated to keep arms flowing across the border and to maintain Villa as a contender for U.S. recognition. Nonetheless, Carranza's gestures towards workers and the agrarian issue also reflected his acknowledgement of the very real popular pressures that gave the Revolution its initial and continuing momentum. In the end, the Constitutionalist movement succeeded, as it had in Coahuila, in attracting a wide range of supporters. As Carranza assumed a position of national leadership, his commitment to the popular voice, as well as the limits of his reformist vision, would become clearer.

Carranza's National Leadership

With the crucial endorsement of the United States in October 1915, Carranza emerged as Mexico's *de facto* leader until he was officially elected president in March 1917. In his quest for national legitimacy, Carranza convoked a constitutional convention in the year prior to his election. Unlike the earlier gathering that gave rise to the Convention government, this meeting excluded Carranza's enemies (especially the supporters of Villa and Zapata). It was not, however, a captive to Carranza's views. In a draft constitution, Carranza emphasized political goals, including municipal freedom, separation between church and state, and a strong executive.[3] The more radical and more numerous delegates, while remaining loyal to Carranza's leadership, were determined to embrace more sweeping changes. The resulting Constitution of 1917 clearly endorsed anticlericalism, land reform, and labour reform. Article 27 called for permanent restoration of lands taken illegally during the Porfiriato. Article 123 formally established the national government as the protector of the Mexican worker, and included a guaranteed eight-hour workday, a minimum wage, and the right of unionization. Article 3, which echoed nineteenth-century liberal efforts to limit the historically strong position of the Catholic Church, significantly curtailed the Church's political, social, and economic power. Church involvement in primary education, for example, was prohibited; clergy were forbidden to vote; and the Church was banned from owning property.

Venustiano Carranza is not recognized in Mexican history as a great champion of the 1917 Constitution. He accepted it with less than enthusiasm, and he faced the difficult task of implementing its broad program of reform within the context of a Mexico spent by civil war and still struggling with unrest.

Particularly in the area of land reform, Carranza's efforts were limited, and often resisted by *hacendados* and local authorities. He distributed a total of 540,000 acres (fewer than some individual *hacendados* owned), most of it in areas where Zapata's movement threatened to undermine Carranza's control. Towards the end of his presidency, Carranza announced that all properties confiscated by his generals during the civil war (including those taken under the 1915 agrarian law) would be returned. Mexico's economic crisis, a product of wartime, compelled this measure, and it helped to temper Carranza's already measured attitude towards serious land reform. In particular, Mexico faced a food shortage that compelled the importation of food and made the resumption of domestic agricultural activity one of the president's top priorities.[4]

Carranza's efforts on behalf of Mexican workers were perhaps more indicative of his awareness of the importance of the popular voice. As he had done as governor of Coahuila, Carranza continued to court workers. He and his generals often became directly involved in labour issues, and Carranza's assertiveness towards foreign-owned companies helped bolster his image as a champion of the working class. That image helped deliver the workers' vote in the 1917 elections. In turn, Carranza supported the establishment of a new union, the Regional Confederation of Mexican Workers (CROM), in 1918. Yet even as Carranza remained a consistent supporter of labour issues, his approach remained cautious. The Casa del Obrero Mundial, which had cast its lot with Carranza during his battle against the Convention, soon incurred his wrath when it added to Mexico's instability by staging a series of strikes. Carranza declared martial law and enlisted the aid of Pablo González in subduing the strikers. The CROM, meanwhile, came to be seen as a more acceptable labour organization, since it was (at least for a time) clearly beholden to the Mexican president. In short, Carranza recognized workers as an important source of support and consistently championed workers' rights. At the same time, his cultivation of labour was highly personalistic and, as with land reform, was tempered by Carranza's desire for order and stability.[5]

Ultimately, as both *de facto* and *de jure* leader of Mexico, Carranza followed a course that was at the same time progressive and aware of popular demands, and moderate in scope. His progressivism was informed by first-hand experience with the revolutionary unrest and dislocations of the Revolution in his native Coahuila. His moderation (though also a product of his own background) was largely dictated by the economic quandary that dogged Mexico in the aftermath of civil war. Food shortages and inflation were the primary problems that Carranza faced as president. Hence, he used his executive power to compel the continued production and distribution of food and to encourage banks to return to a silver standard, eventually ridding Mexico of the inflation and confusion wrought by the wartime circulation of rival currencies.[6] Carranza's struggle to bring about a national reconstruction was replicated on the local level in Coahuila.

Dislocation and Discontent

The arrival of the victorious Constitutionalist troops in Piedras Negras in September 1915 brought an initial surge of optimism among residents in the border region. As the fighting ended and the railroads were repaired, business activity resumed in most areas of Coahuila. U.S. recognition of Carranza's government raised hopes for Coahuila's economic revival, and Americans and other foreigners began to return to their homes and shops in Mexico's interior. As a major railroad centre the Eagle Pass–Piedras Negras area was flooded with Mexican refugees trying to return to their homes after the worst of the fighting. Many had waited out the revolution in the southwestern United States as railroad or agricultural workers. The seasonal round that took some Coahuilans to Texas to pick cotton (a traditional outlet for many of the state's labourers that had been shut down by the economic crisis preceding Madero's revolt) apparently resumed as well.

In Piedras Negras itself conditions also improved. The customs house became increasingly busy, and merchants who had faced rebel attacks and had grappled with an ever-present currency crisis once again began to stock their shelves. The resumption of regular railroad traffic also aided the mining region of central Coahuila, which resumed regular shipments of minerals to the border for export to the U.S. The promise of economic revival, moreover, coincided with the resumption of civilian government. This development, noted one American official, would help the "grafting that has always run hand in hand with military control."[7]

The final Constitutionalist occupation of Piedras Negras also

MUNICIPIO LIBRE

*Detail from a political pamphlet issued in Coahuila after Carranza's national
victory in 1915. The pamplet hails the principle of municipal autonomy,
and depicts Lady Liberty breaking the chains of boss rule.*

Archivo General del Estado de Coahuila: Fondo Revolución.

brought with it the hope of permanent change. Shortly after
driving out the Villistas, Carranza's officials posted several
decrees that the First Chief had issued from Veracruz. Among
them was a pledge to make the *municipio libre*, or independent
municipality, the basis of the political system of the Mexican
states. In Piedras Negras the posted decree included a dramatic
picture of Lady Liberty breaking the chains of boss rule.

High expectations for reform, however, quickly gave way
to the difficult task of reconstructing the war-torn state. That
job fell to Gustavo Espinosa Mireles, a native of southeastern
Coahuila. Trained as a lawyer, the young Espinosa Mireles had
joined the Constitutionalists in 1913 and had become Carranza's
private secretary. In September 1915 Carranza designated him
governor of Coahuila, a post he held until 1917, when he was
officially elected governor. The immediate need to pacify the
state and rebuild the economy ensured that the governorship of
Espinosa Mireles would bring no sweeping changes, particularly
in Coahuila's economic structure. At the same time, however,
Espinosa Mireles recognized the need for viable reforms, especially in the political system.

In his attempts to quell unrest in Coahuila, Espinosa Mireles'
attention was inevitably drawn to the Coahuila-Texas frontier.
Border intrigue as well as continued Villista activity kept northern Coahuila in an uncertain state throughout 1916. Félix Díaz,
nephew of Mexico's former dictator, found adherents in some

Coahuilan exiles when he declared a revolt against Carranza in February 1916. Felicista supporters included Manuel Garza Aldape, former member of the Huerta cabinet; Luis Alberto Guajardo, former Huertista *jefe político;* and Porfirian *cacique* Andrés Garza Galán. By March the Coahuila-Texas frontier was alive with the plotting of Felicistas, Villistas, and Huertistas.[8]

The scheming of various factions along Coahuila's northern border soon coalesced in an anti-Carranza plot that gained a few adherents in the Laguna as well. Originating in El Paso and led by Emiliano G. Saravia, the Legalista (Legalist) movement spoke against the "dictatorship" of Carranza and lamented his pretensions to power. Legalista adherents included old Porfirians, supporters of the now-deceased Huerta, and ex-Villistas. The conspirators organized and equipped small bands of men along the international frontier and planned a seizure of Piedras Negras and Las Vacas. In Coahuila the Legalista plot attempted to play upon Mexico's worsening currency crisis by placing large amounts of silver into circulation in Mexican border towns. Legalistas also lured new recruits by offering payment of wages in silver.

Reports of Legalista activities indicated that the group had established a base at the Hacienda San Carlos of Lorenzo González Treviño. Most *hacienda* workers, who had earlier joined the Constitutionalist movement, continued to support Carranza. The silver offered by the Legalistas, however, proved too tempting for several men who were being paid in Constitutionalist bills that were often of little value. The Legalistas did not succeed in hatching their plot among Coahuilans, but Carranza's officials realized that the seriousness of the economic situation could cause defections from their ranks.[9]

The Legalista movement underscored the fact that Carranza's definitive occupation of the border area did not mean an immediate end to the dislocations caused by the past revolution. Although the end of violence allowed some Coahuilans to find work on both sides of the border with greater ease, unemployment remained a problem in the northern region. Several residents were reduced to hauling small sacks of pecans, corn, istle, and other goods to the international frontier, where they were sold to American merchants. Pilferers and petty thieves abounded in Piedras Negras and became so bold "that no one even dare[d] to place newly washed clothes out to dry for fear of their being stolen by a peon."[10]

The continuing currency crisis was at the heart of much

of the unrest in Coahuila. Once favoured over Villa's bills, Carrancista money left over from the last round of civil war was now continuously devalued, and in Piedras Negras several merchants insisted on payment in gold. Money exchanges closed in anticipation of more devaluation. Local authorities set prices, but businessmen were still forced to buy their goods in the United States, where banks would accept new Mexican money issued by Carranza in 1916, although they exchanged it at less than face value. While some Coahuilan shopkeepers adopted American money as their standard, others simply refused to stock their shelves. Piedras Negras railroad workers soon struck on the currency issue, and by the end of May the strike had spread to include the entire National Railroad. Another railroad strike in November was settled only when Governor Espinosa Mireles agreed to pay a percentage of the workers' salaries in silver.[11]

Constitutionalist soldiers throughout Coahuila were also victims of the currency crisis. Desertions in Saltillo and Torreón were frequent, and many deserters became bandits. After fighting against Villa in Chihuahua, a band of some six hundred Constitutionalists arrived along the Coahuilan border in a state of near-starvation. Famished and paid in worthless money, they killed cattle, raided fields, and soon scattered into the interior of the state.[12]

Workers in central Coahuila's mining region suffered as well. Here, too, many merchants were compelled to charge high prices for basic goods. Local *hacendados* insisted on payment in gold when they sold their goods to the mining communities. Miners shouldered the burden of high prices, and frequent strikes occurred. A strike in Rosita brought the direct intervention of Carranza, who addressed worker demands by ordering an increase in wages. He was helpless, however, to send desperately needed corn to the workers because of the lack of reliable transportation. A similar problem plagued miners in Múzquiz, and because corn shipments were the object of numerous robberies, the Constitutionalist Army had to issue a *salvoconducto*, or safe-conduct pass, in order to guarantee the transport of corn to the area.[13]

The stabilization of the mining industry and attention to the needs of miners were top priorities of Carranza and the Espinosa Mireles administration. Immediately upon assuming office, Espinosa Mireles sent an inspector to Coahuila's coal region. The inspector reported that few of the state's coal mines were operational, lacking the materials needed, while workers went unpaid. Still, support for Carranza continued to be strong among Coahuila's miners.[14]

Peace and stability were likewise slow in returning to the capital of Saltillo. Continuing food shortages and a long drought helped create a situation in which a mob of poor women stoned and sacked several stores. Espinosa Mireles personally dispersed the women and arranged for government distribution of corn. Gradually, however, crops were planted, and with the aid of regular shipments from the border, local stores began to replenish their supplies.[15]

The Laguna region, which was the main area of continued Villista activity throughout 1916, proved the most difficult to pacify and rebuild. Food riots occurred in Torreón, and the continuing flood of refugees from the Laguna brought to the border reports of "deplorable" conditions and banditry. The currency crisis exacerbated the food shortages by encouraging merchants to send their goods to the U.S. for a better price. Shopkeepers in San Pedro began selling staple goods at inflated prices, and some *hacendados* issued provisional coupons as payment for their workers. The military commander of Torreón authorized the issuance of new currency to pay the salaries of agricultural workers and to cover the expenses of stimulating the stagnant economy. Laguna residents, reported Durango consul H.C. Coen, were tired of war and opposed to both Villa and the Constitutionalists. Here too, however, recovery was apparently in the offing. At the end of the summer of 1916, American official Phillip C. Hanna optimistically reported that "in the Laguna, king cotton is saving the situation, for with abundant water all of the ranches are busy and there is employment for everybody."[16]

Recovery, then, was sporadic and setbacks were frequent. Espinosa Mireles, who faced the difficult task of effecting a more permanent restoration, often received direct help from Carranza, who continued to pay close attention to his native state. At the same time, national policies designed to curb inflation and compel food production guided the governor, who followed Carranza's lead by decreeing jail time for any who speculated in the new national currency issued in 1916. He also ordered Coahuilan merchants to reduce their prices in proportion to the value of the new money.[17] Espinosa Mireles likewise addressed the shortage of food and other items in Coahuila by discouraging their export, prohibiting the unauthorized exit of istle, hides, cotton, metals, and other materials, that could be exchanged for better prices outside of Coahuila. To stop the illegal extraction of these items, the governor named fiscal agents to conduct vigilance along the railroad lines from Saltillo to the state's borders with Nuevo León, Chihuahua, San Luis Potosí, and Zacatecas. He also decreed against any extraction of grains and other basic food items. Merchants authorized to export hides, metals, and istle were required to use part of their profits to buy grains and to introduce them into Coahuila's towns at a reasonable price. Several municipal officials issued their own regulations prohibiting the export of food items. In central Coahuila, the municipal president of Progreso declared a fine for any attempting to export wheat or corn from the area.[18]

Cattle rustling continued to be a problem. Espinosa Mireles declared the theft of cattle to be a capital crime and authorized municipal presidents to proceed in summary fashion against cattle thieves. In another attempt to solve the problem of cattle rustling while addressing the needs of local residents, the governor authorized the municipal president of Sabinas to collect all animals of unknown brands found in the pasture of a local cattle company, and distribute them among the region's neediest farmers.[19]

The problems of banditry and vagrancy presented yet another challenge. Both in the Laguna and along the Coahuila-Texas border, robbery and pillaging were common as members of the lower classes took matters into their own hands. In Matamoros municipal president Mariano Chavero took his own steps against banditry and vagrancy, which he equated, with a great deal of justification, with Villismo. All landowners were required to submit a list of their tenants and workers, and any change of residence by these people had to be authorized. Chavero also mandated the vigilance of outsiders, ordered that all ex-Villistas carry a special pass, and required that all weapons be handed over to local authorities, under threat of capital punishment.[20]

Espinosa Mireles' attempts to alleviate the immediate crisis and dislocations that followed on the heels of revolution often had broader implications. Indeed, some of his measures were direct challenges to a traditional economic system characterized by monopoly and entrenched privilege. Through a special commission established in Torreón to address the severe grain shortage, he permitted Laguna farmers to export their cotton seed in exchange for corn. This freed the region's farmers from their long-standing obligation to sell the seed to the Companía Jabonera de la Laguna, a product of the Porfiriato, which had a monopoly on the cotton seed industry.[21]

Plagues and early frosts in 1915 caused a 70 per cent decline in that year's Laguna cotton crop, making the resource more coveted. Speculation in the Laguna's precious cotton encouraged frequent robberies of that item, prompting Espinosa Mireles to order the punishment of thieves and demand steps to ensure the legal procedence of all cotton. The cotton crop of Carlos González (whose lands had been confiscated and rented out during Villa's occupation of the Laguna) awaited harvest and was the object of frequent robberies. So that the harvest would occur and the cotton not be wasted, Espinosa Mireles declared the crop government property.[22] Carranza also acknowledged the seriousness of the situation by decreeing the confiscation of cotton stores where the government was unable to purchase them. The expropriation of foreign-owned cotton, however, generated heated protests from Spaniards and the diplomatic representatives of France and Germany, and finally forced Carranza to reverse his decree.[23]

Espinosa Mireles displayed a willingness to take extraordinary measures to restore Coahuila's economy. In 1916 he decreed a tripling of taxes on all lands not being worked, and authorized municipal presidents to distribute abandoned lands to others so that they could be cultivated. Owners could not reclaim these lands until the harvest was gathered.[24] Such measures mirrored and were encouraged by those of President Carranza. Similarly, Espinosa Mireles' handling of the agrarian question was faithful to Carranza's vision, and constrained by its limits.

Land Reform and the Politics of Reconstruction

The appropriation of lands and other resources in Coahuila for economic and political purposes had begun with Carranza's rebellion against Huerta in 1913. The Carrancista occupation of Piedras Negras in that year was accompanied by confiscations of the properties of declared enemies, on the order of congressman and military commander Gabriel Calzada. During the subsequent occupation by Huerta's soldiers these properties were returned, only to be confiscated again when the Constitutionalists recaptured the plaza. After Huerta's defeat Carranza allowed the use of confiscated lands by others so that the year's harvest could be gathered. Constitutionalist officers also allowed liberal use of lands in areas under their control. In Abasolo General Fortunato Zuazua simply decreed that local residents could plant crops wherever they wished.[25]

As late as 1917 Coahuila's state government was authorizing municipal officials to distribute idle lands and waters temporarily among those who would use them to sustain a harvest.[26] Yet such concessions and government expropriations never amounted to true agrarian reform. Instead, Carranza used confiscations in his native state as a temporary political measure to punish his enemies, and Espinosa Mireles allowed the appropriation of resources only to meet the immediate demands of a wavering economy.

That Carranza intended no significant change in land tenure within Coahuila became apparent immediately after the 1915 expulsion of Villa's forces. The first decree of Espinosa Mireles ordered the return of all properties previously confiscated by Constitutionalists and Villistas. At the same time, the governor authorized the continued appropriation of properties owned by those who had rebelled against the Constitutionalist government.[27]

In Coahuila as in other areas of Carranza's Mexico, the lands and businesses of Huerta and Villa sympathizers were targeted for expropriation. Shortly after assuming office, Governor Espinosa Mireles ordered the confiscation of Luis Alberto Guajardo's *hacienda* in Múzquiz. Several other members of the Guajardo family, all of whom had supported Huerta and subsequently fled Mexico, had their substantial holdings in Múzquiz expropriated. Property confiscations were especially prevalent in this central Coahuilan municipality, which was the centre of the Garza Galán clique during the Porfiriato, and whose *hacendados* had tended to support Huerta. Thus, the lands of brothers Andrés and Juan Garza Galán were intervened, as were the properties of Manuel Garza Aldape.[28]

In the Laguna a special commission administered the properties of Carranza's enemies, while making sure that the lands were planted and harvested. The Torreón properties of Huerta supporter Luis García de Letona, already appropriated during the Villista occupation of the Laguna, continued to be administered by the Constitutionalists despite their owner's insistence that he had been an enemy of Huerta. The split between Carranza and Villa in 1914 complicated the situation in the Laguna.

Carranza and Espinosa Mireles received numerous petitions from owners whose properties had been confiscated immediately after Villa's 1914 occupation of Torreón. Hoping to shield themselves from the appropriations of the Constitutionalists, these owners claimed to be victims of Villismo rather than traitors to the Constitutionalists. In one petition, Torreón merchant Guillermo Valencia disputed the confiscation of his store, insisting that Villistas had pressed him into their ranks, so that his sympathy for Villa had not been genuine. In most cases, local officials were apparently careful to distinguish between Villista confiscations that occurred before and after the split with Carranza.[29]

Several Coahuilans who had fled Mexico during the bloody fighting were also singled out, perhaps by mistake, even if their political loyalties were ill defined. Constitutionalists seized a *hacienda* and two urban plots located in Sabinas and Piedras Negras that were once owned by the late colonel Nicanor Valdés (one of Coahuila's nineteenth-century military colonists and a member of the Federal forces that resisted Porfirio Díaz' 1876 revolt). Although the properties were entrusted to Valdés' widow, Juana, even before Madero's revolt began, they were appropriated when Juana fled to the United States. After the Constitutionalist victory Plutarco Valdés, Juana's son and a major in the Carrancista army, obtained the return of these properties, insisting that his mother had remained aloof from politics during the Revolution.[30]

Not suprisingly, given the fact that brothers Emilio and Raúl had chosen to support Villa, the extensive properties and businesses of the Madero family were targeted for confiscation. In northern Coahuila, for example, the Hacienda Palmira was confiscated and the municipal president given permission to sell its products. Properties and businesses in Parras, centre of the Madero fortune, were likewise appropriated, as were family lands in the Laguna. The Hacienda La Merced, a major focus of Maderista activity in 1910–11, was also appropriated. Interestingly, however, it continued to be administered by Cayetano Trejo, the former president of a local Anti-reelectionist club. Although Constitutionalist confiscations virtually ruined the Madero family's hard-earned fortune, Carranza began to return these intervened properties by 1917.[31]

Municipal officials within Coahuila appear to have had some influence over the confiscation of property after 1915. Some municipal presidents ordered their own confiscations of "enemy" lands. A petition from Sierra Mojada achieved the confiscation of Regulo J. Garíbar's lands by arguing that Garíbar had fought with the Orozquistas and Huertistas. Such requests were frequent, although it is not clear how many received a favourable answer. Just as frequent were local protests against the return of confiscated properties. The municipal president of Torreón advised Espinosa Mireles not to return the property of Federico Reyes, a member of the local Defensa Social who had personally apprehended some Carranza supporters in 1913.[32]

Despite the continued appropriation of properties after 1915, most intervened lands, including those of Carranza's acknowledged enemies, were eventually restored to their owners. The return of lands was as much a political measure as was their confiscation. Through the Administración de Bienes Intervenidos (the office that oversaw confiscated property), Carranza compelled *hacendados* to petition him personally and to explain their behaviour during the Revolution. The restitution of property was contingent upon the petitioner's promise not to sue the Carranza administration for damages. Additional conditions were placed upon the return of some lands. Miguel Cárdenas, a grudging supporter of Huerta in 1913, obtained the restoration of lands and irrigation waters in Sacramento only after paying taxes from which he had been exempt before the Revolution.[33]

The limits of Carranza's agrarian reform in Coahuila may be seen in a case involving the Hacienda San Carlos, located in the northern part of the state. The *hacienda* had provided an important source of recruits for Madero and Carranza and had served as a base for revolutionary activities. It was, however, a property of Lorenzo González Treviño, an uncle of the late Francisco Madero and a man identified by Constitutionalists as an enemy. The *hacienda* was confiscated in 1915, and by 1916 it was being administered by Bruno Neira, future governor of Coahuila. Under Neira's administration an interesting situation developed in which a group of *hacienda* workers, organized as a sharecroppers' league under the leadership of Emeterio Garza, attempted to assert their control over the *hacienda*. Espinosa Mireles, warned by Neira of the spread of "socialist" ideas among these tenants, ordered the arrest of Garza. Neira then ordered the other members of the so-called Unión de Agricultores (Farmers' Union) to abandon the lands that they were working.[34]

Although Carranza may have angered some Coahuilans with his return of confiscated lands, his *Ley Agraria* (agrarian law), issued on January 6, 1915, was calculated to reassure Mexico's peasants of his respect for the agrarian question. Several months after the publication of Carranza's law, Coahuilans began to petition for the return of communal lands taken away during the Porfiriato. By 1920 about twenty-five such requests had been made, but only the *ejido* (communal plot) of Castaños, located in central Coahuila, had been formally returned. Eventually the Carranza administration approved about twelve petitions. Most of those applying for communal lands were from northern and central Coahuila, areas that were given *ejidos* and military colonies during the colonial and Reform eras and subsequently had them taken away during the Porfiriato.[35]

From 1920 until the era of Lázaro Cárdenas, who assumed the presidency in 1934 and embarked upon an ambitious implementation of the 1917 Constitution that included significant and sweeping agrarian reform, little change in land tenure occurred. Coahuila remained one of the states in which *latifundia* was most persistent. In the Laguna *hacendados* successfully worked with political authorities to halt land reform, and in the north members of the Cámara Ganadero de Coahuila (state cattleman's association) fought to keep their titles to communal lands that had been surveyed and privatized during the Porfiriato. In 1933, moreover, Coahuila passed a law against the dissolution of *latifundia* in order to protect the cattle industry, which depended for its survival on large extensions of the dry Coahuilan landscape.[36] Thus, in agrarian matters Coahuila proceeded as Carranza did: in a moderate and measured way. Here, where agrarian grievances were real (but not as central as in Zapata's state of Morelos), land movement adhered more to political exigencies than to a conscious program of change. Only with the administration of Lázaro Cárdenas would Coahuilans finally experience the effects of land reform. Indeed, the Laguna region was one of the centrepieces of Cárdenas' agrarian policy, and in 1936 he redistributed most of that region's irrigated lands, creating 292 *ejidos*.

Political Reconstruction and Reform

In the political arena too, Carranza and Espinosa Mireles proceeded cautiously, convinced of the need for a strong government to aid in the broader task of pacification. At the same time, both men remained aware of the popular sentiment in favour of change and an end to Porfirian patterns. The result was a state government that was authoritarian in its tactics and populist in its rhetoric. In sum, the Espinosa Mireles governorship was reminiscent of Carranza's earlier leadership in Coahuila.

Like many Carrancista governors, Espinosa Mireles sought to manage closely the political process. Free and open elections did not occur, and electoral corruption was apparently common. After 1915 Coahuila's government remained highly centralized, and military officers still held sway over several areas of the state. This was particularly true in the Laguna, which continued to experience banditry. Nor did the end of fighting within Coahuila mean the end of opportunism. Several Constitutionalist officers in the Laguna engaged in their own private businesses and enjoyed duty-free imports, free transportation of goods, and low taxes, which enabled them to sell cheaply and undercut local competition. According to American official William Blocker, General Francisco Murguía was headquartered in Torreón for business purposes. This officer had taken over properties involved in the guayule industry and was "established there in considerable military splendor, in the way of special locomotives, private cars … [and] a staff of gilted officers.…"[37] Murguía's behaviour was not atypical, for Carranza maintained a large army that needed both discipline and rewards. Generals were often granted special favours, and were allowed to generate "unofficial" income.[38]

The authoritarian nature of the Espinosa Mireles administration, as well as Carranza's insistence on maintaining a significant degree of political control over his native state and its military leaders, were not always accepted. General Luis Gutiérrez, another Constitutionalist officer who used his profits from the Revolution to purchase a significant amount of property in the Saltillo area, advanced his candidacy for the governorship in 1917. When the questionable election placed Carranza's favourite, Espinosa Mireles, in office once again, Gutiérrez and his supporters, including General Francisco Coss, immediately cried foul. Despite an attempt to placate Gutiérrez with another post, by the end of the year an armed revolt was underway. Although the supporters of Gutiérrez managed to capture Monclova briefly, their rebellion was quickly crushed with the help of additional troops that Carranza sent to Coahuila. By the beginning of the next year, Espinosa Mireles was securely installed for another term. Sporadic guerrilla activity by

Gutiérrez and a small band of followers continued, however, and Gutiérrez himself remained a player in Coahuilan politics. In 1920, he briefly occupied the governorship after Obregón and other northern leaders, angered at Carranza's attempt to designate Mexico's next president, staged a rebellion that resulted in Carranza's death.[39]

As late as 1920 the state government intervened in municipal elections, voiding their results when necessary. At the same time, Espinosa Mireles was careful to allow at least some popular participation in the political life of several municipalities. Upon assuming his post, the governor named *visitadores políticos* (political inspectors) to organize plebiscites in various areas of the state. Jorge E. von Versen was designated *visitador* for the Monclova and Rio Grande districts. Although new officials had already been chosen by the governor (perhaps with the help of Carranza), von Versen conducted the plebiscites in the form of town meetings, encouraging and usually receiving a popular display of support for the designated officials.[40]

Espinosa Mireles apparently also responded favourably to popular requests for local plebiscites. He received numerous letters from Coahuilans recommending candidates for local offices. Workers from Cuatro Ciénegas insisted that whoever was chosen as municipal president be a native of the area, "a man of energy and noble aspirations," and a person who understood the importance of public education, which had been previously neglected by local officials. Other groups petitioned the governor, urging him to select local officials who were completely loyal to Constitutionalism.[41]

The virtual absence of an open electoral process under Espinosa Mireles thus did not mean a disregard for municipal authority and initiative. Indeed, the governor encouraged municipal activism and local efforts at reform. In an attempt to end corruption and grafting at the local level, the governor raised the salaries of municipal officials. To help municipal presidents in maintaining order and preserving public health and morality, he decreed the creation of a commission for each town with at least twenty thousand inhabitants. This body, selected by the municipal council itself, was entrusted with administration and oversight of duties related to public health and safety, school attendance, prosecution of criminals, and other matters.[42]

Encouraged by the governor's initiative, several municipalities embarked upon ambitious programs of public works and local reform. In Ocampo each councilman took charge of a specific task (education, public health, etc.), a new school was built on community lands taken away during the Porfiriato, and an agrarian committee was established to deal with questions of land and water. The regulation of commerce, including mandated prices on basic items, was one of the local economic measures taken by the town council. Ocampo's council also enacted reforms with a distinctly moral tone. The Reglamento General de Buen Orden Municipal included rules against carrying guns, gambling, and loitering in the streets after 10 p.m. The Reglamento de Policía prohibited policemen from drinking. The local administration of Piedras Negras followed suit by prohibiting the "disgraces" of gambling, cockfights, and open beer halls, while taking steps to punish local officials who indulged in such pleasures.[43] These efforts at moral reform echoed Carranza's earlier efforts as Coahuila's governor. They also mirrored his dubious efforts on the national level to prohibit gambling and discourage drinking and drug use.[44]

In his encouragement of municipal activism, Espinosa Mireles acknowledged the idea of the *municipio libre*, an idea that had been incorporated into the revolutionary plans of both Madero and Carranza and that was subsequently included in the 1917 Constitution. The idea of municipal autonomy was also endorsed, at least on paper, by a new state constitution that was promulgated in 1918 under the guidance of Espinosa Mireles. This document echoed the national one, with articles on land reform and workers' rights. It also included a pledge to the principle of no re-election. In 1919 a series of electoral reforms were added to Coahuila's constitution. Detailed regulations sought to assure secrecy in balloting and the ability of all political parties to participate in the electoral process. Municipal presidents were prohibited from judging the capacity of office seekers, and could only register candidates as they presented themselves. Candidates for municipal councils were required to be native Mexicans with residence in the municipality for at least three years. Re-election of council members was prohibited.[45] Thus, despite the continuing manipulation of the electoral system, Espinosa Mireles did not ignore the popular pressure for more direct participation in the political process.

Another hallmark of the Espinosa Mireles governorship was reform of the state's taxation system. One goal was to equalize the tax burden of Mexicans and foreigners. This was part of the stated justification for a 1915 decree placing higher taxes on istle, hides, guayule, cotton, and minerals, since large numbers of foreign businesses were engaged in the extraction of these products. The extra revenue, moreover, was earmarked to increase the salaries of public officials. Higher taxes were also exacted from *hacendados* and merchants and the revenue was used for public services.[46]

The governor also singled out those previously exempted from taxes because of special concessions. In 1917 he threatened to revoke the concessions of companies that did not re-initiate work within thirty days. But the stronger trend was toward entirely eliminating these tax breaks. Espinosa Mireles pressured individuals and companies enjoying special privileges to begin paying their share, and in some cases he ordered them to pay back taxes. In Múzquiz, for example, the heirs of former Porfirian governor José María Garza Galán were ordered to pay back taxes on their extensive holdings. Finally, the governor clarified the duties of tax officials and elaborated a hearing process in order to end the practice of delaying payment of duties while individuals petitioned for exemptions or discounts.[47] In his efforts to revise Coahuila's tax system, Espinosa Mireles followed the lead of Carranza, who crafted nationalist economic policies designed to undercut foreign privileges and lessen the tax burden of the popular classes.[48]

At the same time that he sought to equalize and streamline taxes, Espinosa Mireles embraced policies designed to aid more immediately in Coahuila's economic recovery. Most significantly, the owners of rural lands not being cultivated were to suffer a tripling of taxes, while municipal authorities were authorized to distribute such lands to local residents for cultivation. At the same time, the governor encouraged the development of urban properties by decreeing temporary tax exemptions to those who repaired or otherwise improved such properties.[49]

In his continued support for Coahuila's workers Espinosa Mireles also proved himself an heir of Carranza. The governor encouraged workers to organize and even donated money to the state's mutualist societies, many of which had been suppressed as "Carrancista" during the era of Villa's domination. Favourable legislation for workers was a hallmark of the Espinosa Mireles administration, and in 1916 the governor decreed the establishment of a separate ministry of labour. This office was entrusted with the gathering of labour statistics, co-ordination of workers' organizations, settlement of labour disputes, and formulation of laws for the state's labourers. In 1918, moreover, Espinosa Mireles hosted the national meeting of labour unions at which the Regional Confederation of Mexican Workers was established.[50]

Educational reform was a hallmark of Carranza's Mexico that received special attention in Coahuila, and the quickness with which Espinosa Mireles acted on the education issue indicated his acknowledgement of its importance. Special state funds were earmarked for education, and the expansion and improvement of schools was a top priority. Teachers' salaries were increased, sometimes by as much as 50 per cent. In addition to reforms in the state tax system designed to create more revenue for schools, Espinosa Mireles decreed a 10 per cent tax on admission to all forms of public entertainment and used the funds for education. In a more creative measure, he ordered a batch of confiscated opium sold and the proceeds given to public schools.[51]

In his attention to local educational needs, Espinosa Mireles was careful to emphasize municipal autonomy. A 1916 decree revised a tax, placed since 1883 on all municipal treasuries, that supported preparatory and professional instruction state-wide. The money now went directly to the municipalities to be used for primary education. Espinosa Mireles stressed that this measure provided greater local autonomy and fulfilled one of the promises of the revolution: to grant municipalities a significant degree of independence. Likewise, in creating a Junta Central de Educación (State Board of Education) with branches in each municipality, the governor was careful to note that municipal autonomy would be preserved.[52]

Efforts to expand the availability of education included requiring all mining, agricultural, and industrial companies to establish at least one primary school in areas where there were over thirty children. Another decree stipulated that there be at least one school for adult men and women for every ten thousand inhabitants in each municipality. Such measures demonstrated Espinosa Mireles' dedication to Coahuila's workers, and he emphasized the need to use education to help workers perform their tasks and better understand and appreciate the laws of the Carranza administration. Finally, more schools were created to train teachers, and a Coahuilan Pedagogical Congress was established to promote good teaching.[53]

In his attention to the expansion of Coahuila's school system,

Espinosa Mireles insisted on the centrality of public schools and liberal education. Even private institutions were prohibited from teaching religion and were compelled to follow the curriculum and use the texts of public schools. Inspectors visited private schools to assure compliance. Only lay schools, insisted the governor, could teach individuals to govern themselves, and uniformity of teaching was necessary for the formation of a "national soul."[54] This aspect of the governor's educational policy echoed the anti-clericalism of Article 3 of the 1917 Constitution. But while several Carrancista governors also endorsed punitive measures against the Catholic Church, Carranza himself rejected such anti-clerical sentiment and did not act upon it.

Espinosa Mireles' efforts in education were ultimately more successful than Carranza's national education program. Despite the president's emphasis on centralization, national education policy was based on the decentralization of power. Carranza sought to replicate Coahuila's educational programs by giving municipalities more control, and through a lessening of federal intervention. While well intentioned, such reforms brought discontent and, with less direct federal support, they actually led to a decline in the number of Mexican schools.[55]

Espinosa Mireles' efforts to bolster Coahuila's educational system and to support the state's workers were in many ways the continuation of policies begun under the Carranza governorship. The emphasis on municipal autonomy and local initiative helped Espinosa Mireles sustain the loyalty of Coahuilan authorities, just as it acknowledged the state's strong heritage of federalism. Changes in the taxation system manifested a clear determination to abolish the privileges of the Porfirian era. At the same time, however, the promise of effective suffrage that had been the banner of Maderismo was not immediately realized. Although he introduced electoral reforms and paid lip service to popular political participation, Espinosa Mireles, often with the help of Carranza, manipulated elections and maintained a largely authoritarian government.

The agrarian policies followed by Carranza and Espinosa Mireles perhaps best demonstrated the limits of Constitutionalist reform. Significant expropriations did occur, and Espinosa Mireles proved himself willing to appropriate lands and resources. Yet such measures were temporary, intended to address immediate economic needs or to punish political enemies. Carranza's

Ley Agraria eventually restored some communal lands taken away during the Porfiriato, but more significant land reform would have to await the era of Lázaro Cárdenas.

Espinosa Mireles' approach to the agrarian issue and his careful manipulation of the political system mirrored Carranza's moderate ideological stance, just as they responded to the more immediate need to reconstruct war-torn Coahuila. At the same time, viable reforms did occur in several areas. In his emphasis on local autonomy, continuing support of Coahuila's workers, restructuring of the tax system, and populist approach to education, Espinosa Mireles acknowledged the significance of the past revolution and the extent to which the demands of the popular classes (while not always articulated) were a central part of that revolution.

Rebel forces near Torreón, 1912.
Courtesy of Richmond Collection.

Venustiano Carranza, First Chief of the Constitutionalist movement,
with General Pablo González.
Center for Southwest Research, General Library, University of New Mexico, 986-035-0005.

Headquarters and fortifications of the early constitutionalist movement in the Sierra Mojada mountains, March 1913.

Centro de Estudios de la Historia de México/CONDUMEX

Forces of General Pablo González in Monclova, March 1913.

CONDUMEX.

*President Victoriano Huerta and military officers during
the campaign against the Constitutionalists, 1913–14.*

Photo Collection, El Paso County Historical Society.

Federal forces entering Torreón as the Constitutionalist rebellion begins, c. 1913.

Frederick Wulff Collection, C.L. Sonnichsen Special Collections Department, University of Texas–El Paso.

Pancho Villa, General of the division of the North,
with supporters and aides Toribio Ortega and Juan Medina.
Horne Collection, El Paso Public Library.

Federal troops and artillery in Torreón, c. 1913.

Frederick Wulff Collection, C.L. Sonnichsen Special Collections Department, University of Texas–El Paso.

Venustiano Carranza with Gustavo Espinosa Mireles and brother Sebastián Carranza (seated and standing left).

Aultman Collection, El Paso Public Library, 2550.

Wealthier residents of Torreón, perhaps including Spaniards,
board a train to escape the violence of the Revolution, c. 1913.
Frederick Wulff Collection, C.L. Sonnichsen Special Collections Department, University of Texas-El Paso.

Spanish refugees expelled from the Laguna by Pancho Villa, disembark in El Paso, 1914.
Aultman Collection, El Paso Public Library, 230.

Rebel cannon fire during the 1914 occupation of Torreón
by the forces of Pancho Villa.
Aultman Collection, El Paso Public Library, 231.

Political rally at railroad station in San Pedro, Coahuila, c. 1915.
CONDUMEX.

Conclusion

When Manuel Sarabia, suspected ringleader of the 1896 Conspiracy of Monclova, predicted a revolution in his native state of Coahuila, he invoked a spirit of independence that had deep historical roots. Coahuila's frontier past, as well as its pattern of development, had evolved traditions of local autonomy, political independence, and economic self-sufficiency. By Sarabia's time, the forces of economic and political integration presented a challenge to Coahuilan habits. Rapid modernization, economic transformation, and social change promised to transform permanently the Coahuilan landscape.

It was the self-proclaimed mission of the Porfiriato to solidify this transformation. Yet while many elites, both native and foreign, as well as members of the rapidly expanding middle class welcomed the economic initiatives of the Díaz administration, development occurred at a price for all social sectors and caused inevitable dislocations. For smallholders in northern and central Coahuila and for the members of the Laguna's independent agricultural communities, modernization meant the loss or threatened loss of communal lands and the end of a self-sufficient and largely self-contained economy. Porfirian policies, moreover, generated increased competition over resources, especially water. This competition affected both smallholders and elite landowners. Moreover, as Coahuila became linked to markets in Mexico and beyond, its mobile workforce and politically disenfranchised middle class were increasingly vulnerable.

By the late nineteenth century Coahuila's political system also reflected the process of a broader transformation. Three *camarillas*, incorporating a small group of extended families and business partners, dominated politics at both the municipal and state level. Beginning with the ouster of Governor Evaristo Madero in 1884 and continuing into the 1900s, Díaz sought to centralize control over Coahuila by balancing the interests of each clique. At the same time, many Coahuilans experienced the imposition of Mexico's central government through the arbitrary use of the *jefatura política*. As Porfirian political machinations continued, political success on the local level was increasingly dependent on a willingness to co-operate with the centre.

Coahuila's experience during the Porfiriato, however, is not as simple as the story of an encroaching central government and an inevitable program of modernization. For Coahuilans of all social classes consistently challenged the Porfirian model even as they adjusted to its dislocations. Their defiance took many forms, and could be seen in disputes over water and rangeland, in rebellion along the international border, in the resistance of Laguna property owners to the federalization of the waters of the Nazas River, in the increasing activism among Coahuila's miners, in economic competition between foreigners and Mexicans, and in the revolt of political elites against the central government in 1893. In each of these challenges can be read a determination to preserve a degree of autonomy in the face of political and economic integration. When the revolution predicted by Sarabia finally emerged, it built upon this determination.

The Madero revolt of 1910-11 was a reaction to two factors: economic crisis and resistance to Porfirian centralization. Although Madero himself envisioned a movement that echoed the largely moderate political aspirations of elites and the middle class, these two factors affected all social groups, and so the revolt had broader implications. A true cross-section of society participated in this phase of the Revolution. Localized outbursts against the symbols of Porfirian control and abuse were common, and several Coahuilans urged President Madero and Governor Carranza to sanction such activities by destroying the old regime in its various guises. Above all, the Madero rebellion gave expression to popular discontent and provided a forum for the articulation of popular demands.

It is in this early phase of the Mexican Revolution that Coahuila's experience was a "northern" one: reaching across class lines and echoing a desire for self-determination. In the patterns of rebellion, targets of violence, petitions for reform, and social bases of support for Madero (and Governor Carranza) Coahuila's *serrano* revolt emerges most clearly. And while the Madero rebellion appears as an unruly movement lacking a unifying theme or purpose, it is the quest to preserve Coahuila's historic autonomy that gave shape (and indeed meaning) to the revolution in that state. Certainly that autonomy could be understood in a variety of ways (as a right to rangeland and water, or freedom of competition in the political arena, for example). But in the final analysis, Coahuila's revolution stands in contrast to the more class-based revolts that characterized southern states such as Morelos, where Emiliano Zapata waged a more clearly single-minded struggle for land.

An explanation of Coahuila's revolutionary experience, however, must go beyond the concept of *serrano* rebellion. For while popular discontent was often expressed in terms of local autonomy (through, for example, attacks against imposed officials), and although acts of banditry sometimes reflected this same urge to local independence, it is clear that Coahuila's economic troubles, which began after 1900 in response to an international recession, also played a crucial role in the Revolution. Economic crisis and dislocation provided recruits for the Maderista rebellion, just as they helped create the conditions conducive to banditry. The persistence of the economic quandary, moreover, presented a chief obstacle to all rebel factions and revolutionary leaders who sought to gain effective control over Coahuila. The momentum of Coahuila's revolution, then, was provided less by *serrano* ideals than by the weight of economic reality. Economic dislocation mobilized many Coahuilans and economic crisis provided an "opening" for the expression of their grievances.

Madero's political victory in 1911 did not end Coahuila's popular revolt. Here, as in the rest of Mexico, Madero's failure to dismantle the old regime had inevitable consequences. President Madero was also powerless to end political factionalism and competition within Coahuila; in addition to rebellions by Reyistas, Orozquistas, and Magonistas, the machinations of the Garza Galán clique contributed to instability in northern Coahuila and the border region. In attempting to manipulate political and military decisions in his native state through the use of relatives and old political allies, Madero revealed his limited understanding of the nature of Coahuila's revolution. Indeed, in the mind of many Coahuilans, Madero simply repeated the mistakes of Porfirio Díaz. For while the rhetoric of Maderismo echoed local demands for autonomy, Madero's leadership largely ignored those demands. Madero became simply another distant leader, attempting to impose his will.

In his attention to the popular undercurrent of the Revolution, Carranza succeeded where Madero had failed. Although his approach to reform was moderate, Carranza continued to gain adherents while Madero's national regime atrophied. Against a backdrop of economic deterioration and continuing unrest, the first Chief built a viable Constitutionalist army. In mobilizing the discontent of many Coahuilans, Carranza at least partially harnessed the popular movement that had been unleashed by Madero's revolt. At the same time he maintained the support of the middle sectors and of several elites.

The Constitutionalist victory in Coahuila thus underscores the continuing importance of the popular movement. It also demonstrates the centrality of the border to the Revolution in northern Mexico. Even before 1910, northern rebels had bene-fited from the long, permeable international frontier. During the Maderista and Carrancista rebellions, it served as a safety valve for insurgents, while providing the arms and revenue needed to wage a successful war against the centre. Above all, the border was crucial to the financing of the Constitutionalist movement, and Carranza's successful manipulation of the Coahuila-Texas zone ensured an eventual military victory in his native state.

By 1915 the Constitutionalist movement had weathered major challenges from the regime of Victoriano Huerta and the pop-ular movement of Pancho Villa. The efforts of Carranza and Espinosa Mireles to pacify and reconstruct Coahuila in the aftermath of the Revolution bore fruit slowly. By 1917 the econ-omy in many areas of the state showed signs of improvement. Progress, however, was uneven and setbacks were frequent. The currency crisis persisted, and some regions of the state continued to feel the dislocations of the Revolution, particularly through unemployment and the scarcity of basic goods.

The end of the fighting in Coahuila thus did not mean the beginning of a new political era within the state. Although he championed electoral reform, Espinosa Mireles retained, with Carranza's help, an authoritarian regime. The principles of effective suffrage and no re-election remained part of revolu-tionary rhetoric. Likewise, Madero's earlier pledge to the con-cept of the *municipio libre*, later endorsed by Carranza and the Constitutionalist movement, found only limited expression. For while Espinosa Mireles fashioned his decrees with an eye towards preserving municipal autonomy, the political system remained highly centralized. It was also increasingly tied to the central government: Espinosa Mireles and his successors would find that their effectiveness as leaders depended (at the very least) on acknowledging the growing power of Mexico's post-revolutionary state.

Although the rebellions of Madero and Carranza did not succeed in reclaiming the state's political autonomy from an encroaching central government, they did alter Coahuila's political profile. The realignment of Coahuilan politics had already begun in 1884, when the removal of Governor Evaristo Madero initiated the gradual decline of the Madero *camarilla* in the state's political life. The Maderista movement, which was at least partly the expression of politically disenfranchised elites, only temporarily halted this decline. Moreover, the failure of the Madero family to sanction Constitutionalism simply hastened the further erosion of the family's economic and political clout.

The national victory of Constitutionalism marked, within Coahuila, the successful ascension to power of Carranza and his followers—heirs of the Porfirian *camarilla* led by Miguel Cárdenas. The political factions of the Porfirian era, however, did not necessarily survive the revolution intact. Miguel Cárdenas, who had once counted the Carranza family among his most important supporters, chose to side, albeit grudgingly, with Huerta and against Carranza. As a result, he became a victim of Carrancista property confiscations.

The phenomenon of Galanismo is perhaps the best example of the persistence of conflict among Porfirian elites during the Revolution. The Madero revolt ousted the Garza Galán clique. Its members worked continuously, sometimes in conjunction with other rebel groups, to undermine Governor Carranza and to restore Galanista dominance. Under Huerta's administration Galanistas enjoyed a brief resurgence in the persons of Luis García de Letona and Miguel Garza Aldape, who became *jefes políticos*. At the same time, the Garza Galán brothers refused affiliation with either Huerta or Carranza and continued their plotting along the border. Such activities continued after 1915 through support for Felicismo and for the Legalista plot of 1916. They helped precipitate Carranza's confiscation of the lands of the Garza Galán family and those of several Galanista adherents. A broader pattern of continuing elite competition, then, may be identified within the context of the Mexican Revolution in Coahuila.

The Constitutionalist victory did not bring about immediate or sweeping reform of the state's economic structure. *Latifundia* persisted, and the return or redistribution of lands occurred on a minimal level. The lack of a traditional, landed peasantry, as in Morelos and elsewhere in Mexico, meant that sentiment for sweeping agrarian reform was not strong. At the same time, however, the return of communal lands, or their opening up by local officials, was not insignificant. The example of Castaños, located in central Coahuila, illustrates that popular demands against the effects of economic development and Porfirian abuses could indeed work their way into the Revolution and effect a positive outcome. Farmers of this independent agricultural community, which was established during the latter nineteenth century and then encroached upon during the Porfiriato, had joined Maderista rebels in 1911 as they opened fire on Monclova's municipal officials. A petition filed after 1915 eventually succeeded in obtaining the return of Castaños' communal lands.

Despite the lack of a significant change in Coahuila's pattern of landholding, the old economic system, characterized by monopolies, entrenched privileges, and generous concessions to a select few, was at least partly eliminated by Espinosa Mireles through tax reform. Significantly, however, such reform was motivated more by economic necessity than by ideological conviction. Here too, the rhetoric of the Revolution did not necessarily become reality.

Fifty years after the beginning of the Mexican Revolution, Alfredo Breceda Mercado and Roque González Garza, natives of Coahuila and among the earliest adherents to Francisco Madero's Anti-re-electionist cause, were interviewed about their experiences during the first few decades of the twentieth century. Both men emphasized the importance of the *municipio libre*, and Breceda Mercado argued that municipal autonomy, although a central part of the Revolution, was an ideal yet to be realized.[1] Indeed, on the national level, Mexico's revolution gave birth to a one-party system that continued a broader trend towards political centralization, and that has only recently (at the end of the twentieth century) met an effective challenge. Still, the events that began with Madero's revolt and ended with the victory of Constitutionalism are significant in a larger historical context. Along with the rebellion of 1893 and the 1896 Conspiracy of Monclova, the movements led by Madero and Carranza were part of Coahuila's broader adjustment to modernization. At the same time, they underscored the persistence of the "spirit of Hidalgo."

Notes

Notes to Introduction

1. An excellent account of the Mexican Revolution as part of an evolutionary process may be found in Jaime Rodríguez O., ed., *The Revolutionary Process in Mexico: Essays on Political and Social Change* (Los Angeles: University of California Press, 1990). The *longue-durée* approach is also adopted by Coahuila historians Eduardo Enríquez Terrazas and Martha Rodríguez García, eds., *Coahuila: Textos de su historia* (Mexico City: Instituto de Investigaciones Dr. José María Luis Mora, 1989), pp. 399–406.
2. Knight's description of *serrano* society and some of his basic ideas of *serrano* revolt may be found in *The Mexican Revolution*, vol. 1 (Lincoln: University of Nebraska Press, 1990), pp. 115–127. Friedrich Katz attempted an earlier explanation of the uniqueness of the northern revolution in *The Secret War in Mexico* (Chicago: University of Chicago Press, 1981), pp. 18–20.
3. In this respect, I accept John M. Hart's presentation of the Mexican Revolution as a result of exogenous economic factors. See *Revolutionary Mexico: The Coming and Process of the Mexican Revolution* (Berkeley: University of California Press, 1989).

Notes to Chapter 1

1. Spiritism is a philosophy focused on communicating with and seeking guidance from the spirit world.
2. Juan J. Villarreal to Bernardo Reyes, Monclova, 7, 11, 13, 17 March 1896, Centro de Estudios de Historia de México, CONDUMEX, Archivo de Bernardo Reyes (hereinafter cited as ABR), carpeta 24, legajo 4771, 4778, 4784, 4792.

3. The pattern of settlement and municipal development in the Rio Grande District is outlined in Esteban López Portillo, *Catecismo geográfico e histórico del estado de Coahuila de Zaragoza*, 2nd ed. (Saltillo: Tipografia del Gobierno en Palacio, 1886), pp. 179-215.

4. Katz, *Secret War*, p. 8.

5. In Mexico, a *municipio* is a political unit consisting of an urban centre and its surrounding area.

6. Manuel Plana, *El reino de algodón en México: La estructura agraria de la Laguna (1855-1910)* (Torreón: Ayuntamiento de Torreón, 1991), pp. 37-38; Eduardo Enríquez Terrazas and José Luis García Valero, *Coahuila: Una historia compartida* (Mexico City: Instituto de Investigaciones Dr. José María Luis Mora, 1989), pp. 79-80, 196, 213.

7. Enríquez Terrazas and García Valero, *Coahuila*, pp. 241-245; Pablo Cuéllar Valdés, *Historia del estado de Coahuila* (Saltillo: Biblioteca de la Universidad Autónoma de Coahuila, 1979), p. 131; Plana, *El reino*, pp. 71-72; Francois Chevalier, "The North Mexican Hacienda: Eighteenth and Nineteenth Century," in Archibald R. Lewis and Thomas F. McGann, eds., *The New World Looks at its History* (Austin: University of Texas Press, 1963), pp. 95-102. For a survey of the development of population centres in northern Coahuila since the colonial era that illustrates this general pattern, see Esteban López Portillo, *Anuario coahuilense para 1886* (Saltillo: Tipografia del Gobierno en Palacio, 1886).

8. Mario Cerutti, *Economía de Guerra y poder regional en el siglo XIX: Gastos militares, aduanas, y comerciantes en años de Vidaurri (1855-1864)* (Monterrey: Archivo General del Estado de Nuevo León, 1983), pp. 133-137.

9. An excellent discussion of the establishment and growth of Evaristo Madero's economic empire is contained in Mario Cerutti, *Burguesía, capitales, e industria en el norte de México* (Mexico City: Alianza Editorial, 1992), pp. 217-251. Additional biographical information may be found in José Vasconcelos, *Don Evaristo Madero (Biografía de un patricio)* (Mexico City: Impresiones Modernas, 1958).

10. William Schuchardt, report from Piedras Negras, 12 April 1869, General Records of the Department of State, Consular Despatches from U.S. Consuls in Piedras Negras, Mexico, 1868-1906 (hereinafter cited as SD-CD/Piedras Negras) Washington DC: National Archives, 1964.

11. Cerutti, *Economía de Guerra*, pp. 196-197; Enríquez Terrazas and García Valero, *Coahuila*, p. 85.

12. Cerutti, *Economía de Guerra*, pp. 17-18, 196-197, 210-211; Enríquez Terrazas and García Valero, *Coahuila*, pp. 82-83. The best book in English on Vidaurri is Ronnie Tyler's *Santiago Vidaurri and the Southern Confederacy* (Austin: Texas State Historical Association, 1973).

13. Plana, *El reino*, p. 39; Cerutti, *Burguesía*, p. 52. Many residents of the northern frontier had apparently argued for such a free zone in order to help attract families to this sparsely settled area. The *Zona Libre* was established first in Tamaulipas and, according to Cerutti, was officially sanctioned by the Mexican government in 1861. Plana and Cerutti indicate that the free zone applied only to northeastern Mexico, yet in 1887 a U.S. consular official described the zone as a fifteen-mile-wide strip reaching from the western mouth of the Rio Grande to the Gulf of California. See consular report of W.G. Allen, Piedras Negras, 26 January 1887, SD-CD/Piedras Negras.

14. Cerruti, *Burguesía*, p. 52; Enríquez Terrazas and García Valero, *Coahuila*, p. 247; Plana, *El reino*, p. 62; Commercial report of J. W. Wadsworth, Saltillo, 31 August 1883, General Records of the Department of State, Consular Despatches from U.S. Consuls in Saltillo, Mexico, 1876-1906 (hereinafter cited as SD-CD/Saltillo). The free zone was also a bane to American merchants outside the zone, who were forced to pay high export duties and thus had to sell their goods at outrageously high prices. See consular report of W. G. Allen, Piedras Negras, 26 January 1887, SD-CD/Piedras Negras.

15. Report of Lewis A. Martin, Ciudad Porfirio Díaz, 1 July 1905, SD-CD/ Piedras Negras. (Note that the name of Piedras Negras was changed to Ciudad Porfirio Díaz in 1888. It regained its former name in 1911).

16. William Schuchardt, Piedras Negras, 15 April and 30 October 1882, SD-CD/Piedras Negras.

17. E. D. Linn, Piedras Negras, 6 March 1886; W. G. Allen, Piedras Negras, 29 January 1887; Schuchardt, Piedras Negras, 30 October 1882, SD-CD/ Piedras Negras. Schuchardt observed that most legitimate export trade went through Laredo, where no special taxes or export fees existed.

18. Col. Pedro A. Valdés to Reyes, San Juan de Sabinas, 12, 15 April 1887, ABR carp. 6, leg. 1171; Col. Nicanor Valdés to Reyes, Piedras Negras, 16 April 1887, ABR carp. 6, leg. 1157; Reyes to Díaz, Monterrey, 21 April and 9 May 1887, ABR carp. 6, leg. 1159, 1181; M. M. Sánchez to Reyes, Piedras Negras, 27 June 1887, ABR carp. 7, leg. 1230.

19. Reyes to Díaz, Monterrey, 9 May 1887, ABR carp. 6, leg. 1181.

20. Schuchardt, Piedras Negras, 15, 27 October, 13 December 1871, SD-CD/ Piedras Negras.

21. Katz, *Secret War*, pp. 8-9.

22. Rita Favret Tondato, *Tenencia de la tierra en el estado de Coahuila (1880-1987)* (Saltillo: Universidad Autónoma Agraria Antonio Narro, 1992), pp. 29-36, 122; Esperanza Fujigaki Cruz, "Las rebeliones campesinas en el porfiriato 1876-1910," in *Historia de la cuestión agraria mexicana*, vol. 2: *La tierra y el poder*, ed. Enrique Semo (Mexico City: Siglo XXI Editores, 1988), pp. 189-191. In his study *Mexico and the Survey of Public Lands: The Management of Modernization 1876-1911* (Dekalb: Northern Illinois University Press, 1994), Robert Holden argues that survey companies did not contribute significantly to land concentration and that Porfirian laws related to *terrenos baldíos* were not a major factor in the Mexican Revolution. I suggest that in the case of Coahuila, which is not one of the states researched by Holden, a combination of factors (survey activities, illegal usurpations, and legal land purchases) contributed to land concentration, and that this in turn became a source of discontent and unrest.

23. Enríquez Terrazas and García Valero, *Coahuila*, pp. 213, 241, 243-245. The lack of specialized studies on land tenure changes during the Porfiriato prevents more precise knowledge of the effect of land concentration on smallholders. Much can be inferred, however, from the document *Carta general de la propiedad rural del estado de Coahuila, 1913* (Saltillo: n.p., 1913). This map, product of a commissioned survey conducted in 1912 and 1913, may be found in the Archivo Municipal de Saltillo.

24. Petition of *vecinos* of Gigedo, 4 January 1909, Archivo General del Estado de Coahuila (hereinafter cited as AGEC): Fondo Siglo XIX, exp. 10,696.

25. Several such complaints from smallholders and large landowners alike are contained in Archivo General del Tribunal Superior de Justicia del Estado de Coahuila: Fondo Histórico 1820-1930 (hereinafter cited as AGJ), Juicio Civil. See, for example, complaints of Fortino Bermea and Patricio Milmo, Rosales, 1901, and complaints of Francisco Ibarra and Manuel B. Dávila, Piedras Negras, 1909.

26. Documents dealing with the 1891-92 activities of Garza and his followers are contained in Archivo de Relaciones Exteriores, Libro Encuadernado (hereinafter cited as ARE-LE), exp. 11-10-44. Gabriel Saldívara has compiled a collection of these documents in *Documentos de la rebellion de Catarino E. Garza en la frontera de Tamaulipas y sur de Texas 1891-1892* (Mexico City: VI Congreso Mexicano de Historia, 1943). A description of Garza's revolutionary plan is given in Ildefonso Villarello Vélez, *Historia de la revolución mexicana en Coahuila*, 2nd ed. (Saltillo: Biblioteca de la Universidad Autónoma de Coahuila, 1983), pp. 17-20.

27. San Antonio Daily Express, 25 September 1891, in ARE, exp. 11-10-44.

28. Plutarco Ornelas to Secretary of Foreign Relations, San Antonio, 13 June 1892, Archivo de Relaciones Exteriores (hereinafter cited as ARE), exp. 11-10-44, part 7.

29. Matías Romero to Secretary of Foreign Relations, Washington, 23 July 1890, ARE, exp. 11-9-35; Secretario de Gobierno to Juez 1a del Distrito en el Estado, Saltillo, 19 August 1893, AGEC: Fondo Copiadores, Secretario de Gobierno, 1893.

30. The definitive study of the Sánchez Navarro estate is Charles H. Harris, *A Mexican Family Empire: The Latifundia of the Sánchez Navarros, 1765-1867* (Austin: University of Texas Press, 1975). Harris rightly points out that more studies are needed in order to ascertain whether the Sánchez Navarro *latifundia* was typical in its business practices.

31. Favret Tondato, *Tenencia*, pp. 31-32, 122, 213; Cerutti, *Burguesía*, pp. 259n, 262n.

32. Enríquez Terrazas and García Valero, *Coahuila*, p. 213.

33. Emilio Carranza to Reyes, Ocampo, 23 May 1895, ABR, carp. 23, leg. 4474; Reyes to Díaz, Monterrey, 12 April 1903; Reyes to Miguel Cárdenas, Monterrey, 29 April 1903, ABR copiador 41, documentos 20174, 20185. Earlier, the Sánchez Navarro family had come to have a near monopoly over the waters of the Sabinas and Nadadores rivers.

34. Petition of Martín Morales and Francisco García Letona, Monclova, 1898, AGJ, Juicio Civil.

35. Enríquez Terrazas and García Valero, *Coahuila*, pp. 181-183; Daniel Cosío Villegas, *Historia Moderna de México* (Mexico City: Editorial Hermes, 1965), vol. 7, 198-200. (Hereinafter cited as *HMM*).

36. Juan Luís Sariego, *Enclaves y minerals en el norte de México: historia social de los mineros de Cananea y Nueva Rosita 1900-1970* (Mexico City: Ediciones de la Casa Chata, 1988), pp. 61-64.

37. Ibid., pp. 72, 82, 99-100.

38. Ibid., p. 60.

39. Favret Tondato, *Tenencia*, pp. 81-83; Ramón Eduardo Ruíz, *The Great Rebellion: Mexico 1905-1924* (New York: WW Norton, 1980), pp. 16-17; Enríquez Terrazas and García Valero, *Coahuila*, pp. 82-83.

40. López Portillo, *Anuario*, pp. 500-501.

41. B. J. Pridgen, Piedras Negras, 20 September 1885, SD-CD/Piedras Negras.

42. Sariego, *Enclaves*, pp. 109-111, 116-128.

43. Secretaría de Hacienda to Governor Jesús del Valle, Saltillo, 5 January 1910; Municipal president of Sabinas to Governor Jesús del Valle, 2, 4 February 1910, AGEC: Siglo XIX.

44. Sariego, *Enclaves*, pp. 118-128, 150.

45. Ibid., pp. 129-131. Little is known about the development of the workers' movement in Coahuila itself, and inferences must be made from the experiences of workers in northern Mexico as a whole. Sariego's interviews with miners of Coahuila's coal region, however, indicate that the PLM was active in this area before the revolution.

46. Ibid., pp. 150-152.

47. Juan J. Villarreal to Reyes, Monclova, 7 March 1896, ABR, carp. 24, leg. 4771.

48. Favret, *Tenencia*, pp. 22-24; Cosío Villegas, *HMM*, vol. 7, p. 73.

49. Plana, *El reino*, pp. 27, 71-72, 106.

50. William K. Meyers, *Forge of Progress, Crucible of Revolt: Origins of the Mexican Revolution in La Comarca Lagunera, 1880-1911* (Albuquerque: University of New Mexico Press, 1994), pp. 24-27; María Vargas-Lobsinger, *La hacienda de "La Concha": Una empresa algodonera de la Laguna 1883-1917* (Mexico City: Universidad Nacional Autónoma de México, 1984), pp. 18-19; Barry Carr, "Las peculiaridades del norte mexicano, 1880-1927: Ensayo de interpretación," *Historia mexicana* 22 (enero–marzo, 1973): 324; Plana, *El reino*, pp. 80-89, 92.

51. Meyers, *Forge of Progress*, p. 26; Vargas-Lobsinger, *La Concha*, pp. 18-19; Favret Tondato, *Tenencia*, pp. 22, 111.

52. Meyers, *Forge of Progress*, p. 26; Vargas-Lobsinger, *La Concha*, pp. 18-19; Favret, *Tenencia*, pp. 22, 111.

53. Meyers, *Forge of Progress*, pp. 32-35.

54. Meyers, *Forge of Progress*, p. 34; Enríquez Terrazas and García Valero, *Coahuila*, pp. 145-146, 165.

55. Documents on the 1881 Nazas dispute and invasion are contained in Archivo General de la Nación (hereinafter cited as AGN): Ramo Gobernación, 2a 881 (10) exp. 4. For an excellent discussion of the Tlahualilo Company and the water issue in the Laguna region, see William K. Meyers, "Politics, Vested Rights, and Economic Growth in Porfirian Mexico: The Cía. Tlahualilo in the Comarca Lagunera, 1885-1911," *Hispanic American Historical Review* 57 (August 1977): 425-454.

56. Katz, *Secret War*, pp. 14-15, 144-146, 175-178; William B. Meyers, "Second Division of the North: Formation and Fragmentation of the Laguna's Popular Movement, 1910-1911," in *Riot, Rebellion, and Revolution: Rural Social Conflict in Mexico*, ed. Friedrich Katz (Princeton: Princeton University Press, 1988), pp. 456, 458-459.

57. Meyers, *Forge of Progress*, pp. 116-117; 122-124; 129, 131.

58. Fukigaki Cruz, "Las rebeliones," pp. 186, 199, 208-210. Enríquez Terrazas and García Valero, *Coahuila*, pp. 20, 58.

59. Fujigaki Cruz, "Las rebeliones," pp. 200-201; Vargas-Lobsinger, *La Concha*, pp. 18, 21, 44, 63-64, 112, 139.

60. Pablo M. Cuéllar Valdés, *Historia de la ciudad de Saltillo* (Saltillo: Fondo Estatal para la Cultura y los Artes de Coahuila, 1998), pp. 17-25, 40-61.

61. Enríquez Terrazas and García Valero, *Coahuila*, pp. 103-113; William Stanley Langston, "Coahuila in the Porfiriato: A Study of Political Elites" (Ph.D. diss., Tulane University, 1980), p. 61; Cuéllar Valdés, *Saltillo*, pp. 69-78, 110.

62. López Portillo, *Catecismo*, pp. 75-102;

63. Romana Falcón, "Raíces de la Revolución: Evaristo Madero, el primer eslabón de la cadena," in *The Revolutionary Process in Mexico: Essays on Political and Social Change, 1880-1940* , ed. Jaime Rodríguez O. (Los Angeles: University of California Press, 1990), pp. 37-39; Romana Falcón, "Logros y límites de la centralización Porfirista: Coahuila vista desde arriba," in *El dominio de las minorías: República Restaurada y Porfiriato*, ed. Ann Staples, Gustavo Verduzco Igartúa, Carmen Blázquez Domínguez, and Romana Falcón (Mexico City: El Colegio de México, 1989).

64. Langston, "Coahuila in the Porfiriato," pp. 130-136. Langston characterizes Coahuilan politics as feudalistic.

65. Ibid.

66. Falcón, "Logros y límites," pp. 119-130.

67. Romana Falcón, "La desaparición de jefes politicos en Coahuila: Una paradoja porfirista," *Historia mexicana* 37 (enero-marzo 1988): 429; Enríquez Terrazas and García Valero, *Coahuila*, p. 100.

68. Alicia Hernández Chávez and Ildefonso Dávila del Bosque, "La querrella de Coahuila: municipios y jefes politicos en el Siglo XIX," in *Archivo Municipal de Saltillo Catálago del Fondo Jefatura Política 1885-1895* (Saltillo: Archivo Municipal de Saltillo, 1985), p. 14. The new *jefaturas* were established in Sierra del Carmen, Ciénegas, Monclova, San Buenaventura, and Candela.

69. Falcón, "La desaparición," pp. 430-431.

70. Hernández Chávez and Dávila del Bosque, "La querella," p. 14; Falcón, "Raíces de la revolución," pp. 45-47; Douglas W. Richmond, *Venustiano Carranza's Nationalist Struggle, 1893-1920* (Lincoln: University of Nebraska Press, 1983), p. 9.

71. Richmond, *Carranza*, pp. 9-10; Langston, "Coahuila in the Porfiriato," pp. 138-142.

72. Richmond, *Carranza*, pp. 11-12; Meyers, *Forge of Progress*, p. 164.

73. Secretario de Gobierno to Juez 1o de Distrito en el Estado, Saltillo, 19 August 1893, AGEC: Copiadores, Secretario de Gobierno, 1893.

74. Falcón, "Logros y límites," pp. 98-99; Richmond, *Carranza*, pp. 4-6.

75. Langston, "Coahuila in the Porfiriato," pp. 96-97.

76. Ibid., pp. 94-95, 118.

77. Ibid., pp. 44, 122-125; Falcón, "Logros y límites," pp. 118-119; Hernández Chávez, "La querella," p. 15; Reyes to Díaz, Saltillo, 8, 24 October 1893, ABR, cop. 14, doc. 8624, 8643.

Notes to Chapter 2

1. The political career of Bernardo Reyes, as well as the growth and decline of Reyismo, is detailed in Anthony T. Bryan, "Mexican Politics in Transition, 1900–1913: The Role of General Bernardo Reyes" (Ph.D. diss., University of Nebraska, 1970), and E.V. Niemeyer, *El General Bernardo Reyes*, trans. Juan Antonio Ayala (Monterrey: Gobierno del Estado de Nuevo León, 1966). A more recent appraisal of Reyismo in Mexico is provided by Alan Knight in *The Mexican Revolution*, vol. I, pp. 47-55.

2. Richmond, *Carranza*, pp. 1–4.

3. Ibid., pp. 4–7.

4. Ibid., pp. 12–13.

5. Ibid., pp. 13–15.

6. Falcon, "Raíces de la Revolución," pp. 47–51.

7. Reyes to Díaz, Saltillo, 21 September 1893, ABR, cop. 14, doc. 8603, 8606.

8. Alberto Guajardo to Reyes, Múzquiz, 12, 23 July 1897; Marcos Benavides to Reyes, Allende, 6 August 1897; Reyes to Juan J. Villarreal, Monterrey, 19 August 1897; ABR carp. 26, leg. 5079, 5104, 5106; cop. 25, doc. 14174.

9. Falcón, "Logros y límites," pp. 121–122.

10. Fructuoso García to Reyes, Ciudad Porfirio Díaz, 25 February 1894, ABR carp. 20, leg. 3929.

11. Reyes to Juan J. Villarreal, Saltillo, 13 September 1893; Reyes to Valeriano Valdés, Monterrey, 13 February 1894; Plutarco Ornelas to Ignacio Mariscal, San Antonio, 12 December 1894; Reyes to Díaz, Monterrey, 22 April, 6 May, 6 September, 26 December 1894; ABR, carp. 22, leg. 4291; cop. 13, doc. 8000, 8493; cop. 14, doc. 8760, 8763, 8767, 8854, 8929.

12. Bryan, "Reyes," pp. 243–250; Villarello Vélez, *Historia de la Revolución*, pp. 116–117; Richmond, *Carranza*, pp. 18–19.

13. Madero's biography is detailed in Stanley R. Ross, *Francisco I. Madero: Apostle of Mexican Democracy* (New York: Columbia University Press, 1955), pp. 3–19.

14. Adrián Aguirre Benavides, interview by Jaime Alexis Arroyo, Mexico City, February 1961, Instituto Nacional de Antropología e Historia, PHO/1/19 (hereinafter cited as INAH, PHO).

15. Ross, *Madero*, pp. 11–14; Vasconcelos, *Evaristo Madero*, pp. 139, 202–203.

16. Francisco I. Madero to Antonio Gurza, San Pedro, 7 August 1906, Museo de Antroplogía e Historia, Archivo de Francisco I. Madero, reel 5 (hereinafter cited as AFM); Meyers, *Forge of Progress*, pp. 162–163.

17. Meyers, *Forge of Progress*, pp. 145–155.

18. Ross, *Madero*, pp. 35–36; Enríquez Terrazas and García Valero, *Coahuila*, pp. 323–324.

19. Ross, *Madero*, pp. 37–39; Enríquez Terrazas and García Valero, *Coahuila*, p. 328. The officers of several Maderista clubs complained of persecution by local officials. See Petition of J.M. Aguirre Hernández and Dámaso C. García, Parras, 25 July 1905, and Petition of Juan Long M. and Eduardo Elizondo, Múzquiz, 28 July 1905, AGN: Gobernación, secc. 1 (905), carp. 7, exp. 1; Madero to Trinidad Garza Cano, Madero to Aniceto Balderas, Madero to Díaz, San Pedro, 26, 27, 28 July 1905, AFM, r. 5; L.A. Guajardo to Reyes, Múzquiz, 2 June 1905, ABR, carp. 36, leg. 7080.

20. Francisco I. Madero, *La sucesión presidencial en 1910* (Mexico City : Librería de la viuda de Ch. Bouret, 1911).

21. Ross, *Madero*, pp. 58–64; 98.

22. Cumberland, *Mexican Revolution*, pp. 62–65, 75–80, 101–107.

23. Bryan, "Reyes," pp. 265, 268, 275.

24. Reyes to Díaz, Monterrey, 14 August 1905, ABR, carp. 36, leg. 7124. See also Reyes to Díaz, Monterrey, 24 August 1905, ABR, carp. 29, leg. 5746; Bryan, "Reyes," pp. 198–199.

25. See, for example, Madero to Carranza, San Pedro, 28 July 1909, AFM, r. 9.

26. Langston, "Coahuila in the Porfiriato," pp. 224–225.

27. The Anti-re-electionist club of Múzquiz, for example, consisted primarily of local *hacendados* or property owners of some means. See L A. Guajardo to Reyes, Múzquiz, 12 June 1905, ABR carp. 36, leg. 7080.

28. Vasconcelos, *Evaristo Madero*, p. 205.

29. Pres. mun. Cuatro Ciénegas to Governor, 7, 8 June 1910, AGEC: Siglo XIX; various correspondence dealing with Maderista rebellions of 19 and 20 November 1910, AGEC: Revolución, exp. 10,962.

30. Langston, "Coahuila in the Porfiriato," pp. 245-247.

31. Knight, *Mexican Revolution*, vol. 1, pp. 62-71.

32. Cumberland, *Mexican Revolution*, pp. 44-45; Ross, *Madero*, pp. 40-42; Alberto Guajardo to Reyes, Múzquiz, 22 March 1901, ABR, carp. 34, leg. 6606.

33. W. Dirk Raat, *Revoltosos: Mexico's Rebels in the United States, 1903-1923* (College Station: Texas A&M Press, 1981), pp. 21, 28-29; Langston, "Coahuila in the Porfiriato," pp. 195-196; Jean Dale Lloyd, "Los levanta-mientos del Partido Liberal Mexicano en 1906," in *Historia de la cuestión agraria mexicana*, vol. 3: *Campesinos, terratenientes, y revolucionarios 1910-1920*, ed. Oscar Betanzos (Mexico City: Siglo XXI Editores, 1988), pp. 48-49.

34. Lloyd, "Los levantamientos," pp. 52-53.

35. Langston, "Coahuila in the Porfiriato," pp. 186-188.

36. Various accounts and correspondence of the Jiménez attack and extradition proceedings may be found in ARE. See, for example, Diligencia practicada en Ciudad Porfirio Díaz, 11 October 1906, ARE, exp. 11-8-164; Francisco Villasana to Secretary of Foreign Relations, Eagle Pass, 8 October 1907, ARE-LE 1243; See also Raat, *Revoltosos*, pp. 37, 129-131.

37. Report of Corl. Fructuoso García, Ciudad Porfirio Díaz, n.d. (1907) and Testimony of Juan José Arredondo, Ciudad Porfirio Díaz, n.d. (1907), ARE-LE 855.

38. Villasana to Secretary of Foreign Relations, Eagle Pass, 8 October 1907; *Rio Grande News*, Eagle Pass, 12 October 1906, in ARE-LE 1242.

39. Enrique Creel to Secretary of Foreign Relations, Washington, 28 March 1907; Villasana to Secretary of Foreign Relations, Eagle Pass, 8 October 1907, ARE-LE 1243.

40. Albino Dorantes to Gen. Jefe de la 3a Zona Militar, Las Vacas, 1 July 1908, in "Diligencias Practicadas por Corl. Antonio Carrión," Ciudad Porfirio Díaz, 19 July 1908, ARE-LE 820; Report of David González Treviño, Juez Primera de Letras del Departamento de Rio Grande, Ciudad Porfirio Díaz, 4 September 1908, ARE, Exp. 15-20-91. American newspaper reports of the Viesca attack may be found in ARE-LE 935. See, for example, *San Francisco Examiner*, 28 June 1908; *San Antonio Daily Express*, 26 June 1908.

41. Testimony of Guillermo Adam in report of David González Treviño, Juez 1o de Letras, Ciudad Porfirio Díaz, 4 September 1908, ARE, Exp. 15-20-91. When questioned, Adam claimed he was coerced into joining the PLM ranks.

42. Raat, *Revoltosos*, pp. 35, 22-40.

43. Ruíz, *The Great Rebellion*, pp. 83-84, 91, 116-118; Pres. mun. Matamoros to Matamoros Ayuntamiento, 1 January 1910, AGEC: Siglo XIX.

44. Ruíz, *The Great Rebellion*, pp. 91, 124-126; Residents of San José del Aura to Governor Cárdenas, 14 September 1904; Residents of Allende, Rosales, and Gigedo to Governor del Valle, 22 August 1910, AGEC: Siglo XIX.

45. See Langston, "Coahuila in the Porfiriato," pp. 198-200.

46. Katz, *Secret War*, pp. 10-11.

47. Madero to José D. Espinosa, San Pedro, 7 July 1908, AFM, r. 7.

Notes to Chapter 3

1. Order of Pres. mun. Saltillo, 5 June 1910, Archivo Municipal de Saltillo, Fondo Presidencia Municipal, carp. 154/2, leg. 7, exp. 1-3. Cumberland, *Mexican Revolution*, p. 110.

2. Cumberland, *Mexican Revolution*, pp. 110-118.

3. For discussions of the Plan of San Luis Potosí, see Ross, *Madero*, pp. 115-116, and Cumberland, *Mexican Revolution*, pp. 121-123.

4. Luther T. Ellsworth to State Department, Ciudad Porfirio Díaz, 3 November 1910, Records of the Department of State Relating to the Internal Affairs of Mexico, 1910-1929, 812/444 (hereinafter cited as NA followed by file number).

5. Pres. mun. Cuatro Ciénegas to Governor, 28 November 1910, exp. 10,962, AGEC: Revolución; Report of Pres.   mun. Cuatro Ciénegas, 14 November 1910, AGN: Gobernación, secc. 1, carp. 3, exp. 2.

6. Pres. mun. Cuatro Ciénegas to Governor, 28 November 1910, exp. 10,962, AGEC: Revolución.

7. Ellsworth to State Department, Ciudad Porfirio Díaz, 19, 20, 21 November 1910, NA 812/428-435; Cuesta to Secretary of Foreign Relations, Del Río, 24 November 1910, ARE-LE 614.

8. Villarello Vélez, *Historia de la Revolución*, p. 187; Richmond, *Carranza*, pp. 22-24.

9. Pres. mun. of Monclova to Governor del Valle, 17 May 1911, AGEC: Revolución; Gerónimo González Treviño to Secretary of War, Monterrey, 16, 20 May 1911, Archivo Histórico de la Defensa Nacional: Fondo Revolución, XI/481.5/28, Tomo II and III (hereinafter cited as AHDN: Revolución).

10. Pres. mun. Monclova to Governor del Valle, 27 March 1911, AGEC: Revolución.

11. Pres. mun. Monclova to Governor del Valle, 27 March 1911, AGEC: Revolución; Favret Tondato, *Tenencia*, pp. 85-87.

12. Jefe Político of Monclova to Governor del Valle, 11 April 1911, AGEC: Revolución; Tte. Ricardo Villegas to Corl. Jefe de la Línea Ricardo Peña, Múzquiz, 10 April 1911, AHDN: Revolución, XI/481.5/28, Tomo I.

13. Villarello Vélez, *Historia de la revolución*, pp. 187-189.

14. Voetter to State Department, Saltillo, 18, 27, 29 March, 3 April, 4, 12 May 1911, NA, 812/1060, 1198, 1199, 1281, 1711, 1828.

15. Exp. 11,097: "Correspondencia varia sobre sucesos ocurridos en Parras los 16 y siguientes del mes de abril 1911," 24 April 1911, AGEC: Revolución; G. Treviño to Secretary of War, Monterrey, 16 May 1911, AHDN: Revolución, XI/481.5/27, Tomo I; Paul Voetter, American Consul in Saltillo to State Department, 20, 21 April, 2, 14 May 1911, NA 812/1415, 1495, 1678, 1855.

16. Meyers, "Second Division," pp. 457, 461, 471-473.

17. Exp. 11,136: "Varia sobre sucesos el 23 de abril en San Pedro," 1 May 1911, AGEC: Revolución; Capt. Luis M. Rivera to Gral. Jefe de la Zona, Monterrey, 8 May 1911, AHDN: Revolución, XI/481.5/27, Tomo III; Rivera to Treviño, Monterrey, 8 May 1911, AHDN: Revolución, XI/481.5/28, Tomo II.

18. C. A. Haberlein, report of Federal evacuation of Torreón, 25 May 1911, NA, 812/2026.

19. Accounts of the capture of Torreón and the Chinese massacre may be found in AGEC: Revolución, exp. 11,145. See, for example, Governor del Valle to Secretary of Foreign Relations, Saltillo, 23 May 1911; Secretary of Foreign Relations to   Governor del Valle, Mexico City, 23 May 1911. See also Gen. Emiliano Lojero to Secretary of War, n.p., 31 May 1911, AHDN: Revolución, XI/481.5/28 Tomo II; J.D. Carothers to State Department, Torreón, 19, 22 May 1911, NA, 812/1895, 1968; C. A. Haberlein, report of Federal evacuation of Torreón, 25 May 1911, NA, 812/2026. An excellent study of the Chinese massacre, including information about the Chinese community itself, is provided by Leo M. Dambourges Jacques in "The Chinese Massacre in Torreón (Coahuila) in 1911," *Arizona and the West* 16 (Autumn 1974): 233-246.

20. Hipólito C. Méndez and Manuel S. Mendoza to Secretary of Foreign Relations, Torreón, 20 July 1934, ARE, Exp. III-294-35.

21. Meyers, "Second Division," pp. 455, 466. In addition to Meyers' profile of the rebels, occupational information and descriptions of family background of some rebel leaders may also be found in Instituto Nacional de Estudios Históricos de la Revolución Mexicana (INEHRM), *Diccionario*, and in the service records of Archivo Histórico de la Defensa Nacional: Fondo Cancelados y Pensionistas (hereinafter cited as AHDN-CP). See, for example, Hoja de Servicios del C. Gen. Brig. Benjamín Argumedo, Mexico City, 19 May 1914; José M. Pérez Treviño, Vista en consejo de Guerra Extraordinaria, Durango, 29 February 1916; Extractos de Antecedentes Militares del C. Extinto Gen. Benjamín Argumedo, Mexico City, 21 April 1941 and 21 February 1945, in "Argumedo, Benjamín," AHDN-CP, XI/III/2-70. Hoja de Servicios del Gen. de Div. Francisco L. Urquizo Benavides, Mexico City, 25 January 1941; Extracto de antecedentes militares del Gen. de Div. Francisco Urquizo Benavides, Mexico City, 9 April 1953; Hechos de Armas del C. Gen. de Div. Francisco Urquizo Benavides, Mexico City, 11 January 1954 and 1 July 1955; Acta de Nacimiento (copy) of Francisco Urquizo Benavides, Mexico City, 11 November 1959; in "Urquizo, Francisco," AHDN-CP, XI/III/1-246, Tomo 5. J. Agustín Castro to Secretary of War, 5 December 1931; Account of military services of Toribio V. de los Santos by Alfredo Breceda, Mexico City, 5 December 1931; E. Aguirre to Secretary of War, Mexico City, 8 December 1931; copy of de los Santos' marriage certificate, San Pedro, 10 March 1917, in "de los Santos, Toribio V.," AHDN-CP, XI/III/3-2789, Tomo 1. Testimonio de la escritura de protocolización de los diligencias de juridsicción voluntaria … por la Señora Sabina García, viuda de Ugalde," Torreón, 15 August 1918; copy of marriage certificate of Sixto Ugalde, Matamoros, 13 November 1873, in "Ugalde, Sixto," AHDN-CP, XI/III/3-1678.

22. Jefe de Seguridad Pública to Governor del Valle, Ciudad Porfirio Díaz, 23 January 1911; letter of Francisco Ríos, administrator of Hacienda San Graciano, 13 January 1911; Pres. mun. of Rosales to Governor del Valle, 13 April 1911; Pres. mun. of Hidalgo to Secretario de Gobierno, 24 April 1911, AGEC: Revolución. G. Treviño to Secretary of War, Monterrey, 11 January 1911; Corl. José Montalvo to Treviño, n.p., n.d., AHDN: Revolución, XI/481.5/28, Tomo 1. Treviño to Secretary of War, Monterrey, 29 May

1911, AHDN: Revolución, XI 481.5/28, Tomo III.

23. Ellsworth to Secretary of State, Ciudad Porfirio Díaz, 16, 20, 26 January 1911, NA, 812/658, 663, 668.

24. Gómez to Secretary of Foregn Relations, Del Rio, 15 January, 27 March, 4, 15 April 1911, ARE-LE 625, 645, 650, 658.

25. Ellsworth to State Department, Ciudad Porfirio Díaz, 22 May 1911, NA, 812/1956.

26. Francisco Villasana to Secretary of Foreign Relations, Eagle Pass, 10 April 1911, ARE-LE 651; Ellsworth to State Department, May 1911, NA, 812/1892.

27. Knight, *Mexican Revolution*, I, pp. 17–18, 35.

28. Villasana to Secretary of Foreign Relations, Eagle Pass, 13 January 1911, ARE-LE 627. Ellsworth to State Department, Ciudad Porfirio Díaz, 26 January 1911, NA, 812/688; General of Third Military Zone to Governor del Valle, 24 March 1911, AGEC: Revolución.

29. Municipal presidents of Sierra Mojada, General Cepeda, and Ramos Arizpe to Governor's Secretary, 5, 20, 21 April, 1911, AGEC: Revolución.

30. Pres. mun. Viesca to Jefe Político Torreón, 21 February 1911; Pres. mun. Rosales to Governor's Secretary, 15 March 1911; Francisco del Palacio to Governor's Secretary, Torreón, 3 May 1911; Pres. mun. San Pedro to Governor's Secretary, 29 May 1911, AGEC: Revolución.

31. Unnumbered expediente and various correspondence of the State Treasury, 26 April 1911, AGEC: Revolución; Decree no. 1152 and unnumbered decree, 10 January and 7 April 1911, AGEC: Fondo Decretos.

32. Ellsworth to State Department, Ciudad Porfirio Díaz, 29 October 1910; Wilson to State Department, Mexico City, 8 February 1911, NA, 812/354, 797.

33. Biographical treatements of Orozco and Villa include Michael C. Meyer, *Mexican Rebel: Pascual Orozco and the Mexican Revolution* (Lincoln: University of Nebraska Press, 1967) and Friedrich Katz, *The Life and Times of Pancho Villa* (Stanford, CA: Stanford University Press, 1998).

34. Cumberland, *Mexican Revolution*, pp. 125–129.

35. Cumberland, *Mexican Revolution*, pp. 141–151.

Notes to Chapter 4

1. Francisco Villasana to Secretary of Foreign Relations, Eagle Pass, 5 June 1911, ARE-LE 663; Luther T. Ellsworth to State Department, Ciudad Porfirio Díaz, 2, 3 June 1911, NA 812/2064, 2068; Voetter to State Department, Saltillo, 3 April 1911, NA 812/1281.

2. See Vélez, *Historia de la revolución*, pp. 191–192; account of *El Nacional*, 5 May 1911, in AGEC: Revolución, exp. 11,136.

3. Ellsworth to Secretary of State, Ciudad Porfirio Díaz, 18 June 1911, NA 812/2159.

4. See, for example, People of Las Esperanzas to Carranza, 13 July 1911, AGEC: Revolución.

5. People of Gigedo to Ayuntamiento, 10 July 1911; Alberto Santos to Francisco Madero, Del Rio, 2 February 1912, AGEC: Revolución. Colonel Fructuoso García, Reyes' appointed leader in northern Coahuila, had also

appropriated land in the Rio Grande District.

6. Demarcation of *ejidal* lands of Abasolo Nuevo, 7 September 1912, exp. 11,192, AGEC: Revolución.

7. Pres. mun. San Juan de Sabinas to Carranza, 20 January 1912, AGEC: Revolución.

8. Petition of people of Abasolo for return of ejidal property, 20 August 1911, exp. 10,998; Opening of a road from Candela to Progreso, 9 February 1912, unnumbered exp., AGEC: Revolución.

9. Ayuntamiento of Matamoros to Carranza, 25 September 1912, AGEC:Revolución.

10. Richmond, *Carranza*, pp. 37-38.

11. Pres. mun. Nadadores to Governor's Secretary, 22 July 1911; Complaint of Ismael Castro against Mayor of Abasolo, Abasolo, 2 January 1913, Exp. 11,340; Reports of Andrés G. García, 1 September 1911, AGEC: Revolución, Exp. 11,177.

12. Exp. 11,124: Protection for Spanish residents of Torreón, 6 July 1911; Unnumbered exp.: Death of Spaniard Gumersindo Solares in Torreón, 23 October 1911; Gobernación to Carranza, Mexico, 26 July 1912, AGEC: Revolución. See also Freeman to State Department, Durango, 9 September 1911, NA 812/2360. There is some indication that Spanish landowners in the Laguna were especially resented because of their harsh treatment of workers. See Adrián Aguirre Benavides, interview by Jaime Alexis Arroyo, Mexico City, February 1961, INAH/AP, 1/19; and Mayor of Torreón to Carranza, 17 October 1911, AGEC:Revolución.

13. Richmond, *Carranza*, pp. 27-30. See Pres. Mun. of Zaragoza to Governor's Secretary, 1, 9, 21, June 1911, AGEC: Revolución.

14. Mining community of El Menor to Carranza, n.d. (1911); Pres. mun. Monclova to Governor's Secretary, 5 July 1911, AGEC: Revolución.

15. Pres. mun. Sacramento to Governor's Secretary, 12 July 1911, AGEC: Revolución.

16. Workers of Palau to Carranza, 30 June 1911; Workers of Companía Carbonífera Rio Escondido to Carranza, 18, 20 May 1911; Unión de Mineros Mexicanos, El Menor, to Companía Carbonífera del Norte, 8 February 1912; UMM Palau to Manager of Coahuila Coal Company, 24 February 1912, AGEC: Revolución.

17. See, for example, UMM Rosita to Carranza, 14 November 1911, AGEC: Revolución

18. Club Benjamín Canales, Rosita to Carranza, 20 November 1912; Miners of Palau to Carranza, 7 November 1911; UMM Rosita to Carranza, and Señoras y Señoritas of Rosita to Carranza, 2 April 1911; Ejército Restaurador Puerto del Carmen to Carranza, 16 June 1911, AGEC: Revolución.

19. People of Cloete Mine, Agujita to Carranza, 6 December 1911, AGEC: Revolución; Pres. mun. Sabinas to Governor's Secretary, 6 December 1911, 7, 19 September 1912, AGEC: Revolución; Circular no. 119, section 3, Saltillo, 4 December 1911, AGEC: Fondo Circulares.

20. Richmond, *Carranza*, pp. 31-34; Reglamento sobre Prostitución, in Pres. mun. Saltillo to Governor's Secretary, 6 March 1912, AGEC: Revolución.

21. Pres. mun. Torreón to Carranza, Pres. mun. Torreón to Governor's Secretary, 4, 10, October 1911, AGEC: Revolución. Opium was imported through

several commercial houses in Torreón to be sold by Chinese dealers. See Richmond, *Carranza*, p. 33.

22. Richmond, *Carranza*, pp. 39, 56; Unnumbered decree, Saltillo, 22 March 1912; Decrees 1298, 1393, Saltillo, 19 July, 12 November 1912, AGEC: Decretos.

23. People of Esmeralda to Juan B. Silva, 11 June 1911; People of Sacramento to Carranza, 14 June; Pres. mun. Esmeralda to Governor's Secretary, 18 June 1911; Club Antireelecionista "Evaristo Madero," and Club Antireelecionista "Igualdad" to Carranza, 30 September 1911, AGEC: Revolución.

24. Club Liberal Progresista to Carranza and Pres. mun. of Juárez to Governor's Secretary, 5, 6, January 1913; Residents of Abasolo Nuevo to Carranza, 1 Jaunuary 1912, AGEC: Revolución.

25. Cumberland, *Mexican Revolution*, p. 144.

26. Knight, *Mexican Revolution*, vol. 1, pp. 248–251.

27. Bryan, "Reyes," pp. 282–286, 293–308; Knight, *Mexican Revolution*, vol. 1, pp. 251–254, 256.

28. Pres. mun. Viesca to Governor's Secretary, Complaint of Emilio Castañeda and Francisco Luna to Judge of Viesca, 21, 25 August 1911; Exp. 11,163: Complaint of Reyista club of Viesca, 8 September 1911, AGEC: Revolución. See also Exp. 11,104: Political demonstration in favour of Carranza, 24 August 1911, and Pres. mun. Saltillo to Governor's Secretary, 15 September 1911, ibid.

29. Reyes to Ysidro Yruegas, Mexico City, 16 August 1911; Reyes to Eduardo Lobatón, Mexico City, 17 August 1911; Reyes to Francisco Luna, Mexico City, 18 August 1911; Reyes to Dr. Ignacio Alcócer, Mexico City, 31 August 1911, ABR, cop. 46, docs. 21221, 21231, 21238, 21490.

30. Cumberland, *Mexican Revolution*, p. 187.

31. Governor's Secretary to Secretary of Foreign Relations, Saltillo, 14 October 1911, ARE-LE 675.

32. Manuel Piña to Justice Secretary, San Antonio, 17 December 1911, ARE-LE 850.

33. John Womack, Jr., *Zapata and the Mexican Revolution* (New York: Random House, 1968), pp. 401–413.

34. Knight, *Mexican Revolution*, vol. 1, pp. 295–301.

35. Pres. mun. Sierra Mojada to Carranza; Teodoro Elizondo to Carranza, 27 May, 15, 18 June 1912, AGEC: Revolución.

36. R.E. Múzquiz to Secretary of Foreign Relations, Eagle Pass, 6 September 1912, ARE-LE 759; Múzquiz to Carranza, 11 April 1912; R.S. Bravo to Múzquiz, Del Rio, 19 April and 10, 21 May 1912; Múzquiz to San Antonio Consul, Eagle Pass, 15 May 1912, ARE-LE 856. See also G. Treviño to Secretary of War, Monterrey, 6, 27 March 1912; Report of F. Trucy Aubert, n.p., 11 March 1912; Report of F. Trucy Aubert, Campamento "El Sacramento," 10 May 1912; A. Blanquet to Secretary of War, Sabinas, 9, 13 October 1912, AHDN: Revolución XI/481.5/29, Tomo I.

37. Arturo Lozano to Secretary of Foreign Relations, 28 August 1911; José O. Flores to Manuel Esteva, San Antonio, 29 August 1911, ARE-LE 674; Informe, 9 May 1912, ARE-LE 741(9); Bravo to Secretary of Foreign Relations, Del Rio, 21, 23 September 1912, ARE-LE 759(8); unsigned report, El Paso, 2 January 1912 ARE-LE 857(3). See also Ellsworth to State Department, 20 February 1912, NA 812/2891.

38. San Antonio Consul to Secretary of Foreign Relations, 1 September 1911; A.B. Martínez to Esteva, Guerrero, 25 August 1911; J. Pérez Rodríguez to A.B. Martínez, Guerrero, 18 September 1911, ARE-LE 674.

39. See, for example, L.A. Guajardo to Francisco Madero, Torreón, 5 April 1912, ARE-LE 744(1).

40. Gobernación to Carranza, Mexico, 29 June 1911, AGEC: Revolución; Ellsworth to State Department, Ciudad Porfirio Díaz, 28 June 1911, NA 812/2191.

41. R.S. Bravo and Rafael E. Múzquiz to Mexican Consul, Del Rio and Eagle Pass, 30 January 1913, ARE-LE 832.

42. R.E. Múzquiz to Secretary of Foreign Relations, Eagle Pass, 23 October 1912, ARE-LE 743(5).

43. Madero to Francisco León de la Barra, Tehuacán, 25 July 1911, Centro de Estudios de Historia de México, CONDUMEX, Archivo de Venuistiano Carranza (hereinafter cited as AVC), carp. 1, leg. 37. See also F.R. Villavicencio to Esteva, San Antonio, 1, 2 August 1911; Esteva to Secretary of Foreign Relations, ARE-LE 672.

44. Gobernación to Carranza, Mexico, 16 April 1912; R.S. Bravo to Carranza, Del Rio, 1 August 1912, AGEC: Revolución.

45. Pres. mun. San Pedro to Carranza; Pres. mun. Torreón to Carranza, 27 June, 3 July 1911, AGEC: Revolución.

46. Pres. mun. Torreón to Carranza, 13 October 1911; Exp. 11,180: Events of 31 October in Torreón, 3 November 1911, AGEC: Revolución; G. Treviño to Secretary of War, Monterrey, 12 November 1911, AHDN XI/481.5/28, Tomo II; Treviño to Secretary of War, Monterrey, 16, 27 March, 12 June, 25 August 1912; Gen. Brig. Jefe de Dto. to Secretary of War, Torreón, 22 May 1912, in Report of Gen. Aureliano Blanquet, Mexico, 31 May 1912, AHDN: Revolución, XI481.5/29, Tomo I.

47. Pres. mun. Torreón to Carranza, Joaquín Serrano to Carranza, Torreón, 9, 28 January 1912, AGEC: Revolución; Treviño to Secretary of War, Monterrey, 23, 27 February, 5, 11 October 1912; Gen. J. Tellez to Secretary of War, Torreón, 9 March 1912, AHDN: Revolución, XI/481.5/29, Tomo I.

48. Meyers, "Second Division," pp. 480-481.

49. Antonio F. Farías to Madero, San Pedro, 4 February, 14 April, 4 May, 29 July 1912, AGN: Ramo Francisco Madero, carp. 321, fojas 10290, 10292-10299.

50. Cesáreo Castro to Madero, Cuatro Ciénegas, 1 February 1912; Encarnación Domínguez and others to Madero, Del Rio, 31 December 1911; Pedro Márquez to Madero, Matamoros, AGN: Madero, carp. 290-2, f. 9165-75; caja 64, exp. 2875, 2848.

51. Gobernación to Carranza, Mexico, 8 February 1912, AGN: Gobernación, unclassified telegrams, caja 907.

52. Helena Herrmann to Fomento, San Pedro, 1 July 1912, AGN: Madero, carp. 18-3, f. 593-598; Carlos A. Fuentes Borrega to Madero, San Pedro, 28 May 1912, ibid., carp. 942-3, f. 27088. Uncle Marcos Benavides was offered the position of chief consular agent in Los Angeles, ibid., carp. 688, f. 19997-98.

53. José María Rodríguez to Madero and Andrés L. Farías to Madero, Torreón, 15, 21 December 1911, AGN: Madero, caja 62, f. 1475-1477, 1482.

54. José María Rodríguez to Madero, Torreón 30 June 1912, AGN: Madero, carp. 1221, f. 3980.

55. F.R. Villavicencio to Manuel Esteva, San Antonio, 9 August 1911, ARE-LE 673; AGN: Gobernación, caja 907, unclassified telegrams (1911-1912). Andrés Garza Galán helped with the smuggling of arms for the Reyes' revolt of 1911. See unsigned police report, Douglas, Arizona, 9 May 1912, ARE-LE 741(9).
56. C. Garza to Madero, Saltillo, 13 September 1912, AGN: Madero, carp. 270-1, f. 8350.
57. Richmond highlights several differences between the two men in *Carranza*, pp. 1-4, 17-21, 42. Alfonso Junco provides insights into Carranza's relationship with Madero in his study and personal collection of documents from Carranza's contemporaries in *Carranza y los orígenes de su rebelión* (Mexico: Editorial Jus, 1955).
58. Junco, *Carranza y los orígenes*, pp. 23-27.
59. Catarino Benavides to Emilio Madero, Allende, 22 September 1911; Emilio Madero to Catarino Benavides, Torreón, 28 September 1911; Marcos Benavides to Emilio Madero, Allende, 8 October 1911, AGN: Gobernación, unclassified correspondence to/from Emilio Madero, caja 1003.
60. Carranza to Madero, Saltillo, 25 November 1911, AGN: Ramo Revolución, caja 1, carp. 12, exp. 291.
61. Ernesto Madero to Carranza, Mexico, 18 April 1912, AGEC: Revolución.
62. Junco, *Carranza*, pp. 29-39; Knight, *Mexican Revolution*, I, pp. 478-479. See also Phillip C. Holland to State Department, Saltillo, 3 February 1913, NA 812/6051.
63. Exp. 11,148: Agreements between Compañía Carbonífera Ajujita y Anexas and its workers, 1911; Fomento to Carranza, 18 March, 1912, AGEC: Revolución; AGN: Departmento de Trabajo, 4 March 1912, caja 5 exp. 6; Report of Ellsworth, Piedras Negras, 4, 6 March 1912, NA 812/3112, 3150.
64. Holland to State Department, Saltillo, 3, 18 October 1912; 3, 24 January 1913, NA 812/5222, 5323, 5825, 5935.
65. J.D. Carrothers to State Department, Torreón, 28 February 1911; Charles M. Freeman to State Department, Durango, 6 March 1911, NA 812/890, 935.
66. Pres. mun. San Pedro to Governor's Secretary, Pres. mun. Torreón to Carranza, 18, 28, November 1911, AGEC: Revolución; Ellsworth to State Department, Piedras Negras and Hamm to State Department, Durango, 16, 17, 27 November 1911, NA 812/2508, 2516, 2518, 2586; unsigned memo, Mexico, November 1911, ARE-LE 850.
67. Phillip C. Hanna to State Department, Monterrey, 3 March 1912, NA 812/3085; Pres. mun. San Pedro to Governor's Secretary, L.A. Guajardo to Carranza, Hornos, and Gobernación to Carranza, Mexico, 6, 10, 14 March 1912, AGEC: Revolución; Gen. J. Tellez to Secretary of War, Torreón, 9 March 1912, AHDN: Revolución XI/481.5/29, Tomo I.

Notes to Chapter 5

1. Junco, *Carranza*, p. 43; Cuéllar Valdés, *Historia*, p. 208; Richmond, *Carranza*, p. 43. Junco and Cuéllar Valdés include the state of Chihuahua in the governor's meeting.

2. Carranza to Gobernación, Saltillo, 7 February 1913, AGEC: Revolución.

3. Ross, *Francisco Madero*, pp. 218-221, 236-248.

4. The details of the conservative plot, Madero's fall, and the murders of Madero and Pino Suárez are detailed in Ross, *Francisco Madero*, pp. 280-286, 295-301, 309-329.

5. Holland to State Department, Saltillo, 11 March 1913, NA 812/6968; Richmond, *Carranza*, pp. 43-44; Cuéllar Valdés, *Historia*, pp. 208-209, 212.

6. Postal Inspector to General Postal Inspector, San Pedro, 11 March 1913, Report of General Arnoldo Casso López, Saltillo, 24 March 1913, AHDN: Revolución, Exp. XI/481.5/30, Tomo I; unspecified newspaper report, Saltillo, 26 March 1913, NA 812/10937.

7. Villarello Vélez, *Historia de la revolución*, pp. 241-244; Richmond, *Carranza*, p. 45.

8. Ellsworth to State Deparment, Ciudad Porfirio Díaz, 24 April 1913, NA 812/7247; Joaquín Maass to Secretary of War, Monclova, 11 July 1913, AHDN: Revolución, Exp. XI/481.5/30, Tomo II; Michael C. Meyer, *Huerta: A Political Portrait* (Lincoln: University of Nebraska Press, 1972), pp. 91-92.

9. P. Ramos to Governor, Saltillo, 6 and 12 May 1913; Pres. mun. Torreón to Governor's Secretary, 1 May 1913; Pres. mun. Arteaga to Governor's Secretary, 2 May, 1913; Juan Peña to Governor, Saltillo, 24 February 1914; Cosme Gallardo, Amado and Francisco Martínez, and José Rojas to Governor, Saltillo, 25 February 1914, AGEC: Revolución.

10. Alcocer to Governor's Secretary, Saltillo, 12, 13 May 1913, Report of Major Liviano Domínguez, Torreón, 21 August 1913, AHDN: Revolución, Exp. XI/481.5/30, Tomos II and III; General Arnoldo Casso López to Secretary of War, 22 April 1913, Colonel Ricardo Peña to Secretary of War, Reata, 22 April 1913, General Ignacio A. Bravo to Secretary of War, Torreón, 6 May 1913, AHDN: Revolución, Exp. XI/481.5/30, Tomo I; Silliman to Secretary of State, Saltillo, 16 October 1913, NA 812/9555.

11. Alcocer to Governor's Secretary, Saltillo, 19 April and 6 May 1913, AGEC: Revolución; Pres. mun. Torreón to Governor, 17 May 1913, AGEC: Revolución; Continental Mexican Rubber Company to R. Dávila de la Peña, Torreón, 30 September 1913, AGEC: Revolución; Exp. 11,618, "Referente al circular núm. 186..", 6 December 1913, AGEC: Revolución; R.S. Bravo to A.M. Elias, Eagle Pass, 8 July 1913, ARE-LE 769(14).

12. Silliman to Secretary of State, Saltillo, 30 June, 6 September 1913, NA 812/8074, 8884.

13. Silliman to Secretary of State, Saltillo, 22 November 1913, 12 January 1914, NA 812/10032, 10633.

14. R.S. Bravo to A.M. Elias, Eagle Pass, 12 July, 4 August 1913, ARE-LE 763(21), 832.

15. J.D. Carothers to Secretary of State, Torreón, 7 May 1913, NA 812/7586; Secretario de Fomento to Secretario de Trabajo, Mexico City, 18 August 1913, AGN: Ramo Trabajo, caja 46, exp. 3; H. Boardman to Secretario de Trabajo, Ramos Arizpe, 11 October 1913, AGN: Trabajo, c. 41, exp. 14..

16. Federico Villarreal to Governor, Monclova, 6 September 1913; Pres. mun. Monclova to Governor's Secretary, 18 September 1913; José María Siller to Governor, Saltillo, 23 September 1913; León de la Garza to Governor, Monterrey, 1 April 1914; L.A. Guajardo to Governor's Secretary, Ciudad

Porfirio Díaz, 9 January 1914; Cayetano Villaseñor to Governor, Ciudad
Porfirio Díaz, 13 January 1914; Pres. mun. Morelos to Governor's Secretary,
20 November 1913; Pres. mun. San Juan de Sabinas to Governor, 29
November 1913, AGEC: Revolución.

17. Felipe de la Garza to Governor, Ciudad Porfirio Díaz, 19 January
1914; Merchants of Piedras Negras to Governor, 15 January 1914; E.H.
Schmidt to Governor, Piedras Negras, 23 March 1914; Farmers, merchants,
and industrialists of San Pedro to Governor, 12 March 1914, AGEC:
Revolución; Unnumbered decree, Saltillo, 22 April 1914, AGEC: Decretos.

18. Silliman to Secretary of State, Saltillo, 12 June 1914, NA 812/10633.; José
Refugio Velasco to Secretary of War, Torreón, 20 February 1914, AHDN:
Revolución, Exp. XI/481.5/31, Tomo I; Exp. 11,625, "… casas de juego
en el estado," 14 January 1914, AGEC: Revolución; Meyer, *Huerta*, pp.
182–184

19. Jefe Armas San Pedro to Governor's Secretary, 1 April 1913; Pres. mun.
Matamoros to Governor, 8 April 1913, AGEC: Revolución.

20. Luis García de Letona to Governor, Torreón, 1 March 1913; Alcocer to
Miguel Garza Aldape, Saltillo, 7 July 1913; Exp. 11,430: "Nombramiento de
jefe Político …," 27 July 1913; Unnumbered decree, Saltillo, 6 September
1913, AGEC: Revolución.

21. Ballesteros to Governor, Monclova, 24 September 1913, Guajardo to
Governor's Secretary, Ciudad Porfirio Díaz, 10 January 1914, AGEC:
Revolución; Silliman to Secretary of State, Saltillo, 16, 28 October 1913,
NA 812/9555, 9774.

22. Exp. 11,604: "Varios vecinos de Torreón solicitan no entre en función el
Jefe Político…," 18 February 1914, AGEC: Revolución; Samuel Guy Inman
quoted in Knight, *Mexican Revolution*, vol. 2, p. 92.

23. Citizens of Candela to Gobernación, Candela, 15 July 1914, AGN:
Gobernación, Período Revolucionario, c. 33, exp. 7; Unnumbered decrees,
Saltillo, 3 April, 9 February 1913, AGEC: Decretos.

24. Exp. 11,343: Merchants of Saltillo to Governor, 1 April 1913; Pres. mun.
Torreón to Governor, 20 April 1913; Miguel Garza Aldape to Governor,
Torreón, 7 September 1913; Exp. 11,446: "Formación de un cuerpo
rural …", 28 March 1913, AGEC: Revolución.

25. Exp. 11,608: "La defensa y ataque de la ciudad de Monclova," 16 March
1914; Knight, *Mexican Revolution*, vol. 2, pp. 83–84.

26. Silliman to Secretary of State, Saltillo, 8 August 1913, NA 812/8459.; A.M.
Elias to Secretary of Foreign Relations, Eagle Pass, 28 March 1914, ARE-LE
792(2); Knight, *Mexican Revolution*, vol. 2, pp. 136–137.

27. Lozano to Secretary of Foreign Relations, Laredo, 15, 16 February 1913,
ARE-LE 782(10); R. S. Bravo to Consular Inspector, Eagle Pass, 25 July
1913, ARE-LE 859(1).

28. Mexican Embassy to Secretary of Foreign Affairs, Washington, 24 February
1913, ARE-LE 785(24); A.M. Elias to Secretary of Foreign Relations,
Laredo, 2 August 1913, ARE-LE 788(15); Knight, *Mexican Revolution*, vol.
2, pp. 19, 47.

29. Juan Hernández García to Carranza, Rosita, 28 February 1912, AGEC:
Revolución; García to Secretary of War, Relación de servicios prestados a
la revolución durante seis años, Mexico City, 24 October 1917; Pres. mun.
Sabinas to Gen. Jesús J. Madrigal, Sabinas, 30 April 1930, in "Hernández

García, Juan," AHDN–CP, Exp. XI/111/4-3053.

30. Ricardo Castillo to Carranza, Montoya, New Mexico, 18 May 1913, AVC, carp. 2, leg. 202; Del Rio Consul to A.M. Elias, 1 July 1913, ARE–LE 749(10); Consular Inspector to Secretary of Foreign Relations, 11 March 1914, ARE–LE 787(8); Del Rio Consul to Inspector General, 28 March 1914, ARE–LE 716(2).

31. Ildefonso M. Castro to Carranza, Múzquiz, 25 May 1913, AVC carp. 2, leg. 263; ibid., 6 June 1913, AVC, carp. 3, leg. 388; Carranza to Castro, Piedras Negras, 30 May, AVC, carp. 3, leg. 309; ibid., 12 June 1913, AVC, carp. 4, leg. 439; A.M. Elias to Secretary of Foreign Relations, n.p., 19 June 1913, ARE–LE 763(7).

32. Secretary of Foreign Relations to Secretary of War, Mexico, 12 June 1913, AHDN: Revolución, Exp. XI/481.5/30, Tomo II; R.S. Bravo to Secretary of Foreign Relations, Eagle Pass, 12 June 1913, ARE–LE 782(9).

33. R.S. Bravo to Consular Inspector, San Antonio, 28 July 1913, ARE–LE 763(20); R.S. Bravo to A.M. Elias, Eagle Pass, 30 July , 3 October, 1913, ARE–LE 751, 842(9).

34. Faustino S. Villarreal to Carranza, Palau, 13 June 1913; José Domínguez to Carranza, Matamoros, 18 December 1913; Carranza to Pres. mun. Sabinas, Piedras Negras, AVC, carp. 4, leg. 456; carp. 5, leg. 658; carp. 3, leg. 313.

35. Juan Martínez to Carranza, Eagle Pass, 29 December 1913, AVC, carp. 5, leg. 708; Juan S. Hernández to Carranza (?), Palau, 18 July 1914, AVC, carp. 11, leg. 1098.

36. This profile is the product of a sampling of 32 names gleaned from muster rolls contained in AGEC: Revolución, and from lists of military leaders contained throughout Villarello Vélez, *Historia de la revolución*. Information on occupation and political antecedents for each man was extracted from individual service records in AHDN-CP, and from INEHRM, *Diccionario*.

37. R.S. Bravo to Secretary of Foreign Relations, Eagle Pass, 14 March 1913, ARE–LE 765(1); A.M. Elias to Secretary of Foreign Relations, San Antonio, 17 July 1913, ARE–LE 788(7); Consular Inspector to Secretary of Foreign Relations, San Antonio, 1 October 1913, ARE–LE 778(14); Sebastián Carranza to Carranza, Hacienda San Carlos, 4 April 1913, AVC, carp. 1, leg. 98.

38. An assessment of the nature of Huerta's support may be found in Knight, *Mexican Revolution*, vol. 2, pp. 1–11. See also Richmond, *Carranza*, pp. 46–47.

39. Richmond, *Carranza*, p. 58; Knight, *Mexican Revolution*, vol. 2, pp. 167–171.

40. Mexican Embassy to Consular Inspector, Washington, 26 March 1914; Diebold to Secretary of Foreign Relations, El Paso, 8 April 1914, ARE–LE 795(1); Theodore Hamm to Secretary of State, Durango, 19 April 1914, NA 812/11703; Secretary of Foreign Relations to Secretary of War, Mexico, 15 April 1914, and General Carlos García Hidalgo to Secretary of War, Saltillo, 21 April 1914, AHDN: Revolución, Exp. XI/481.5/31, Tomo I.

41. Katz, Villa, pp. 242–244; Silliman to Secretary of State, Saltillo, 25 October 1913, NA 812/9391; Secretary of War to Secretary of Foreign Relations, Mexico, 21 October 1913, ARE–LE 791(1); George C. Carothers to Secretary of State, El Paso, 3, 23 February and 6 April 1914, NA 812/10820, 10953, 1419.

42. Diebold to Secretary of Foreign Relations, El Paso, 10 April 1914, Diebold to Secretary of War, El Paso, 11 April 1914, ARE–LE 793(2).

43. A.M. Elias to Secretary of Foreign Relations, San Antonio, 4 May 1914, ARE-LE 747(16); Blocker to State Department, Piedras Negras, 24 April 1914, NA 812/11681; Coerver and Hall, *Texas and the Mexican Revolution*, p. 77.
44. Blocker to State Department, Ciudad Porfirio Díaz, 21, 22, 23, 29 April 1914, NA 812/1158, 11624, 11648, 11808; Blocker to State Department, Eagle Pass, 30 April 1914, NA 812/11779.

Notes to Chapter 6

1. R.S. Bravo to Elías, Eagle Pass, 4 August 1913, ARE-LE 832; A.M. Elías to Secretary of Foreign Relations, San Antonio, 17 April 1913, R.S. Bravo to A. M. Elías, Eagle Pass, 15 September 1913, ARE-LE 778(14).
2. Decree of Venustiano Carranza, Piedras Negras, 26 April 1913, ARE-LE 750. Alvaro Obregón, Pancho Villa, and Pablo González all issued paper money.
3. Holland to State Department, Saltillo, 11 March 1913, NA 812/6968; R.S. Bravo to Secretary of Foreign Relations, Eagle Pass, 24 March 1913, ARE-LE 764(2); ibid., 4 June 1913, ARE-LE 750; A.M. Elías to Secretary of Foreign Relations, San Antonio, 22 August 1913, ARE-LE 765(1); Juez Auxiliar to Governor, Mina La Palma, 18 November 1913, AGEC: Revolución.
4. M.E. Diebold to Secretary of Foreign Relations, El Paso, 13 April 1914, ARE-LE 784(2); ibid., 6 May 1914, ARE-LE 797(23); Ellsworth to State Department, Ciudad Porfirio Díaz, 16 April, 6 May 1913, NA 812/7193, 7447.
5. Ellsworth to State Department, Ciudad Porfirio Díaz, 27 January 1911, NA 812/689; Carlos Pereyra to Secretary of Foreign Relations, Washington, DC, 4 February 1911, ARE-LE 629; M. Cuesta to Secretary of Foreign Relations, Del Rio, 22 June 1910 and 6 May 1911, ARE-LE 689(15).
6. Ellsworth to State Department, Ciudad Porfirio Díaz, 28 November, 5 December 1910, NA 812/523, 547.
7. R.S. Bravo to Secretary of Foreign Relations, Eagle Pass, 4 March 1913, ARE-LE 767(1); Ellsworth to Secretary of State, Ciudad Porfirio Díaz, 27 February and 5 April 1913, NA 812/6400, 7029; Ildefonso Villarello Vélez, *Historia de la revolución mexicana en Coahuila*, 2nd ed. (Saltillo: Biblioteca de la Universidad Autónoma de Coahuila, 1983), p. 244.
8. R.S. Bravo to Secretary of Foreign Relations, Eagle Pass, 7 April 1913; J.A. Fernández to Secretary of Foreign Relations, San Antonio, 1 May 1913, ARE-LE 765(1), 758(1).
9. R.S. Bravo to Secretary of Foreign Relations, 4 March 1913, ARE-LE 767(1); J.A. Fernández to Secretary of Foreign Relations, San Antonio, 10 April 1913, ARE-LE 758(1).
10. Ellsworth to State Department, Ciudad Porfirio Díaz, 5, 24, 25, 30 March 1913, NA 812/6503, 6917, 6918, 6919, 6937; Treasury Secretary to Secretary of War, Mexico, 7, 14 March 1913, AHDN: Revolución, Exp. XI/481.5/30, Tomo I; R.S. Bravo to Inspector of Consuls, 5 August 1913, ARE-LE 832; A.M. Elías to Secretary of Foreign Relations, 19 September 1913, ARE-LE 765(1).

11. A.M. Elías to Secretary of Foreign Relations, San Antonio, 30 July 1913, ARE-LE 751; R.S. Bravo to Secretary of Foreign Relations, Eagle Pass, 4 and 7 April 1913, ARE-LE 765(1).
12. Ellsworth to State Department, Ciudad Porfirio Díaz, 16 May 1913, RDS-IA 812/7541; R.S. Bravo to Secretary of Foreign Relations, Eagle Pass, April 1913, ARE-LE 732(11); R.S. Bravo to Secretary of Foreign Relations, Eagle Pass, 31 March 1913, ARE-LE 765(1).
13. Francisco B. Barrón to Secretary of Foreign Relations, Del Rio, 4 June 1913 and 16 December 1913; José Martínez Garza to Secretary of Foreign Relations, Del Rio, 30 December 1913, ARE-LE 747(11,12,14); A.M. Elías to Secretary of Foreign Relations, 16 July 1913, ARE-LE 868(3); E.A. Benavides to José Quevedo, Eagle Pass, 3 January 1914, ARE-LE 760(2); A.M. Elías to Visitador Consulados, San Antonio, 28 February 1914, ARE-LE 781(3); Report of Eagle Pass Consul, February 1914, ARE, Exp. 28-9-125.
14. R.S. Bravo to Consular Inspector, Eagle Pass, 12 August 1913, ARE-LE 832; A.M. Elías to Secretary of Foreign Relations, 13 September 1913; F. Barrón to Secretary of Foreign Relations, 1 October 1913, ARE-LE 765(1); Bravo to Elías, Eagle Pass, 30 September 1913, ARE-LE 842(9); Elías to Secretary of Foreign Relations, San Antonio, 5 October 1913, ARE-LE 758(1); A.M. Elías to Eagle Pass Consul, San Antonio, 2 October 1913, ARE-LE 770(1).
15. A.M. Elías to Secretary of Foreign Relations, San Antonio, 10 October 1913, ARE-LE 761(40); Blocker to Secretary of State, Ciudad Porfirio Díaz, 11 October 1913, NA 812/9230; Fernando Serrano to Secretary of Foreign Relations, San Antonio, 20 November 1913, ARE-LE 747(16); Blocker to Secretary of State, Ciudad Porfirio Díaz, 7 November 1913, NA 812/9682; Visitador Consulados Diebold to Secretary of Foreign Relations, n.p., 18 February 1914, ARE-LE 784(2).
16. Fernando Serrano to Secretary of Foreign Relations, San Antonio, 20 November 1913, ARE-LE 747(16).
17. J.D. Bravo to Consular Inspector, San Antonio, 28 November 1913; Fernando Serrano to Consular Inspector, San Antonio, 1 December 1913, ARE-LE 715(1); Consular Inspector to Secretary of Foreign Relations, San Antonio, 28, 29 November 1913, ARE-LE 716(2); Castillo to Secretary of Foreign Relations, 30 November 1913, ARE-LE 792(9).
18. G. Carello to Guillermo Seguín, Nogales, 19 January 1914, ARE-LE 760(2); G.M. Seguín to E. Llorente, Eagle Pass, 21 March 1914, ARE-LE 789(7); Consular Inspector to Secretary of Foreign Relations, El Paso, 2 April 1914, ARE-LE 787(8).
19. Mexican Consul to Visitador General de Consulados, Del Rio, 17, 21, 24 March 1914, ARE-LE 781(3); Visitador General Diebold to Secretary of Foreign Relations, El Paso, 26, 27 March 1914, ARE-LE 787(8).
20. Don M. Coerver and Linda B. Hall, *Texas and the Mexican Revolution: A Study in State and National Border Policy 1910-1920* (San Antonio: Trinity University Press, 1984), p. 19; Ellsworth to State Department, Ciudad Porfirio Díaz, 15 October and 28 November 1910, NA 812/409, 523; Telegram of Francisco León de la Barra, Mexico, 18 November 1910, ARE-LE 611(1); Jesús Valle to Porfirio Díaz, Saltillo, 19 November 1910, ARE-LE 611(1); Villasana to Secretary of Foreign Relations, Eagle Pass, 19

November 1910, ARE-LE 611(1); Andrés Garza Galán to Rosendo Pineda, Ciudad Porfirio Díaz, 16 November 1910, ARE-LE 611(2).

21. Samuel R. Salazar to Francisco Madero, Monclova, 18 June 1912, AGN: Madero, carp. 218-3, fojas 6356-6361.

22. Linda B. Hall and Don M. Coerver, *Revolution on the Border: The United States and Mexico, 1910-1920* (Albuquerque: University of New Mexico Press, 1988), pp. 52, 150.

23. R.S. Bravo to Secretary of Foreign Relations, Eagle Pass, 2 March 1913, ARE-LE 765(1); R.E. Múzquiz to Carranza, El Paso, 31 December 1913, AVC, carp. 5, leg. 717.

24. Secretary of War to Secretary of Foreign Relations, Mexico, 25 March 1913, ARE-LE 767(1); R.S. Bravo to Customs Official, Eagle Pass, 24 and 25 June 1913, ARE-LE 856(5); A. M. Elias to Bravo, San Antonio, 30 June 1913, ARE-LE 856(5); Barrón to Secretary of Foreign Relations, Del Rio, 13 June 1913, ARE-LE 748; Ellsworth to State Department, Ciudad Porfirio Díaz, 29 and 31 May 1913, RDS-IA 812/7644, 7645; William Blocker to State Department, Ciudad Porfirio Díaz, 2 September 1913, NA 812/8755.

25. A.M. Elías to Secretary of Foreign Relations, San Antonio, 12 June 1913, ARE-LE 749(10).

26. Guillermo M. Seguín to Carranza, Eagle Pass, 3 February 1914, ARE-LE 780(2).

27. Ellsworth to State Department, Ciudad Porfirio Díaz, 25 July 1913, NA 812/8181; J.A. Fernández to Secretary of Foreign Relations, San Antonio, 1 May 1913, ARE-LE 763(6); A.M. Elias to Secretary of Foreign Relations, San Antonio, 10 May 1913, ARE-LE 762(3).

28. See A.M. Elías to Secretary of Foreign Relations, San Antonio, 21 April 1913, ARE-LE 761(27). Arce also served as a contraband agent for Madero's revolt of 1910-11.

29. E.M. Gómez Maillefert to Consul General, Del Rio, 23 October 1913; "Consulado de Mexico en Eagle Pass, Texas. Pruebas presentadas en contra del Señor don Lorenzo González Treviño," 9 October 1913; A. M. Elías to Secretary of Foreign Relations, San Antonio, 16 April 1913 and 9 December 1913, ARE-LE 758(1); Lorenzo González Treviño to Carranza, Parras, 2 September 1914, AVC, carp. 14, leg. 1419.

30. Unsigned letter (A. Treviño?) to Carranza, Boquillas, 5 January 1913, AVC, carp. 1, leg. 65; A. Treviño to Carranza, Boquillas, 20 March 1913, AVC, carp. 1, leg. 89; R.E. Múzquiz to Carranza, Campamento Colombia, 16 May 1913, AVC, carp. 2, leg. 184; A. Treviño to Carranza, Marathon, 23 May 1913, AVC, carp. 2, leg. 250; Miguel Cárdenas to Carranza, San Antonio, AVC, carp. 2, leg. 257; ibid., carp. 13, leg. 1386. As early as May 1911, the Mexican National Bank in Ciudad Porfirio Díaz began sending its funds to Eagle Pass for safekeeping. In addition, many Mexicans moved their belongings to Eagle Pass daily, anticipating attack by revolutionaries. See Ellsworth to State Department, Ciudad Porfirio Díaz, 16 May 1911, NA 812/1864.

31. Assistant Attorney General to Secretary of State, Washington, DC, 30 January 1914, NA 812/10751.

32. A.M. Elías to Secretary of Foreign Relations, San Antonio, 7 January 1914; Consul Eagle Pass to Gen. Arturo A. Alvarez, Eagle Pass, 8 January 1914, ARE-LE 792(16), 758(7).

33. Bravo to Secretary of Foreign Relations, Eagle Pass, 6 May 1913, ARE-LE 750.
34. Unnumbered decree, Saltillo, 15 January 1914, AGEC: Decretos.
35. A lengthy account of the cattle ring may be found in an unsigned report (probably authored by Piedras Negras customs official Antonio Villarreal Cerda) on events along Coahuila's border from 14 May to 11 July 1914, AVC, carp. 10, leg. 1034.
36. "Por que de seguir aquí, en muy pocas meses más, todas las poblaciones tendrán que cambiar de alimentación y ser vegetarianos por que se acabaran los ganados," ibid. Pablo González also recognized the dangers inherent in the mass exodus of cattle from the border states; in May 1914 he issued a decree forbidding the export of all cattle through the customs houses and other ports in Coahuila, Nuevo León, and Tamaulipas. See Blocker to State Department, Ciudad Porfirio Díaz, 14 October 1914, NA 812/13541.
37. Blocker to State Department, Piedras Negras, 23 January 1915, NA 812/14298; Blocker to State Department, 27, 30 September 1916, NA 812/19323, 19425.

Notes to Chapter 7

1. Blocker to State Department, Ciudad Porfirio Díaz, 26 September 1914, NA 812/13360.
2. Blocker to State Department, Eagle Pass, 19 December 1914; Blocker to State Department, Ciudad Porfirio Díaz, 21 December 1914, NA 812/14045, 14135.
3. James A. Sandos, *Rebellion in the Borderlands: Anarchism and the Plan of San Diego, 1904-1923* (Norman: University of Oklahoma Press, 1992), pp. 63-84.
4. Blocker to State Department, Eagle Pass, 26, 28 August 1915; Blocker to State Department, Piedras Negras, 28 August 1915, NA 812/15941, 15947, 16011; Sandos, *Rebellion in the Borderlands*, pp. 131-140, 150.
5. Katz, *Pancho Villa*, pp. 215-218; 306-308; 354-355.
6. Friedrich Katz, "Pancho Villa, Peasant Movements, and Agrarian Reform in Northern Mexico," in *Caudillo and Peasant in the Mexican Revolution*, ed. David A. Brading (Cambridge: Cambridge University Press, 1980), p. 64.
7. Katz, *Villa*, pp. 330-336.
8. Ibid., pp. 336-337; 343-348.
9. Carothers to State Department, El Paso, 25, 28 April 1914; Carothers to State Department, Gómez Palacio, 10 June 1914, NA 812/11704, 11755, 12219.
10. Katz, *Villa*, pp. 361-362.
11. Ibid., pp. 364-370.
12. Ibid., pp. 358, 370; Richmond, *Carranza*, pp. 62-63.
13. Katz, *Villa*, 375-384; Knight, *Mexican Revolution*, vol. 2, pp. 256-263; Richmond, *Carranza*, p. 60.
14. Quirk, *Mexican Revolution*, pp. 37, 41-43; Katz, *Villa*, pp. 384-385; Knight, *Mexican Revolution*, vol. 2, pp. 262-263.
15. Cuéllar Valdés, *Historia*, p. 221; Blocker to State Department, Eagle Pass, 19 August 1914; Blocker to State Department, Ciudad Porfirio Díaz, 26

September 1914; Blocker to State Department, Eagle Pass, 31 December 1914, NA 812/12941, 13360, 14117.

16. Blocker to State Department, Ciudad Porfirio Díaz, 26 September 1914, NA 812/13298, 13360; R.E. Múzquiz to Carranza, Piedras Negras, 6 October 1914, AHDN: Revolución, Exp. XI/481.5/31, Tomo I; R.S. Bravo to Secretary of Foreign Relations, San Antonio, 10 June 1914, ARE–LE 792(9).

17. A.M. Elías to Secretary of Foreign Relations, San Antonio, 15 June 1914, ARE–LE 795(4).

18. Jesús Acuña to Carranza, Saltillo, 10 December 1914, AVC, carp. 22, leg. 2198.

19. Blocker to State Department, Eagle Pass, 16 January 1915; Blocker to State Department, Ciudad Porfirio Díaz, 13 January 1915; Blocker to State Department, Eagle Pass, 21 January 1915, NA 812/14214, 14251, 14255.

20. Report of Guillermo Seguín, Eagle Pass, 16 January 1915, AGN: Gobernación, caja 1049, leg. 873, exp. 2; Blocker to State Department, Eagle Pass, 29, 30 January and 5, 9 March 1915, NA 812/14334, 14318, 14505, 14539; Serapio Aguirre to Carranza, Piedras Negras, 8 March 1915, AHDN: Revolución, Exp. XI/481.5/32, Tomo I.

21. Blocker to State Department, Eagle Pass, 16, 22 March 1915, NA 812/14656, 14662, 14666, 14706; Blocker to State Department, Eagle Pass and Piedras Negras, 11, 15, 17 March, 4, 18, 25, 29 May 1915, NA 812/14562, 14599, 14620, 14990, 15058, 15033, 15090, 15110.

22. Blocker to State Department, Eagle Pass, 12 September 1915; Blocker to State Department, Piedras Negras, 13 September 1915, NA 812/16122, 16218.

23. R.E. Múzquiz to Carranza, Piedras Negras, 7 October 1914, AHDN: Revolución, Exp. XI/481.5/31, Tomo I; Jesús Acuña to Carranza, Piedras Negras, 5 March 1915, AHDN: Revolución, Exp. XI/481.5?32, Tomo I; J. Martínez to Governor, Sabinas, 15, 26 September 1915, Exp. 11,870: "Escritos y oficios diversos 1915 a 1916," AGEC: Revolución.

24. Blocker to State Department, Eagle Pass, 1, 6, 10 April 1915, NA 812/14763, 14872; Decreto núm. 6, Departamento de Hacienda y Fomento, Aguascalientes, 4 May 1915, AGEC: Revolución; Exp. 11,735: " ... ha ordenado el establecimiento de una oficina en Torreón," 6–24 March 1915, AGEC: Revolución.

25. Blocker to State Department, Piedras Negras, 10, 28 July 1915, NA 812/15499, 15612.

26. H. C. Coen to State Department, Durango, 24, 31 May, 13, 22 July 1915, NA 812/15117, 15140, 15507, 15586.

27. Exp. 11,727: " ... la supresión de la compra de agua que hace el municipio de Piedras Negras ...," 4 January 1915; Exp. 11,706: "Con el Decreto núm. 9 que declara nulas e insubsistentes las billetes de emisión carrancista," 1 April 1915; Exp. 11,643: " ... ordenes de multa por infracciones al Decreto núm. 9 ...," 24 June 1915, AGEC: Revolución.

28. Decréto núm. 6, Departamento de Hacienda y Fomento, Aguascalientes, 4 May 1915; Miners and merchants of Palau to Juex Auxiliar, 25 October 1915 in Exp. 11,870: "Escritos y Oficios sobre asuntos diversos 1915 a 1916," AGEC: Revolución.

29. Decreto núm. 4: "Ley de suspención de plazos para el pago de intereses

y créditos a los Bancos," Monterrey, 19 March 1915, AGEC: Revolución; Cuéllar Valdés, *Saltillo*, pp. 73–78.

30. Exp. 11,720: "… con la circular núm. 2, fijando lo que deben ganarse …," Saltillo, 17 April 1915; Exp. 11,719: "… Presidente Municipal de Viesca pidiendo pasar a Zacatecas para comprar maíz …," 8 May 1915; Santiago Ramírez to Gen. Macrino J. Martínez, Saltillo, 27 June 1915; Exp., 11, 703: "… relativo al enganche de 500 trabajadores para los ranchos de la Comarca Lagunera," 1 May 1915; Ramírez to Pres. mun. Monclova, Saltillo, 27 June 1915, AGEC: Revolución.

31. Capt. Josafat Ramón to Governor, Múzquiz, 7 May 1915; Pres. Mun. Piedras Negras to Governor's Secretary, 12 April 1915; Exp. 11,682: "… Decreto núm. 13, aumentando los sueldos …," 29 June 1915, AGEC: Revolución.

32. Katz, *Villa*, pp. 209–212.

33. Blocker to State Department, Ciudad Porfirio Díaz, 26 September 1914, NA 812/13298.

34. Exp. 11,752: "Junta Interventora," Saltillo, 7 April 1915, AGEC: Revolución; Richmond, "Factional Political Strife," pp. 63–64; Katz, *Secret War*, pp. 65, 282–284; Friedrich Katz, "Pancho Villa, Peasant Movements and Agrarian Reform in Northern Mexico," in *Caudillo and Peasant in the Mexican Revolution*, ed. David A. Brading (Cambridge: Cambridge University Press, 1980), pp. 65–70.

35. Exp. 11,721: "… El Mayor Jefe de Armas de Sierra Mojada que debe hacer respeto de los ranchos…," 5 April 1915, AGEC: Revolución.

36. Exp. 11,722: "… la solicitud del Señor Pedro Cuéllar …," 19 February 1915, AGEC: Revolución.

37. Exp. 11,723: "La consulta que hace a este gobierno el Presidente Municipal de Villa Acuña …," 6 January 1915; Exp. 11,724: "… una consulta que hace el Presidente Municipal de Piedras Negras …," 6 January 1915, AGEC: Revolución.

38. Katz, *Pancho Villa*, pp. 476–478.

39. Knight, *Mexican Revolution*, vol. 2, p. 310.

40. Of the sampling of thirty-two members of Coahuila's irregular forces prior to Carranza's rebellion, presented in Chapter 4, twenty had Maderista antecedents. Of these, only four defected to Villa's ranks. They included Sixto Ugalde, Catarino Benavides (Francisco Madero's uncle), Lucio Blanco (who only briefly sided with the Convention), and Eulalio Gutiérrez Ortiz (who became the first president of the Convention government).

41. Blocker to State Department, Eagle Pass, 24 October, 13, 17, 18 November 1916, NA 812/19678, 19852, 19853, 19894, 19907.

42. Consul General to Secretary of State, San Antonio, 12 January 1917, NA 812/20271.

43. Blocker to State Department, Eagle Pass, 1 January 1917, NA 812/20188; Report of Patrick O'Hea, quoted in Blocker to State Department, Eagle Pass, 17 January 1917, NA 812/20414.

44. Report of Patrick O'Hea, quoted in Blocker to State Department, Eagle Pass, 17 January 1917, NA 812/20414.

45. Blocker to State Department, Eagle Pass and Piedras Negras, 8, 9 May and 23 June 1916, NA 812/18090, 18101, 18591; Silliman to State Department, Saltillo, 8 June 1916, NA 812/18357.

46. Silliman to State Department, Saltillo, 30 June, 6 July, 1916, NA 812/18623, 18662; Blocker to State Department, Eagle Pass, 15 July 1916, NA 812/18735.

47. Espinosa Mireles to Carranza, Saltillo, 6, 10, 11 April 1916; General Jacinto B. Treviño to Carranza, n.p., 15 April 1916; Treviño to Obregón, n.p., 20 April 1916; Espinosa Mireles to Carranza, Saltillo, 8, 10 May and 1 June 1916; Gen. Arnulfo González to Obregón, Torreón, 1, 2 November 1916, AHDN: Revolución, Exp. XI/481.5/33, Tomo I.

Notes to Chapter 8

1. Richmond, *Carranza*, p. 61.
2. Ibid., pp. 66–69; 71–74.
3. Ibid., pp. 108–110.
4. Ibid., pp. 113–118; 121–124.
5. Ibid., 124–134.
6. Ibid., pp. 83–92.
7. Blocker to State Department, Piedras Negras, 25 September, 6, 12, 17, 24 November, 16 December 1915, NA 812/16328, 16763, 16806, 16879, 16841, 16980.
8. Blocker to State Department, Piedras Negras and Eagle Pass, 6, 30 March, 3, 4, 7, 11, April 1916, NA 812/17381, 17726, 17746, 17731, 17816.
9. Blocker to State Department, Eagle Pass, 27, 28 October 1916, NA 812/19709, 17676, 17671; Andrés García to Secretary of Foreign Relations, El Paso, 14 September 1916; Espinosa Mireles to Secretary of Foreign Relations, Saltillo, 7 December 1916, ARE-LE 799(17).
10. Blocker to State Department, Eagle Pass, 24 October 1916, NA 812/19678; Blocker to State Department, Piedras Negras, 24 October, 31 January 1916, NA 812/19678, 17223.
11. Blocker to State Department, Piedras Negras, 22 February 1916, NA 812/17327; Blocker to State Department, Eagle Pass, 12, 17 May 1916; Blocker to State Department, Piedras Negras, 27 May 1916, NA 812/18146, 18183, 18282; Exp. 11,993: "Escrito de los comerciantes de Piedras Negras," 25 November 1915, AGEC: Revolución; Blocker to State Department, Eagle Pass, 27 November 1916, NA 812/19964.
12. Blocker to State Department, Eagle Pass, 11, 14 October 1916, NA 812/19544, 19529.
13. Pres. mun. Sabinas to Governor, 1 March 1916, Exp. 221: "Oficios Diversos … San Juan de Sabinas"; Exp. 12,390: "Presidente Municipal … San Juan de Sabinas," 19 October 1915; Exp. 12,163: "Comunicaciones diversos girados entre este gobierno y la Presidencia municipal de Múzquiz," 27 October 1915, AGEC: Revolución.
14. J. Martínez to Governor, Sabinas, 15, 26 September 1915, Exp. 11,870: "Escritos y oficios sobre asuntos diversos 1915 a 1916," AGEC: Revolución.
15. Silliman to State Department, Saltillo, 19 April, 12 June 1916, NA 812/17932, 18398; Silliman to State Department, Eagle Pass, 29 July, 2 August 1916, NA 812/18821, 18843.
16. Manuel Cepeda to Secretario de Gobierno, Saltillo, 12 November 1915, Exp. 12,291: "Presidencia Municipal de San Pedro," 7 October 1915,

Pedro Franco Ugarte to Governor, Torreón, 5 October 1915, AGEC: Revolución; Blocker to State Department, Eagle Pass, 20 March 1916; H.C. Coen to State Department, Durango, 31 March 1916; Blocker to State Department, Eagle Pass, 30 September, 24 October 1916, NA 812/17544, 17756, 19425, 19678; Hanna to State Department, San Antonio, 4 August 1916, NA 812/18853.

17. Circular of 10 May 1916 in Exp. 125: "Papel Moneda," AGEC: Revolución; Richmond, *Carranza*, pp. 87–92.

18. Decreto núm. 4, Saltillo, 2 October 1915, in Exp. 12,338: "Tesorería General del Estado ... correspondencia"; Exp. 12,308: "Agentes Fiscales," 27 September 1915; Circular núm. 1760, Saltillo, 3 April 1916, in Exp. 12,166: "Oficios diversos Ramos Arizpe;" Pres. mun. Progreso to Governor, 30 December 1915, in Exp. 12,165: "Diversos asuntos ... Progreso," AGEC: Revolución.

19. Decreto núm. 6, Saltillo, 16 November 1915, Exp. 12,161: "Nombramiento de Presidente Municipal en matamoros ... y oficios cambiados ..."; Espinosa Mireles to Pres. mun. Sabinas, Saltillo, 29 February 1916, Exp. 221: "Oficios Diversos girados entre este Gobierno y la Presidencia de San Juan de Sabinas," AGEC: Revolución.

20. Exp. 12,292: "Recaudación de Rentas, San Pedro," 18 October 1915; F. Peraldi to Governor, Piedras Negras, 6 May 1916, Exp. 12,318: "Jefatura de Armas, Piedras Negras Coahuila"; Pres. mun. Matamoros to Governor, 27 September 1915, Exp. 12,161: "Nombramiento de Presidente Municipal en Matamoros ... y oficios cambiados ...," AGEC: Revolución.

21. Report of Special Commission, Torreón, 30 March 1916, Exp. 12,173: "Oficios ... cambiados entre este Gobierno y la Presidencia Municipal de Torreón ... octubre de 1915 hasta ... junio de 1916," AGEC: Revolución.

22. Pedro Francisco Ugarte to Governor, Torreón, 7 August 1916, Exp. 208: "Escritos y oficios sobre diversos asuntos"; memoranda, "Saltillo, November and December 1915," in Exp. 12,283: "Archivo General," AGEC: Revolución.

23. Report of Special Commission, Torreón, 7 December 1915, Exp. 12,315: "Comisión Algodonera de la Laguna," AGEC: Revolución; Blocker to State Department, Eagle Pass, 10 January 1916, Williams to State Department, Torreón, 15, 27 January 1916, NA 812/17077, 17107, 17166.

24. Decreto núm. 19, Saltillo, 11 March 1916, AGEC: Revolución.

25. Pres. mun. Nava to Ventura González, 21 September 1914; Salvador Chacón to Governor, Abasolo, 18 October 1915, Exp. 11,929: "Presidencia municipal de Abasolo Viejo," AGEC: Revolución.

26. Decreto núm. 4, Saltillo, 26 November 1917, AGEC: Decretos. Lands and waters were to revert to their original owners after the gathering of one harvest.

27. Decreto núm. 1, Saltillo, 14 September 1915, AGEC: Decretos.

28. Espinosa Mireles to Recaudador de Rentas, Saltillo, 20 Setpember 1915, Exp. 12,271: "Recaudación de Rentas, Múzquiz"; Fernando Peraldi to Governor's Secretary, Monclova, 10 December 1915, Exp. 12,244, AGEC: Revolución.

29. Exp. 12,316: "Comisión Interventora de la Laguna," 20 November 1915; Exp. 12,240: "... solicitud para que se le devuelvan las propiedades ... en Torreón," 19 November 1915, AGEC: Revolución; President of Junta

Intervetora de la Comarca Lagunera to Gobernación, Torreón, 4 April 1916, AGN: Gobernación, Período Revolucionario, caja 6 exp. 21; petition of Miguel Bernardini, Torreón, 26 June 1917, AGN: Gobernación, Período Revolucionario, caja 187, exp. 57.

30. Dirección de Bienes Intervenidos, Mexico, 31 March 1919, "Relación de las Propiedades Intervenidas que existen actualmente bajo el control de la Administración de Bienes Intervenidos en el Estado de Coahuila," AGN: Gobernación, Período Revolucionario, caja 184, exp. 38, fs. 19–21; Hoja de Servicio of Corl. de Cab. Nicanor Valdéz, AHDN: Cancelados y Pensionistas, D/111/4/6407.

31. Governor to Pres. mun. Rosales, 19 October 1915, in Exp. 12,386: "Presidencia Municipal Rosales," Espinosa Mireles to T.V. Santos, Saltillo, 11 December 1915, in Exp. 12,218: "Telegramas ... 1915 a 1916," Order of Jesús Acuña, n.p., 5 April 1916, AGN: Gobernación, Período Revolucionario; Tesorero General to Rubén Rodríguez, Saltillo, 31 January 1916, Exp. 12,338: "Tesorería General del Estado ... correspondencia," AGEC: Revolución; Petition of Manuel Madero and others to Gobernación, 22 June 1917; AGN: Gobernación, Período Revolucionario, caja 7, exp. 2.

32. Pres. mun. Sierra Mojada to Governor, 9 December 1916, Exp. 141: "... causas que motivaron la intervención de las propiedades de varios personas ..."; Pres. mun. Allende to Governor, 21 November 1915; Pres. mun. Torreón to Governor, n.d. (1916), Exp. 12,220: "... solicitud de Federico W. Reyes ...," AGEC: Revolución.

33. Richmond, *Carranza*, pp. 51–52; Katz, *Secret War*, pp. 145–146, 288–293; "Copia del Acta de Entrega de La Concha y Anexas," 23 February 1916, "Copia del Acta de Entrega de La Fe Fábrica de Hilados y Tejidos," 18 March 1916, AGN: Gobernación, Período Revolucionario, caja 6, exp. 83; Pres. mun. Sacramento to Governor's Secretary, 19 October 1915, Exp. 12,403: "Presidencia Municipal Sacramento," AGEC: Revolución.

34. Bruno Neira to Espinosa Mireles, Piedras Negras, 15 August, 20 September 1916, Exp. 208: "Escritos y oficios sobre diversos asuntos," AGEC: Revolución.

35. Pres. mun. San Juan de Sabinas to Governor, 23 February 1916. Rita Favret has studied the effect of Carranza's *Ley Agraria* on Coahuila in, *Tenencia*, pp. 137–139, 142–143.

36. Favret, *Tenencia*, pp. 216–217; 153–155.

37. Coen to State Department, Durango, 4 August 1917, NA 812/21178; Blocker to State Department, Piedras Negras, 9 February 1918, NA 812/21738.

38. Richmond, *Carranza*, pp. 154–159.

39. Cuéller Valdés, *Historia*, pp. 225–226; Hanna to State Department, San Antonio, 9, 17 February 1917 and 23 October, 7 November 1918; Blocker to State Department, Eagle Pass and Piedras Negras, 6, 7, 8, 10 September, 13 November, 11, 13, 15, 16, 17, 18 December 1917 and 8 April 1918, NA 812/20505, 20533, 22338, 21245, 21248, 21252, 21261, 21478, 21535, 21536, 21538, 21543, 21551, 21552, 21559, 21562, 21652, 21878.

40. Decreto núm. 223, Saltillo, 27 November 1918, Decreto núm. 345, Saltillo, 1 March 1919, Decreto núm. 319, Saltillo, 4 February 1919, Decreto núm. 46, Saltillo, 9 January 1920, Decreto núm. 3, Saltillo, 19 November 1919, Decreto núm. 320, Saltillo, 6 December 1920, Decreto núm. 341, Saltillo, 31

December 1920, AGEC: Decretos; Jorge E. von Versen to Espinosa Mireles, n.p., 30 January 1916, in Exp. 12,175: "... elecciones y plebescito verificados en el Estado ...," AGEC: Revolución.

41. Segundo Guajardo and others to Governor, Cuatro Ciénegas, 27 December 1915; Marcos Flores and others to Espinosa Mireles, Morelos, 8 October 1915; V. de la Garza and others to Governor, Nava, 6 December 1915, Exp. 12,175: "... elecciones y plebescito verificados en el Estado el mes de septiembre de 1915 hasta el de junio 1916," AGEC: Revolución.

42. Unnumbered decree of 25 September 1915 in exp. 12,157, AGEC: Revolución; Decréto núm. 8, Saltillo, 7 January 1916, AGEC: Decretos.

43. Report of Pres. mun. Ocampo, 1916, Exp. 12,172: "Comunicaciones diversos girados entre este gobierno y las presidencias municipales ... año fiscal de 1915 a 1916," AGEC: Revolución; Blocker to State Department, Eagle Pass, 8 January, 7 February 1917, NA 812/20261, 20511.

44. Richmond, *Carranza*, pp. 166-167.

45. This latter rule was apparently modified by the state congress in 1920, allowing the re-election of council members who vacated their posts ninety days before the election (Decréto núm. 375, Saltillo, 30 March 1919; Decréto núm. 189, Saltillo, 30 June 1920, AGEC: Decretos. See also Villarello Vélez, *Historia de la revolución* , pp. 311-314).

46. Decréto núm. 4, 2 October 1915 in AGEC: Revolución.

47. Decréto núm. 32, Saltillo, 8 February 1917, Decréto núm. 153, Saltillo, 13 November 1918, AGEC: Decretos; Espinosa Mireles' order of 31 January 1916 in Exp. 12,338: "Tesorería General del Estado ... correspondencia," AGEC: Revolución.

48. Richmond, *Carranza*, pp. 92-105; 169.

49. Decréto núm. 14, Saltillo, 28 February 1916; Decréto núm. 19, Saltillo, 11 March 1916, AGEC: Decretos.

50. Exp. 12,220: "Documentos Diversos relacionados con las sociedades mutualistas en el estado," 10 March 1915, AGEC: Revolución; Villarello Vélez, *Historia de la revolución*, pp. 305-308; Richmond, "Factional Politica Strife," p. 65.

51. Circular 5, Sección de Contaduría, Saltillo, 15 January 1918, AGEC: Circulares; Espinosa Mireles to Pres. mun. Saltillo, 15 October 1916, Exp. 210: "Presidencia Municipa de Saltillo, Oficios diversos," AGEC: Revolución.

52. Decréto núm. 20, Saltillo, 15 March 1916; Decréto núm. 11, Saltillo, 18 January 1916, AGEC: Decretos.

53. Circular 1240, n.d., in Exp. 12,166: "Oficios Diversos ... Ramos Arizpe," 14 September 1915, AGEC: Revolución; Decréto núm. 5, Saltillo, 5 October 1915, Decréto núm. 18, Saltillo, 10 March 1916, Decréto núm. 7, Saltillo, 1 December 1915, AGEC: Decretos.

54. Decréto núm. 16, Saltillo, 2 March 1916, AGEC: Decretos.

55. Richmond, *Carranza*, pp. 171-178.

Notes to Conclusion

1. Alfredo Breceda Mercado, interview by Manuel Arellano, Mexico City, April 19, 1961, INAH PHO/1/15; Roque González Garza, interview by Daniel Cazos, Mexico City, August 1960, INAH PHO/1/18.

Bibliography

Archival Sources

Mexico City

Archivo General de la Nación: Archivo de Gobernación, Ramo de Madero,
    Ramo de Trabajo.
Archivo Histórico de la Defensa Nacional: Fondo Revolución, Archivo
    Cancelados y Pensionistas.
Centro de Estudios de Historia de México, CONDUMEX: Archivo del General
    Bernardo Reyes, Archivo de Venustiano Carranza.
Museo de Antropología e Historia: Archivo Francisco I. Madero, Archivo de la
    Palabra.
Secretaría de Relaciones Exteriores: Archivo de Relaciones Exteriores.

Saltillo, Coahuila

Archivo General del Estado de Coahuila: Fondo Siglo XIX, Fondo Revolución,
    Fondo Decretos, Fondo Circulares, Fondo Copiadores.
Archivo General del Tribunal Superior de Justicia: Fondo Histórico.
Archivo Municipal de Saltillo: Fondo Presidencia Municipal.

United States

Department of State. *Records of the Department of State Relating to the Internal
    Affairs of Mexico, 1910-1929.*
Department of State. *Consular Despatches from U.S. Consuls in Piedras Negras,
    Mexico, 1868-1906.*
Department of State. *Consular Despatches from U.S. Consuls in Saltillo, Mexico,
    1876-1906.*

Secondary Sources

Books

Alessio Robles, Vito. *Coahuila y Texas. Desde la consumación de la independencia hasta el tratado de paz de Guadalupe Hidalgo.* 2 vols. 2nd ed. Mexico City: Editorial Porrúa, 1979.

Carman, Michael Dennis. *United States Customs and the Madero Revolution.* El Paso: Texas Western Press, 1976.

Cerutti, Mario. *Burguesía, capitales e industria en el norte de México.* Mexico City: Alianza Editorial, 1992.

———. *Economía de Guerra y poder regional en el siglo XIX: Gastos militares aduanas y comerciantes en años de Vidaurri (1885-1864).* Mexico City: Archivo General del Estado de Nuevo León, 1983.

———. *Monterrey, Nuevo León, el Noreste: Siete Estudios Históricos.* Mexico City: Universidad Autónoma de Nuevo León, 1987.

Coahuila: Reseña geográfico y estadística. Mexico City: Librería de la Vda. de C. Bouret, 1909.

Cockroft, James D. *Intellectual Precursors of the Mexican Revolution 1900-1913.* Austin: University of Texas Press, 1968.

Coerver, Don M., and Linda B. Hall. *Texas and the Mexican Revolution: A Study in State and National Border Policy 1910-1920.* San Antonio: Trinity University Press, 1984.

Cosío Villegas, Daniel, ed. *Historia moderna de México: El Porfiriato: La vida económica.* 2 vols. Mexico City: Editorial Hermes, 1965.

———. *Historia moderna de Mexico: El Porfiriato: La vida política interior.* 2 vols. Mexico City: Editorial Hermes, 1970.

Cuéllar Valdés, Pablo M. *Geografía del Estado de Coahuila.* Saltillo: Universidad Autónoma de Coahuila, 1981.

———. *Historia de la ciudad de Saltillo.* Edición fascimilar. Saltillo: Fondo Estatal para la Cultura y los Artes de Coahuila, 1998.

———. *Historia del Estado de Coahuila.* Saltillo: Biblioteca de la Universidad Autónoma de Coahuila, 1979.

Cumberland, Charles C. *Mexican Revolution: The Constitutionalist Years.* Austin: University of Texas Press, 1972.

———. *Mexican Revolution: Genesis under Madero.* Austin: University of Texas Press, 1952.

———. *Mexico: The Struggle for Modernity.* New York: Oxford, 1968.

Enríquez Terrazas, Eduardo, and José Luis García Valero. *Coahuila: Una historia compartida.* Mexico City: Instituto de Investigaciones Dr. José María Luis Mora, 1989.

Enríquez Terrazas, Eduardo, and Martha Rodríguez García, eds. *Coahuila: Textos de su historia.* Mexico City: Instituto de Investigaciones Dr. José María Luis Mora, 1989.

Favret Tondato, Rita. *Tenencia de la tierra en el estado de Coahuila (1880-1987).* Saltillo: Universidad Autónoma Agraria Antonio Narro, 1992.

Guerra, Eduardo. *Historia de la Laguna: Torreón, su origen y sus fundadores.* Saltillo: Imprenta de Coahuila, 1932.

Guerra, Francois-Xavier. *México: Del Antiguo Régimen a la Revolución.* 2 vols. Mexico City: Fondo de Cultura Económica, 1988.

Hall, Linda B., and Don M. Coerver. *Revolution on the Border: The United States and Mexico, 1920-1920.* Albuquerque: University of New Mexico Press, 1988.

Harris, Charles H. *A Mexican Family Empire: The Latifundia of the Sánchez Navarros, 1765-1867.* Austin: University of Texas Press, 1975.

Hart, John M. *Revolutionary Mexico: The Coming and Process of the Mexican Revolution.* Berkeley: University of California Press, 1989.

Instituto Nacional de Estudios Históricos de la Revolución Mexicana. *Diccionario Biográfico de la revolución mexicana.* Vol. 1. Mexico City: Instituto Nacional de Estudios Históricos de la Revolución Mexicana (INEHRM), 1990.

Junco, Alfonso. *Carranza y los orígenes de su rebellion.* 2nd ed. Mexico City: Editorial Jus, 1955.

Katz, Friedrich. *The Life and Times of Pancho Villa.* Stanford: Stanford University Press, 1998.

———. *The Secret War in Mexico.* Chicago: University of Chicago Press, 1981.

Kerig, Dorothy Pierson. *Luther T. Ellsworth: U.S. Consul on the Border during the Mexican Revolution.* El Paso: Texas Western Press, 1975.

Knight, Alan. *The Mexican Revolution.* 2 vols. Lincoln: University of Nebraska Press, 1990.

Lieuwen, Edwin. *Mexican Militarism: The Political Rise and Fall of the Revolutionary Army 1910-1940.* Albuquerque: University of New Mexico Press, 1968.

López Portillo, Esteban. *Anuario coahuilense para 1886.* Saltillo: Tipografia Del Gobierno en Palacio, 1886.

———. *Catecismo geográfico, politico, e histórico del estado de Coahuila de Zaragoza.* 2nd ed. Saltillo: Tipografía del Gobierno en Palacio, 1897.

Meyer, Michael C. *Huerta: A Political Portrait.* Lincoln: University of Nebraska Press, 1972.

Meyers, William K. *Forge of Progress, Crucible of Revolt: The Origins of the Mexican Revolution in La Comarca Lagunera 1880-1911.* Albuquerque: University of New Mexico Press, 1994.

Moreno, Pablo C. *Torreón: Biografía de la más jóven de las ciudades mexicanas: La Comarca Lagunera.* Saltillo: Talleres Gráficos Coahuila, 1951.

Niemeyer, E.V. *El General Bernardo Reyes.* Trans. Juan Antonio Ayala. Monterrey: Gobierno de Nuevo León, 1966.

Perkins, Clifford Alan. *Border Patrol: With the U.S. Immigration Service on the Mexican Boundary 1910-1954.* El Paso: Texas Western Press, 1978.

Plana, Manuel. *El reino de algodón en México: La estructura agraria de La Laguna (1855-1910).* Torreón: Ayuntamiento de Torreón, 1991.

Quirk, Robert E. *The Mexican Revolution 1914-1915: The Convention of Aguascalientes.* Bloomington: Indiana University Press, 1960.

Raat, W. Dirk. *Revoltosos: Mexico's Rebels in the United States, 1903-1923.* College Station: Texas A&M Press, 1981.

Reed, John. *Insurgent Mexico.* New York: International Publishers, 1969.

Richmond, Douglas W. *Venustiano Carranza's Nationalist Struggle, 1893-1920.* Lincoln: University of Nebraska, 1983.

Ross, Stanley R. *Francisco I. Madero: Apostle of Mexican Democracy.* New York: Columbia University Press, 1955.

Ruíz, Ramón Eduardo. *The Great Rebellion: Mexico 1905-1924.* New York: W.W. Norton, 1980.

————. *Labor and the Ambivalent Revolutionaries 1911-1923*. Baltimore: Johns Hopkins University Press, 1976.

Sandos, James A. *Rebellion in the Borderlands: Anarchism and the Plan of San Diego, 1904-1923*. Norman: University of Oklahoma Press, 1992.

Sariego, Juan Luís. *Enclaves y minerals en el norte de México: Historia social de los mineros de Cananea y Nueva Rosita 1900-1970*. Mexico City: Ediciones de la Casa Chata, 1988.

Vargas-Lobsinger, María. *La hacienda de "La Concha": Una empresa algodonera de la Laguna 1883-1917*. Mexico City: Universidad Autónoma de México, 1984.

Valdés, José de la Luz. *Monografía del municipio de Arteaga, Coahuila*. Saltillo: Talleres Gráficos del Gobierno del Estado, 1966.

Vasconcelos, José. *Don Evaristo Madero: Biografía de un patricio*. Mexico City: Impresiones Modernas, 1958.

Villarello Vélez, Ildefonso. *Historia de la revolución mexicana en Coahuila*. 2nd ed. Saltillo: Biblioteca de la Universidad Autónoma de Coahuila, 1983.

Articles and Chapters in Books

Beezley, William H. "Governor Carranza and the Revolution in Coahuila." *Americas* 33 (October 1976): 50-61.

Carr, Barry. "Las peculiaridades del norte mexicano, 1880-1927: Ensayo de Interpretación." *Historia mexicana* 22 (enero-marzo, 1973): 320-346.

Chevalier, Francois. "The North Mexican Hacienda: Eighteenth and Nineteenth Century." In *The New World Looks at its History*, ed. A.R. Lewis and T.F. McGann, 95-102. Austin: University of Texas Press, 1963.

Falcón, Romana. "La desaparición de jefes políticos en Coahuila. Una paradoja Porfirista." *Historia mexicana* 37 (enero-marzo 1988): 423-467.

————. "Raíces de la Revolución: Evaristo Madero, el primer eslabón de la cadena." In *The Revolutionary Process in Mexico: Essays on Political and Social Change, 1880-1940*, ed. Jaime Rodríguez O., 33-56. Los Angeles: University of California, 1990.

————. "Logros y límites de la centralización Porfirista. Coahuila vista desde arriba." In *El dominio de las minorías: República Restaurada y Porfiriato*, ed. Anne Staples, Gustavo Verduzco Igartúa, Carmen Blázquez Domínguez, and Romana Falcón, 95-135. Mexico City: El Colegio de Mexico, 1989.

Fujigaki Cruz, Esperanza. "Las rebeliones campesinas en el porfiriato 1876-1910." In *Historia de la cuestión agraria mexicana*. Vol. 2, *La tierra y el poder*, ed. Enrique Semo, 175-264. Mexico City: Siglo XXI Editores, 1988.

Harris, Charles H., and Louis R. Sadler. "The Plan of San Diego and the Mexican-United States War Crisis of 1916: A Reexamination." *Hispanic American Historical Review* 58 (August 1978): 381-408.

Hernández Chávez, Alicia, and Ildefonso Dávila del Bosque. "La querella de Coahuila: Municipios y jefes politicos en el Siglo XIX." In *Archivo Municipal de Saltillo. Catálogo del Fondo Jefatura Política 1885-1895*, 1-16. Saltillo: Archivo Municipal de Saltillo, 1985.

Jacques, Leo M. Dambourges. "The Chinese Massacre in Torreón in 1911." *Arizona and the West* 16 (Autumn 1974): 233-246.

Katz, Friedrich. "Pancho Villa, Peasant Movements, and Agrarian Reform in Northern Mexico." In *Caudillo and Peasant in the Mexican Revolution*, ed.

David A. Brading, 59-75. Cambridge: Cambridge University Press, 1980.

Kroeber, Clifton B. "La cuestión del Nazas hasta 1913." *Historia mexicana* 20 (enero 1971): 412-427.

Lloyd, Jean Dale. "Los levantimientos del Partido Liberal Mexicano en 1906." In *Historia de la cuestión agraria mexicana.* Vol. 3, *Campesinos, terratenientes, Y revolucionarios 1910-1920,* ed. Oscar Betanzos, 37-59. Mexico City: Siglo XXI Editores, 1988.

Mecham, J. Lloyd. "The Jefe Político in Mexico." *Southwestern Social Science Quarterly* 13 (June 1933): 333-352.

Meyers, William K. "Politics, Vested Rights, and Economic Growth in Porfirian Mexico: The Cía Tlahualilo in the Comarca Lagunera, 1885-1911." *Hispanic American Historical Review* 57 (August 1977): 425-454.

————. "Second Division of the North: Formation and Fragmentation of the Laguna's Popular Movement, 1910-1911." In *Riot, Rebellion and Revolution: Rural Social Conflict in Mexico,* ed. Friedrich Katz. Princeton: Princeton University Press, 1988.

Pompa y Pompa, Antonio. "Estructura de la sociedad coahuilense en la segunda mitad del siglo XIX y la primera del siglo XX." *Humanitas* 10 (1969): 629-639.

Richmond, Douglas W. "Factional Political Strife in Coahuila, 1910-1920." *Hispanic American Historical Review* 60 (February 1980): 49-68.

Unpublished Sources

Bryan, Anthony T. "Mexican Politics in Transition, 1900-1913: The Role of General Bernardo Reyes." Ph.D. diss., University of Nebraska, 1970.

Langston, William Stanley. "Coahuila in the Porfiriato: A Study of Political Elites." Ph.D. diss., Tulane University, 1980.

Index